W9-AXK-271

*Immortal Longings*

# Immortal Longings

*Versions of Transcending Humanity*

**Fergus Kerr**

University of Notre Dame Press

NOTRE DAME, INDIANA

Published in the United States in 1997 by
University of Notre Dame Press
Notre Dame, Indiana 46556
and in Great Britain in 1997 by
Society for Promoting Christian Knowledge
Holy Trinity Church
Marylebone Road
London NW1 4DU

Library of Congress Cataloging-in-Publication Data
A catalog record for this book is available
from the Library of Congress

ISBN 0-268-01180-X

Typeset by Wilmaset Ltd, Birkenhead, Wirral
Printed in Great Britain by
Redwood Books, Trowbridge, Wiltshire

*For Timothy*

# CONTENTS

Give me my robe. Put on my
crown. I have
Immortal longings in me.
*Antony and Cleopatra*, Act 5,
Scene 2: 275–6


For the true way of going, or of
being led by another, to the
mysteries of love, is to begin with
examples of beauty in this world
and to keep climbing for the sake
of that absolute beauty, using them
as steps ... *Symposium*, 211E

# PREFACE

Having been invited to give a set of Stanton Lectures in the Philosophy of Religion in the University of Cambridge in the academic year 1994-95, I chose to focus on the religion in some recent philosophy.

As customarily practised in Anglo-American universities, the philosophy of religion has its own agenda. Philosophers in general seldom show much interest in the philosophy of religion (even when they have religious commitments in private life). For all its thoroughly secular form, however, a good deal of recent philosophical work incorporates religious motifs in a much more important way than might at first appear. The God who has died remains a presence between the lines of many recent texts. The agenda in the philosophy of religion, then, might profitably be extended to include consideration of the *religion* in recent *philosophy*.

Uncovering the theological conceptions at work in the projects of these philosophers, as well as sometimes clarifying what they are up to, often reveals the inadequacy of their assumptions about theology – Christian theology in all these cases. (That in itself is a measure of the vaunted pluralism and openness of modern Western culture.) It is chastening for theologians to discover how little many of their contemporaries, in what were related fields of study not so long ago, know about Christianity, and how deeply they sometimes misconceive it.

My starting point was Stanley Cavell's remark that, for the later Wittgenstein, the metaphysical tradition 'comes to grief not in denying what we all know to be true, but in its effort to escape those human forms of life which alone provide the coherence of our expression'.[1] What Wittgenstein wanted, by contrast, was 'an acknowledgment of human limitation which does not leave us chafed by our own skin, by a sense of powerlessness to penetrate beyond the human conditions of knowledge'. That is to say, the limitations on our knowledge would no longer feel like 'barriers to a more perfect apprehension' – they would simply be accepted as 'conditions of anything we should call "knowledge"'.

Thus – is there a way, are there ways, of acknowledging the limitations of human existence without regarding them, perhaps with a certain resentment, as *barriers*, but which, on the other hand, would not simply *eliminate* our desire to transcend our finitude?

In her Gifford Lectures at Edinburgh in 1993, Martha Craven Nussbaum tackled the notion of our transcending our finitude – the aspiration, perhaps rather the *temptation*, inscribed in so much Western metaphysical and religious thinking, to go beyond our humanity – inviting us to eradicate the whole idea. She seemed to want to endorse the warnings of the poets whom Aristotle cites at the end of the *Nicomachean Ethics* – that 'being human we should think human and being mortal we should think mortal'.[2] Some of her earlier writings suggest, however, that, far from recommending that we should learn simply to give up our immortal longings, Nussbaum offers four or five interesting and (to some extent) incompatible stories about how to deal with them.

But there are totally self-consistent, even dauntingly monolithic projects for dealing with the age-old metaphysical longing to transcend humanity. Karl Barth is of course a Christian theologian, but his work can easily be read as turning the traditional story about transcending our finitude on its head: he simply puts the singular human being Jesus Christ in place of that which human beings desire, so that transcending our humanity, far from depriving us of our nature, only makes us more human than ever (Chapter 2). Martin Heidegger, determined to dislodge what he takes to be a theologically generated ideal of an unmediated communion of soul and deity which neglects the world, tries to equate finitude and transcendence in his remythologized cosmogony (Chapter 3). Iris Murdoch, in contrast, seeks to persuade us that the only way of saving our humanity is by returning to Plato's vision of the sovereignty of the form of the good (Chapter 4). Luce Irigaray, in a feminist-theoretical rereading of the Platonistic tradition, substitutes the sovereignty of sexual difference for that of the form of the good (Chapter 5).

All four of these utterly different ways of dealing with our immortal longings seem to offer extremely self-confident grand narratives, monolithic and totalizing – radically Christocentric with Karl Barth, wholly cosmo-mythopoetic with the later Martin Heidegger, good old-fashioned Platonist metaphysics with Iris Murdoch, and submission to the still hardly acknowledged authority of sexual difference with Luce Irigaray.

With Stanley Cavell and Charles Taylor, we have major philosophers on the Anglo-American scene whose work exhibits none of the internal inconsistency of Nussbaum's as regards religion, but none of the monomania of Barth, Heidegger, Murdoch and Irigaray either. Cavell, who regards religion as no longer a possibility for intelligent people, certainly operates with a highly disputable account of religion in his profound discussion of scepticism as an attempt to go beyond humanity (Chapter 6). Taylor, who does not disguise his Catholic Christian commitments, works with a surprisingly pared-down theology in his equally profound attempt to rehabilitate an understanding of sources for the self that are irreducibly other (Chapter 7).

Finally, in Chapter 8, we have to cross the border from the philosophy of religion into more explicitly theological territory. This takes us into the most acrimonious, but surely the most important argument in recent Catholic theology – the question of natural desire for God. In Catholic theology, as elsewhere, we are in thrall to and assailed by antinomies and dichotomies, between reason and faith, law and love, fact and value, monotheism and value-plurality, nature and grace, and so on, and seek a middle ground where reconciliation becomes feasible. This is no mere academic debate, as a glance at its historical setting would show. Playing two theologians off against one another, Hans Urs von Balthasar and Karl Rahner, I unexpectedly found my sympathies returning to the latter, in the light of the most recent studies of his work. But I have no conclusion to offer, except to repeat what I said at the start: even if all philosophy is not at bottom theology, as von Balthasar once claimed, the theological preconceptions in much modern philosophy deserve a good deal of attention.

I have to thank Professor Nicholas Lash for suggesting that I should enter the race for the Stanton Lectureship 1994–95. The lectures were delivered in February 1995, when I enjoyed the hospitality of Blackfriars, Cambridge, for three weeks, and had many conversations with old and new friends in the Cambridge Divinity School.

Versions of some chapters have been read as papers in the University of Wales, at Swansea and Lampeter. Chapter 1 was presented as the 1996 Aquinas Lecture at St Mary's Priory,

Tallaght; and a conflation of Chapters 1 and 5 as the 1996 Aquinas Lecture at Blackfriars, Oxford. Chapter 3 goes back to the Gunning Victoria Jubilee Lectures which I delivered at the University of Edinburgh in 1977.

More people than I care to remember have listened patiently to the main themes of this or that chapter, or to the thesis of the book as a whole. Telling others how the story was going was always the best stimulus to shaping it and sometimes even the most effective way of changing my mind. The drafting of the lectures was greatly helped by Professor Richard H. Bell, of The College of Wooster, Ohio, when he and Barbara stayed with us in Edinburgh for a few days in 1994. The plot also developed during discussion with the graduate seminar conducted by Dr Kevin Vanhoozer of the Faculty of Divinity in the University of Edinburgh. I am grateful to my friend Jacinta O'Driscoll for transferring my notes from Amstrad to Apple, and to Roger Ruston for turning them into better prose. Finally, nothing would ever have emerged but for the generosity of my colleagues at 25 George Square, Edinburgh, and the peace and quiet in the house.

# CHAPTER ONE

# TRANSCENDING HUMANITY: NUSSBAUM'S VERSIONS

In her Gifford Lectures at Edinburgh in 1993 Martha Craven Nussbaum sought to develop what she labelled a neo-Stoic theory of the emotions.[1] Her thesis was to the effect that emotions are forms of evaluative recognition that ascribe to external things and persons beyond the agent's control great importance for the agent's own flourishing. She sought, secondly, to enquire about the place of the emotions, so understood, in a good human life. Thirdly, among much else, she paid a great deal of attention to the longing – the temptation – inscribed in so much Western metaphysical and religious thinking over the centuries, to transcend the limits of our finite condition.

According to Adam Gifford's will, the lecturers are expected 'to promote and diffuse the study of Natural Theology in the widest sense of that term – in other words, the knowledge of God'. Given that Karl Barth as well as A. J. Ayer have delivered Gifford lectures, the one attacking the very idea of *natural* knowledge of God and the other displaying contempt for the very idea of *any* knowledge of God at all, the terms of reference are plainly very wide. Nussbaum referred little (if at all) to God, but the agenda of her course of lectures seemed to be to bring the emotions back into relationship with the rational nature of the human beings that we are, and then to persuade us to rid ourselves once and for all of the metaphysical and religious desires that make us so discontented with our human lot that we keep striving to transcend it in some (as she would expect) self-destructive and dehumanizing way.

In the first six of her lectures, that is to say, she offered a cognitivist theory of the emotions. In the remaining four she seemed to set herself the task of liberating us from the desire to transcend human finitude which (it may reasonably be said) has motivated a great deal of natural theology from its beginnings in ancient Greece. Essentially, Nussbaum was attacking the Platonic project for self-transcendence, as traditionally understood.

## Ascents of love

How Nussbaum did this was by taking her audience through three accounts of what she called the ascent of love – in Plato's *Symposium*, Dante's *Divine Comedy*, and Emily Brontë's *Wuthering Heights*, demonstrating that each of these versions of self-transcendence involves self-destruction, partial if not radical denial of our full humanity – clearing the way, in her final lecture, for a brilliant reading of James Joyce's *Ulysses*, in which she argued that Molly and Bloom in bed together at the end of the day, imperfect unromantic creatures, sweating and smelly, somewhat unfaithful to one another, no doubt self-deceiving, and so on, nevertheless offer a paradigm of a love that turns the ascent downwards, so to speak, into the everyday world, the only place where our humanity would not be eliminated.

In effect, Nussbaum seemed to be recommending repudiation of the ancient aspiration to transcendence in favour of our simply accepting the humanity of ordinary life. She invited us to free ourselves, to free our culture, from aspiring to a perfection the fulfilment of which would inevitably deprive us of our humanity.

Nussbaum's seventh lecture, then, was largely a recapitulation of her well-known reading of the *Symposium*.[2] Throughout the history of Western philosophy, she argued, we find recurrent attempts to describe an 'ascent' of love, showing how we can retain the energy of erotic desire while removing from it all the pain of jealousy, betrayal, grief and so on. In the *Symposium*, in Diotima's speech as reported by Socrates, we have a proposal to convert erotic desire into contemplation of the good and the beautiful – enabling the creativity of eros to be preserved and enhanced by freeing it of its dependence on particular objects and their vicissitudes in order to focus on a perfectly abstract object. The young lover begins by loving a single body, or rather the beauty of a single body: 'Then he must see that the beauty in any one body is family-related to the beauty in another body; and that if he must pursue the beauty of form, it is great mindlessness not to consider the beauty of all bodies to be one and the same.' The lover then 'must consider that the beauty in souls is more honourable than that in the body'. Having advanced so far, he may then be constrained to contemplate the beautiful in the observances and laws of the civilized community.

Eventually, 'looking towards the vast amount of the beautiful, he will no longer, like some servant, loving the beauty of a particular boy or a particular man or of one set of customs, and being the slave of this', remain vulnerably captivated by particularity. Rather, 'turned towards the vast sea of the beautiful', he will contemplate 'the beautiful itself – unalloyed, pure, unmixed, not stuffed full of human flesh and colours and lots of other mortal rubbish'.[3]

That sounds like a way of transcending one's dependence on the pleasures and pains of involvement with others, though by losing all that characterizes human life, to end in self-abandonment to a totally non-human other – a recipe for losing one's real humanity, Nussbaum would think.

In her eighth lecture, Nussbaum said that, while in early writings Augustine did indeed have a Platonist version of the ascent of love (as thus described), he came to see that there had to be room in Christian life for passionate longing and deep need for other human beings. The self-sufficiency which comes from radical detachment from all particular objects of desire, as in Diotima's programme, could not be a Christian ideal. But this lecture – on Christian love – focused principally on Dante because Nussbaum believes his to be 'among the most defensible and beautiful Christian conceptions of love'.[4] In this version of the ascent of love, Dante's Thomistic view 'must argue against an Augustinian view, according to which the particularity of persons, their flaws and faults, their neutral idiosyncrasies, their very bodies, their history – are all incidental accretions from the world of sin, to be disregarded in the context of redeemed love'.[5] In the poem, Beatrice's love for Dante embraces his faults, as well as his virtues, and his love for her, even before he sees her face again, is roused by the power of her very presence. There is a respect for the loved one's particularity that we do not find in Diotima's programme. Indeed, Dante includes passionate love for the body of the loved one (at any rate for her face and eyes) – the body, as Aquinas holds, that belongs essentially to the human being, including in his or her redeemed condition. Yet in the end, Nussbaum has to say, Dante can accept the body's sexual desires only in the context of a doctrine according to which their fulfilment is always sinful apart from a marriage open to procreation: 'The idea that sex is delightful in itself, and a great human good is foreign to the poem and to its conception of love'.[6]

Thus, powerful though Dante's conception of individual love is, he falls short of holding that in order to love a human individual, even in parental and friendly love, we have to acknowledge the other as a sexual being – and, for Nussbaum, we have to love the sexual body, acknowledging it, without shame, as the embodiment of the soul.[7] In the end, though Dante's conception of love, unlike Plato's in the *Symposium*, is respectful of our human particularity, Nussbaum concludes that he takes the eroticism out of our bodiliness.

In her ninth lecture Nussbaum showed how, in *Wuthering Heights*, Emily Brontë depicts a passionate relationship in which two very particular individuals certainly transcend themselves (Cathy and Heathcliff) – but only by consuming one another in an ecstatic frenzy. On this characteristically Romantic version of love, the one is not lost in some non-human other, as in Plato, and the human beings are not deprived of their sexuality, as in Dante. What happens, however, so Nussbaum argues, is that the ascent here takes love right out of the world of social compassion, which is caricatured as a hollow mediocre world (Thrushcross Grange), in comparison with the lovers' demonic intensity. (Her reading of the novel is perhaps a little too dependent on the Samuel Goldwyn film of 1939, with Laurence Olivier as Heathcliff and Merle Oberon as Cathy, reunited at the end as carefree ghosts skipping merrily over Penistone Crags.)

Classical Greece, medieval Christianity, the Romantic movement – each era has its own paradigm of the ascent of love, its own method of dealing with the natural longing to transcend finite humanity, yet each diminishes and distorts our characteristically human way of being.

In her tenth and final lecture, Nussbaum offered her own version, or so it seemed, of the only self-transcendence available for finite human beings which does not deprive them of their individuality. The ascent of love needs to be turned downwards, so to speak, and become a descent into the mundane realities of the everyday world. Here Nussbaum offered her brilliant reading of Joyce's *Ulysses*, with copious quotations, arguing that, in the relationship between Molly and Leopold Bloom, with all their faults, failings and grubby little deceptions, we have, unmistakably, two richly created individuals with their imperfections, immersed in their much less than grandly romantic daily round, achieving the only kind of self-transcendence that respects the finitude of mortal beings. Finally, that is to say, we simply have to accept our imperfection and celebrate that. Or rather, we have to free ourselves from a certain notion of perfection – an ideal of perfection according to which we should always have to find ourselves inadequate and defective. In the touching loveliness of the mutual vulnerability that these two frail creatures display, in Joyce's novel, the inhuman aspiration to transcend humanity is revealed as obsolete.

Thus Nussbaum's Gifford Lectures, as delivered in May 1993, at least as heard by one listener; but reconsideration of themes in some of her earlier writing suggests that this, although it is her latest word to date, is not the only story she has to tell about transcending human finitude. Paradoxically, the essays, touching on themes related to our immortal longings, which no doubt prompted the Gifford lectureship committee to invite her to contribute to a series on natural theology (however generously defined), turn out to venture much further into theological matters than the Gifford Lectures as delivered ever did.

## Complications in Nussbaum's view

In his long and interesting review of *The Fragility of Goodness*, Charles Taylor invited Nussbaum to say what she really thought about the human aspiration to transcend humanity – an invitation she took up in the William James Lecture at the Harvard Divinity School, where she offered a very different version of transcending humanity from the one just summarized from her Gifford Lectures.[8]

One thing Nussbaum does not do on this occasion is take up Taylor's invitation to say more about her views about 'Judeo-Christian religion' (his term) and what strikes him (as she agrees 'not without reason') as her liking for for 'Greek polytheism'. In the Gifford Lectures, she did not say any more about Christianity than she said in the lecture on Augustine and Dante. That *was* Christianity, in the Gifford Lectures. In the William James Lecture, however, given four years previously, she says that, while there are no doubt 'some deep differences' between herself and Taylor as regards religion – 'it would be interesting to investigate them' – she prefers to direct him to essays in which she has attacked ideas about human limits and transcendence that have (as she believes) their roots in 'the Augustinian idea of original sin'.[9]

Objecting, to Taylor's phrase, surely rightly, she disentangles Christianity from 'Judeo-Christian religion'. Rightly again, she notes that Christianity is 'a protean religion'. Her objections to what she thinks of as a version of Christianity decisively influenced by Augustine may well not have much (if any) force, that is to say, against other versions of Christianity. Indeed, she refers us to what she regards as the 'convincing' claim by Elaine Pagels that it was only when Christianity ceased to be an illegal sect and became a respected imperial institution that it abandoned its characteristic celebration of human freedom in favour of a doctrine that emphasizes the universal bondage of original sin.[10] However that may be, the point that matters here is that Nussbaum is prepared to envisage a version of Christian transcendence of humanity which would be non-Augustinian: free, then, of what she would regard as the Augustinian obsession with the universal state of our being born in sin. Indeed, 'many of [Christianity's] forms have, in fact, begun from an idea of human helplessness that lies closer than Augustine's does to ancient Greek thought, and especially to Aristotle' – perhaps Thomist Catholicism, for instance.[11]

But she chooses to 'defer serious engagement on that issue' – which certainly sounds as if she meant to return to it one day – although her discussion here of 'the aspiration to transcendence', as she calls it, in ('for the most part') purely philosophical terms, is illuminating enough. It has to be said, however, that if the treatment of the paradigms of the ascent of eros in the Gifford Lectures is meant to fulfil her promise to return to the issue, the story that culminates with Molly and Bloom as exemplars of 'transfiguration of everyday life' (the title she gave to that lecture) lacks the complexity of the issues raised in the William James Lecture.

Nussbaum refuses to take up Taylor's invitation to consider the value, within our human this-worldly life, of allowing the aspiration to transcendence to be an aim of one's life as a whole. According to Taylor, having this aspiration to transcend one's humanity as an aim 'can turn us towards this life with a new attention and concern, as has undoubtedly been the case with the Judeo-Christian tradition, with decisive consequences for our whole moral outlook'. That 'undoubtedly' strikes Nussbaum as 'certainly too strong'. True, Taylor says only that the aspiration to transcend humanity 'can' turn human beings to attend to this life with new concern. He does not say that it does so necessarily. He is surely only saying that this valuable new concern with life in this world, no doubt over against platonizing or gnostic spiritualizations of religion, is 'undoubtedly' to be found in 'the Judeo-Christian tradition', but he is not saying that it always or even often has been. (Charles Taylor always looks on the bright side.) He need not be denying the dark and sinister consequences of the aspiration to transcending humanity in certain forms of Christianity. But they are the ones, plainly, that frighten Nussbaum. Her scepticism about his optimistic assessment is connected, as she says, with the sympathy she has with Nietzsche's analysis of the many ways in which the aspiration towards a 'true world' has led to denigration of our actions and relationships in this one.[12]

## Nietzschean hatred of religion

This takes us back to Nussbaum's first substantial set of thoughts about religion prior to her Gifford Lectures. Her two major references are Lucretius and Nietzsche, both of whom believed that seeing the world in a religious perspective 'had deeply poisoned human desires ... constructing deformed patterns of fear and longing'.[13]

Lucretius (c.100–c.55 BC) knew nothing of Christianity – Augustinian Christianity, in particular – which is why Nietzsche, brought up as a Lutheran, had a much more pessimistic view about the extent to which patterns of feeling and structures of sensibility are corrupted by religious teaching: 'Now the human being is so radically alienated from natural bodily humanity, so thoroughly immersed in longing for a happy ending in another world, by contrast to which this one is seen as poor and loathsome, that the removal of religious hope creates a crisis of nihilism.' On Nietzsche's view, the 'teleological patterns of desire', 'the horror of the body', invented and maintained by religion – the Christian religion – are so deep in us that 'it is not clear that there is any vivid life in us that is not made in religion's image – nothing, therefore, to motivate us to construct a new life after its demise'. In fact, as Nussbaum goes on to say, Nietzsche was able to sketch an account of a human life after the demise of religion – 'he believed his task as a writer to be the creation of that hope as a vivid possibility'; but he was in no doubt about the threat of what he called nihilism – 'the prospect of the collapse of the will, the refusal to continue ordering and valuing'.[14]

Nussbaum's Nietzschean rage against what she regards as Augustinian Christianity comes out most clearly in her essay on Samuel Beckett. Her focus in this essay is on the connection between emotion and narrative form – she wants to show how 'we learn our emotional repertory, in part at least, from the stories we hear'.[15] Her text is the dark and sinister conception of Christianity that she reveals in Beckett's *Molloy* trilogy.[16]

The question that Beckett raises for the moral philosopher – 'Do the emotions upon which our interest, as readers, depends themselves embody questionable beliefs, defective forms of life' – is to be answered in the affirmative. The emotions that Beckett's fiction call up, as it happens, embody very sick beliefs springing from belief in the Christian doctrine of original sin – so Nussbaum will say. But this question needs to be asked as well about philosophical writing – about the metaphysical tradition – 'for much of the interest readers have had in a certain style of philosophical writing has traditionally been connected with an interest in transcending everyday humanity, an aspiration problematic at best'.[17]

Nussbaum quotes a great deal from Beckett's novel, very graphically. Molloy's life is pervaded by his sense of being covered in excrement from birth. 'The emotion story that is Molloy's life', Nussbaum summarizes, is 'the story of original sin'.[18] The experience of fear and love voiced in Beckett's fiction, 'differs from the experience of those emotions in a non-Christian culture'. What the novel reveals, is 'the particular and highly specific learned tonality that makes the Christian world of these people a world of highly concrete and distinct form and feeling, in which the ubiquity of guilt and an anal form of disgust (and humour) colour every emotion and perception'. The characters in Beckett's fiction are represented as feeling 'guilt at a parental sexual act that is seen as immersing the mother in excrement and causing the birth of the child through excrement'. It is not just that they feel disgust and loathing, in some theoretical and cerebral way. Their disgust is focused: 'their disgust has as its object, above all, the female body' – but also their own bodies – 'seen ... as mortal', 'since mortality is seen as itself the punishment for sexual guilt'.[19] In the detail of his fiction – and Nussbaum quotes enough to make her thesis credible – Beckett is exploring – revealing, rather – certain connections between birth, copulation and death which are heavily pervaded by disgust of the body. The emotion of erotic love, for example, in the novel, 'becomes a peculiar, highly specific mixture of longing for bliss with loathing and disgust, both toward the object and toward oneself'. 'The vagina ... just is a rectum.'

All of this is 'a view of love' – 'a view taught by a certain concrete society at a certain point in history'. It is a view of love that 'forms a seamless unity with the society's other views or stories of emotion, with its cosmology, its shared forms of life'.[20] In Beckett's fiction we are offered 'a structure of feeling' – ' forms of feeling act themselves out in forms of life, as the characters play out ... the paradigm scenarios their culture and its stories have taught them'.

What happens in the course of the novel is that a massive

critique of this 'Christian' structure of feeling develops. The narrative, indeed, has the power to liberate us as readers from the 'pollution' of religious meanings. Moran, late in the trilogy, rediscovers his bees, for example, as creatures whose lives are not polluted: their dances display a 'different way' from human communication. Yet, unlike human activity under God's eye, these dances have no significance – or anyway an alien significance – 'too novel ever to be sullied by the cogitations of a man like me, exiled in his manhood', as Moran is made to say. Moran regards the life of the bees as a life apart from the life of the emotions. His relation to the bees is the one relationship in his life that is exempt from mediation by emotion: 'I would never do my bees the wrong I had done my God, to whom I had been taught to ascribe my angers, fears, desires, and even my body.'

Gradually, Moran is identified as the author of the entire novel, and indeed of the rest of Beckett's fiction until this point. His exemplary indifference to religious meanings becomes 'the happy discovery that the world does not need to be interpreted' – 'it can simply be lived in, accepted, trusted as the birds trust'. What the novel opens up, for Nussbaum, is 'a clearing beyond disgust and guilt': 'an acceptance of nature and body that does not ask them to be redeemed by any beyond' – 'a relation with living beings that no longer requires to be mediated by religious emotions or even by the language in which they are constructed'.[21]

In fact, by this point in the novel, the central character is refusing to inhabit human language altogether. The novel reaches a climax of anguished solipsism, with the narrator, up to his neck in a jar by a shambles, elaborating almost unstoppably upon 'the inability to speak, the inability to be silent, and solitude'. At this point, Nussbaum hopes for 'a patient therapeutic criticism of the emotions that society has taught us, to live a life free from religious fear and longing, and the love that is based upon these'. She concludes, in a very Nietzschean way: 'Animals have forms of life apart from the pollution of religion; they show us what it could be to be alive without hope or fear or disgust or even love.'[22]

'We can be redeemed only by ending the demand for redemption, by ceasing to use the concepts of redemption'[23] – but, Nussbaum goes on to suggest, again in detailed citation from Beckett's text, the disgust at disgust at the body, the longing for redemption from the longing for redemption, are perhaps just new versions of the same old temptation: our desire being once again to imagine what would, this time, be a real 'happy ending'. Liberation from the desire for an end seems to betray itself.

Thus there is more than one conception of Christianity operating in Nussbaum's work. In the Christian ascent of love as she finds it in Dante she is fairly positive about Christianity as a stage in the history of overcoming the Platonic demand for an ascetical striving to escape the chances and changes of human life by means of concentrating on the eternal form of the good. One might even say, going somewhat beyond what she said in the Gifford Lectures, that the impact of the Christian doctrine of the incarnation of the transcendent God, and the related insistence on loving one's neighbour, has been, historically, a bringing down to earth of metaphysical desire so that we can at last see that the only self-transcendence for mortal human beings is in a certain kind of love, a human way of transcending self in the practice of forbearance, compassion and so forth – in principle at least, then, bringing human beings back from these ancient and inveterate estrangements from themselves in illusory ventures of submission to non-human perfection.

In the essay on Beckett, on the other hand, Nussbaum takes a thoroughly negative Nietzschean line, tracing the 'sickness' and excremental vision of human life to its origin in the Christian doctrine of original sin (as she conceives it). On this story, human beings have been taught by religion to regret that they ever were born; our very existence is made to seem culpable, loathsome to itself, unappeasably guilt-ridden. The doctrine of original sin so eats into people's lives that they find themselves and others disgusting, physically and sexually especially. From this conception of religion it would be preferable to escape into the innocence of the animals.

## Original sin in Henry James

Contrarily enough, in a still earlier essay, Nussbaum has a very different, entirely positive treatment of the concept of original sin.[24] In The Golden Bowl, according to Nussbaum, Henry James is offering us a 'secular analogue of original sin' – her phrase. What we are shown, in the detail and complexity of the novel, is that a human being's relation to moral value in the world is one of imperfect fidelity and therefore of guilt. We turn out to be 'valuing beings who, under the strains imposed by the intertwining of our routes to value in the world, become cracked and flawed'. That is to say, 'guilt toward value', in Nussbaum's strange phrase, while it may not be 'literally a priori', is nevertheless disclosed to be 'a feature of our humanness which attaches to us as a structural feature of our situation in nature and in the family' – 'prior to the specific choices and failures that we enter upon in a particular life'.[25]

Thus, in *The Golden Bowl*, the doctrine of original sin is secularized – brought down to earth – in the slow and painful process by which Maggie Verver learns how flawed human perfection always is. Her initiation into knowledge of a fallen world finally takes the form of telling a lie to her old friend, her husband's ex-girl-friend, in order to gain him irrevocably for herself. In the end, however, recognizing how cruel she is being towards Charlotte, she offers her husband the chance to meet her once more before she departs into exile in America; but he refuses to do so. To love his wife, now, he has to blind himself to his former lover's need to take farewell. The novel concludes with Maggie's burying her face in her husband's breast – unable, 'for pity and dread', to look him in the eyes. On Nussbaum's reading, she sees that he sees only her – that fidelity to her means obliviousness to Charlotte's need. As lovers, Nussbaum concludes, we may have to become grossly insensitive and careless as regards others – there is no other way, in this imperfect life, of dealing with their incompatible claims on us. To maintain purity of love in one direction may necessitate blindness in another.

Here, whatever the rights and wrongs of her reading of the novel, Nussbaum is getting something very positive out of the Christian doctrine of original sin. Far from generating the self-loathing exemplified in the reading of Beckett's fiction, the religious notion of original sin turns out to contribute to, perhaps even actually to constitute, the experience of self-knowledge which for Nussbaum plainly marks the most civilized kind of human life. Moral knowledge, self-knowledge, always involves discovery of one's guilt – of one's implication in ambiguity and deceit. Moral judgements are not the result of applying some overriding principle or rule, as perhaps in utilitarianism or Kantian deontology (Nussbaum no doubt means). Moral growth has to do with a move from innocence to experience – and we live amid bewildering complexities, so that obtuseness and refusal of vision inevitably best us. 'Responsible lucidity can be wrested from the darkness only by painful vigilant effort, the intense scrutiny of particulars'.[26]

In brief: Nussbaum sees human beings as suffering from the effects of original sin (although of course there has been no 'fall'). She sees moral growth very much in terms of remorse and sacrifice, responsibility and self-examination, with unexpected moments of illumination and what might even be called moments of grace. The language of the ancient religious myth of human finitude as marked by guilt (our being created as our being inescapably culpable) is here seen as an important element in the emergence of a certain kind of sophisticated self-consciousness – of how to be 'finely aware and richly responsible', in the phrase she quotes from Henry James.[27]

## The human god of the Christian religion

There is yet another set of considerations about transcending humanity in Nussbaum's work. In her reply to Charles Taylor, she notes that our image of human self-transcendence has always been 'the image of an anthropomorphic perfection made visible by imagining the removal of constraints that make human life a brief, chancy, and in many ways miserable existence'. In many of the ancient Greek myths, for example, translation to immortal life is the supreme reward. 'Unencumbered by the excessive self-hatred that belief in original sin has so frequently brought with it,' the Greeks could view the way of life of the gods as 'not so much better than [ours] as totally, strangely different.'

That is not such an attractive thought as Nussbaum might be expected to entertain. On the contrary, 'lacking the constraints imposed by mortality, lacking vulnerabilities of many kinds', the way of life of the gods 'will of necessity lack, as well, some of the forms of life that we now find valuable and pursue as ends'. In fact, it now turns out, Nussbaum is not so keen on Greek polytheism as opposed to biblical monotheism as she allows Taylor to say. There is no place for athletics, nor for politics, in the life of the gods. Excluding such possibilities, Nussbaum argues, excludes any form of life that human beings would find natural, congenial and inhabitable. What Nussbaum's Aristotle would show us, however, is that we should resist the very idea of transcending humanity if by that we mean the possibility of a good life that does not need other human beings – that does not have the forms of dependency and neediness that lead human beings to reach out to others. Aristotle simply denies that such a life could count as a completely fulfilled human life.[28]

The self-sufficiency that Aristotle regards as appropriate for human beings is a self-sufficiency achieved in company with family, loved ones and fellow citizens, 'since the human being is by nature a political being'.[29] A human life without such ties, and the trouble and grief they may involve, would not be worth living. And these goods, as Aristotle sees, are goods only from within the human form of life. The gods will not come asking for advice about athletics or politics. Here, for Nussbaum, the crucial point is that Aristotle does not denigrate athletics or politics with all their excellences and skills because the gods never go in for them. Rather, good activity for and with others is intrinsically fine and noble, as are the relationships of love and care that bind citizens together in families, not to mention friendships of several kinds.[30]

Indeed, Aristotle says that there is no place for the moral virtues in a divine life. In a god's way of life most if not all of the virtues would be pointless, simply unintelligible. A god cannot have the virtue of courage – there is no risk for a god to face. And so on. The gods with whom Aristotle was acquainted, Nussbaum now says, were frivolous and irresponsible – 'just plain callous, lacking totally in the painstaking effort of mind and desire that is involved in human justice' – 'they simply don't fully see what is going on in our lives, they lack compassion, an essential ingredient of any human justice'. What comes out in the ancient Greek myths is 'the carelessness of the gods ... a carelessness inseparable from their transcendence of our whole needy way of life'. They are, after all, 'the Olympian gods'. 'Their social life is free-floating, amorphous, uninspired by need' – we are confronted with 'their failure, in consequence, to see what is at stake for us'. As we reflect on these points, Nussbaum says, 'we should notice what a profound response to this problem is embodied in Christianity'.[31]

Having started her response to Charles Taylor by saying that she was not going to get into all this, Nussbaum now admits that the temptation to do so is irresistible: 'For Christianity seems to grant that in order to imagine a god who is truly superior, truly worthy of worship, truly and fully just, we must imagine a god who is human as well as divine, a god who has actually lived out the non-transcendent life and understands it in the only way it can be understood, by suffering and death.' If that is what Charles Taylor means when he speaks of Christianity as turning us back to our own world 'with new attention and concern', then 'he is undoubtedly pointing to something important'.[32]

What is important, here, is 'the universal compassion for human suffering which one associates with Christianity at its best' – something which is 'difficult to imagine apart from the paradigm of human suffering and sacrifice exemplified in Christ'. At this point Nussbaum has a footnote reminding us that Christianity is not alone in having a god who dies – 'but it is Christianity, above all, that links this conception to a new idea of the moral example God provides to humans'.

Among the Greek gods, again, there is no room for taking risks or making sacrifices for the people one loves – 'no room for loyalty so strong that it confronts death itself'. And here again, in a parenthesis, Nussbaum allows that 'the Christian idea that god (sic) is also fully human and has actually sacrificed his life' – 'if it can be made coherent' – is 'a most important element in the thought that god (sic) actually loves the world'.

'If it can be made coherent' – here she refers us in a footnote to *The Heart of the Matter*, Graham Greene's novel, where the hero Scobie realizes that his sense of pity and responsibility towards the two women who depend on him is a moral attitude rooted in his years of meditation on Christ's compassion. It seems to Scobie that he is not as responsible to Christ as he is to his fellow human beings – these women need him and Christ surely does not:

> He was desecrating God because he loved a woman – was it even love, or was it just a feeling of pity and responsibility? He tried again to excuse himself: 'You can look after yourself. You survive the cross every day. You can only suffer. You can never be lost. Admit that you must come second to these others' ... and looking up towards the cross on the altar he thought savagely: 'Take your sponge of gall, You made me what I am. Take the spear thrust'.

This is a 'remarkable reflection', Nussbaum says, on the tensions between the idea that God has suffered and sacrificed himself out of love for the world and the idea that God is self-sufficient, eternal and so on.[33]

She takes this no further, but this set of reflections, with all their guarded qualifications, parenthetical asides and cautiously lower-case allusions to the deity, surely takes us some distance from the three we have examined: Christian self-transcendence as (1) an improvement on the Platonic ascent of love because there is at least some recognition of the importance of some other human being (the Dante essay); as (2) 'Augustinian' Christianity with its doctrine of original sin immersing us in self-disgust (the Beckett essay); and as (3) secularized 'guilt toward value', providing us with the possibility of always deeper understanding of one's flawed complex self (the Henry James essay). Now, (4) 'if it can be made coherent', we have a story about a god who is in our history of suffering and death.

## The inescapable longing

There is actually no question of giving up metaphysical longings. Explicitly, in her William James Lecture, Nussbaum denies that she should be understood as meaning that 'in order to pursue appropriately the whole human good, we must leave aside our desire for transcendence'. It may look as if that is what she means, she allows – indeed that is what Charles Taylor may take her as meaning, as it was what many of us took her to be saying in her Gifford Lectures – 'But I believe that matters are more complex'.[34]

It depends what you mean by transcendence – 'there is a great deal of room, within the context of a human life . . . for a certain sort of aspiration to transcend our ordinary humanity'. Nussbaum insists that she does not believe that human beings are originally evil or sinful. That is clearly the 'Augustinian' version of Christian self-transcendence as she (mis)understands it in the essay on Beckett. But most of the time most of us are 'lazy, inattentive, unreflective, shallow in feeling' – quite an interesting list! That is to say: 'most human action falls well short of the fully human target of complete virtue set up by Aristotle's view' – a view which she aligns here, very instructively, with the writings of Henry James and indeed Marcel Proust because of 'their explicit claim that the artist's fine-tuned attention and responsiveness to human life is paradigmatic of a kind of precision of feeling and thought that a human being can cultivate, though most do not'. This is what Nussbaum proposes to call 'transcendence . . . of an *internal* and human sort'.[35]

It is particularly attractive to her because neither Henry James nor Proust 'has the slightest interest in religion or otherworldly or even contemplative transcendence'. In their fiction, however, they offer their readers 'a glimpse of a more compassionate, subtler, more responsive, more richly human world', 'above the dullness and obtuseness of the everyday' – and 'that is a view of transcendence'.

Need we have any grander a view? 'There is so much to do in this area of human transcending (which I imagine also as a transcending by descent, delving more deeply into oneself and one's humanity, and becoming deeper and more spacious as a result) that if one really pursued that aim well and fully I suspect that there would be little time left to look about for any other sort.'

Fine – in her reflections on Henry James but also on Proust, Dickens and others, Nussbaum summons up a sometimes moving and illuminating picture of human life, a life of moral growth, of risk, of disillusionment, much along the lines suggested by her account of Maggie Verver's development in *The Golden Bowl*. But are Molly and Bloom in all their glorious mediocrity great exemplars of this more richly human world above the dullness and obtuseness of the everyday? Moreover, fine as Nussbaum's readings of Proust and James certainly are, can the ancient metaphysical desire for self-transcendence really be transformed into Proustian and Jamesian cultivation of a certain self-awareness – subtle and compassionate as it may well be as one discovers one's own imperfection? And above all – perhaps Nussbaum's Achilles' heel – how easy is it to think of Aristotle as a precursor of Proust and Henry James?

## Dealing with Aristotle's theology

On the one hand, Aristotle surely has a very bluff and uncompli-cated kind of sensibility compared with Proust and Henry James. On the other hand, does Aristotle not have a good deal of interest, if perhaps not in religious or otherworldly transcendence, certainly in contemplative transcendence – far more than Nussbaum is willing to allow?

For Nussbaum has a problem – for which she offers an ingenious solution – with the remarkable passage in the *Nicomachean Ethics* where Aristotle prescribes a Platonic quasi-divine intellect-centred life as best for human beings:

> We must not follow those who urge us, being human, to reason and choose humanly, and, being mortal, in a mortal way; but insofar as it is possible we must immortalize and do everything in order to live in accordance with the best part of ourselves.[36]

That sounds very much like a refusal to accept that we do best to settle for the finitude of our mortal condition. It is pure Platonism, Nussbaum concedes – the only passage in which Aristotle endorses what she calls the Platonism of the middle dialogues. It does not fit with its context, it is in flat contradiction with several important positions and arguments in the *Ethics* as a whole.[37] 'On the other hand, it cannot simply be dismissed'.[38] There is no strong reason to believe this passage was not composed by Aristotle – no reason to rule out forgery either. But the passage expresses a view about ethics, human nature, and so on, that Aristotle vigorously attacks elsewhere. On the other hand, she insists, this suprahuman mortality-transcending intellectualism – a kind of Platonism – clearly gripped Aristotle's imagination, as various other texts show.

Nussbaum's way of dealing with this passage, and similar ones, is

16

to argue that it is 'a serious working-out of elements of a position to which Aristotle is in some ways deeply attracted'. Sometimes he is 'rather quick and dismissive with Platonist positions'. It is surely 'far more worthy of him, and of his method' that, just this once at least, he should allow himself seriously to feel the force of this conception of self-transcendence, this aspiration to transcend mortality by contemplative activity. This is Aristotle either trying hard to imagine why the Platonist ascent of love is so attractive or perhaps even voicing his own deep sense of its attractions. Mostly Aristotle expounds the thoroughly anthropocentric vision of human life that Nussbaum invites us to endorse, but just this once, she concludes, he articulates the Platonist view – 'not attempting to harmonize it with the other view, but setting it side by side with that one ... the other view remains, not fully dismissed, exerting its claim as a possibility'. 'This seems to be a worthy way for a great philosopher to think about these hard questions, and therefore worthy of Aristotle'.[39]

Nussbaum's claim is that Aristotle, in offering a pretty high doctrine of the human mind transcending its mortality in acts of contemplating the good, the true and the beautiful – a doctrine that is quite incompatible with what he shows himself elsewhere to believe – is simply offering us as strong an account as he can of the doctrine he rejects.

This way of dealing with the passage has attractions. It is admirable, if very unusual, for a philosopher to make a serious attempt to present a deep line of thought with which he is in radical disagreement in as sympathetic a light as possible. On the whole, philosophers (and theologians!) set out the views they oppose as polemically and unsympathetically as possible. It is an attractive thought that Aristotle was a generous enough philosopher to be able to articulate with such clarity a view that he rejected. But is this really credible?

Nussbaum is commendably unwilling to deal with this alien text (alien on her reading of Aristotle as a thoroughly anthropocentric thinker) simply by saying it cannot have been written by Aristotle. But surely her way of dealing with it, by suggesting that Aristotle was deliberately expounding, as powerfully as possible, exactly the sort of self-transcendence doctrine he was out to discredit, is rather far-fetched. Aristotle is a great philosopher, there is plenty of evidence in his work of his sense of indebtedness to predecessors from whom he differs, but is it really believable that this embarrassing passage – embarrassing for Nussbaum – is a kind of thought-experiment? Surely Aristotle would have signalled a bit more clearly that this passage articulates precisely the opposite of what he himself thinks?

Suppose, on the other hand, that such passages are not so inconsistent with the rest of Aristotle's thought as Nussbaum believes – suppose, even, that his anthropocentric ethics culminates in this endorsement of immortal longings? Why is Nussbaum so sure that it is incompatible with the rest of Aristotle's thought?

Nussbaum is certainly not out on her own in wanting to eliminate the 'Platonism' in the *Ethics*, though the present trend, certainly in Anglo-American scholarship, seems to be back to the traditional reading.[40] For Nussbaum, at any rate, Aristotle is committed to the view that it is simply incoherent to aspire to the good life of a god – that would mean wanting to become another kind of being altogether. We do not want our friends to become divine – we wish them only the greatest goods compatible with their remaining human.[41] Such remarks are decisive for Nussbaum's interpretation. Her Aristotle is not to be allowed to depart from them.

Nussbaum's Aristotle offers a conception of human life in which we flourish only in relationship to one another, in which practical reason is more important than theorizing, and in which above all we resist the temptation to pass beyond our nature, to denature ourselves, in favour of something allegedly better – something divine, something *ipso facto* destructive of our humanity.

## The inescapability of religion

But it is surely prejudice – anti-theological prejudice, understandable anti-theological prejudice, given her Nietzschean hatred of religion (as in the Beckett essay) – that drives Nussbaum to treat the theology in the *Ethics* as such an implausibly sophisticated thought-experiment.

We can trace at least five different sets of theological considerations in Nussbaum's philosophical work, most of which she acknowledges for what they are, though there is no sign that she is aware of how heterogeneous and even incommensurable they are. (But she might respond by saying that the legacy of religion in philosophy is bound to be confusing and contradictory.)

First there is self-transcendence as in the ascent to love in the *Symposium* – the cure for one's vulnerability is to be found in departing altogether from one's humanity into identification with the form of the good. Over against this, Nussbaum celebrates the

ersonal moral sensibility of the flawed beings about
James and Proust write. Finally, in her references to
conception of a god who has in some sense become
baum is surely not very far away from at least
he idea of a transcendence for human beings into
ion with the divine which might be an affirmation
rather than a denial of our humanity – which takes us
rl Barth's way of dealing with our immortal longings.
to Barth, we might even find ourselves provoked to
ssbaum gets the motivation for her opposition to the
transcendence that destroys our humanity. She
nores religious traditions in which the individual
become something else, be reincarnated in another
ple. But is her inspiration solely from Aristotle? Is her
istotle not influenced, partly at least, perhaps even
he legacy in Western philosophy and culture of the
asis on the unique once-for-all particular individual?
fers Molly and Bloom in bed to Diotima's ascent of
heir comfortable mundaneity compatible with the
Proustian sensibilities? She prefers the innocent play
the birds to the excremental wallowings of a certain
-disgust – but is the 'innocence of becoming'
hrase) reconcilable with Proustian self-awareness
izably human? She exhibits Nietzschean horror of
ivated self-disgust, but otherwise, with her affirma-
life, her admiration for self-discipline and growth in
ty, her social conscience and compassion, all three
constitutive elements of her philosophy, Nussbaum
reat deal to religion – the religion that has played
part in the formation of Western philosophy.

descent of love in the affirmation of ordinary lives like those of
Molly and Leopold Bloom in Joyce's *Ulysses*. The place of religion,
or anyway of the Christian religion, here, is as a stage on the way
from self-transcendence conceived as denying one's humanity to a
conception of self-transcendence as taking place in the very bodily
and incarnational exchange of very ordinary married life.

Secondly, there is self-transcendence as guilt-ridden self-disgust
generated by the Augustinian-Christian doctrine of original sin as
perceived by Nietzsche and Beckett. Over against this, Nussbaum
seems to some extent attracted by the innocence of the animals –
why can we not live like the birds and the bees? Here religion, and
especially the Christian religion, are taken to be body-hating and
sexuality-hating denaturing of our humanity. It would be more
graceful to see human life like the playful innocence of the other
animals.

Thirdly, there is self-transcendence as in the Augustinian-
Christian life-long self-examination that flawed beings have
been trained to go in for – transformed, secularized, demythologized, in a Jamesian moral sensibility, fine, subtle, nuanced and so
forth. Here, incompatibly with the previous version of self-
transcendence, the Christian religion, with its doctrine of our
sinfulness, is taken to have generated something very positive:
sensitivity to moral issues in the endless complexity of personal
relations between flawed and vulnerable human beings.

Fourthly, over against the ancient Greek gods and their blissful
ignorance of the real conditions of finite bodily human life,
Nussbaum favours the Christian story of the god who has
become human, mortal, vulnerable and so forth, 'if it can be
made coherent' – if only it were believable, she no doubt means.

And fifthly, the most pervasive consideration in Nussbaum's
work from her studies of Aristotle onwards, the one that highlights
his remarks about our not wanting happiness for ourselves or others
if it means our becoming something non-human, is the consideration that pushes her into her surely fanciful way of sidelining the
metaphysical theology in Aristotle, and sustains her determination
'to reject as incoherent . . . the aspiration to leave behind altogether
the constitutive conditions of our humanity . . . to seek for a life that
is really the life of another sort of being'.[42]

The one central consideration for Nussbaum is that any conception of self-transcendence that means leaving behind this
human way of life for some radically different form of existence
is a totally unacceptable project. She wants us, rather, 'to bound our

aspirations' – 'by recalling that there are some very general conditions for the values that we know, love, and appropriately pursue'. If we can recognize how bound we are to these conditions, we should at least moderate our rage at these limiting features and thus lose all incentive to transcend them. Realizing this would, she thinks, undercut the negative motivation to pursue various forms of alleged transcendence within human life – 'forms that involve withdrawing love and concern from that which cannot be stably controlled'.

Nussbaum allows that there is not, and never can be, a sharp line to be drawn between the dehumanizing self-transcendence which she seeks to expose and eliminate, and the internal sort of transcendence that she favours, for example in Jamesian moral sensibility. More than that: 'Human striving for excellence involves pushing, in many ways, against the limits that constrain human life.' There is room for striving to surpass what might seem pretty formidable intellectual, emotional, physical and material limits. Her worry is about some forms of aspiration to 'extrahuman transcendence' that undermine people's determination to improve material and social conditions: 'If one thinks that the really important thing is to get over to a different sort of life altogether, then this may well make one work less hard on this one' – though here Nussbaum concedes to Taylor that Nietzsche overstated this point 'against the Christians'.[43] The puzzle is: 'When does the aspiration to internal transcendence become the aspiration to depart from human life altogether?' – a question, she thinks, to which there can be no clear answer, if we want a theory. The only answer has to be given in human life itself – 'as human beings look at the limits as their own struggles have constituted them' – in medical and scientific progress, for example.

'It would be a disaster for humanity' if her attack on the Platonic ascent of love was 'taken to imply that the desire to push our limits back further was an illegitimate desire, and that we should just live on the earth as we find it'. 'We shouldn't, perhaps, imagine that we can coherently wish for immortality' – but that does not mean that we should cease the struggle to transcend the limitations of our condition.

Nussbaum invokes the paradox of the athlete: he or she cannot wish to be without the human body and its limits altogether because then there would be no goal or athletic achievement, but in any particular case it will always be right to keep pushing against these limits: 'It is the paradox of a struggle for victory in which

complete "victory" would be
rate, a life so different from c
ourselves and our valued act

Thus, what Nussbaum is
transcending human finitud
balancing act between the cl
push outward, and the nece
pushes us back in'. 'There is a
human life; and there is ano
trying to depart from that life
conception of *hubris* is what w
pride towards the gods: 'the f
one has actually got' – 'the f
are also possibilities)' – 'the
thoughts'. But the injunction
'is not a penance or denial –
valuable things for us are to

She advocates internal tra
the limit in all sorts of ways, c
relationships with Proustian a
not a little difficult to hold t
ideals of excellence, particul
to be the paradigm in the ba

Whatever doubts one may
baum's internal transcenden
several versions of projects to
always to the sorts of aspirat
would deprive us of our huma
particular sort, beings who g
immersed 'in the characterist
adventures of human finitud

Transcending humanity ou
bodies, is what Nussbaum s
ascent of love. She also has a
religious guilt-free animal in
Nietzsche – a longing which
guilt-ridden body-hating w
stemming from the doctrine
misinterpreted). But it is
differently understood, that
Aristotle's conception of the
also social and emotional

inward and
whom Henr
the Christia
human, Nu
entertaining
some comm
and fulfilme
to consider

In movin
ask where N
aspiration
completely
might indee
form, for ex
reading of
decisively,
biblical em
Nussbaum
eros – but
inwardness
of the bees
Christian
(Nietzsche'
or even rec
religion as
tion of ordi
moral sensi
deeply root
surely owes
such a deci

# CHAPTER TWO

# KARL BARTH'S CHRISTOLOGICAL METAPHYSICS

Martha Craven Nussbaum's work exhibits a variety of ways in which human beings might deal with longings to transcend humanity, not easily harmonizable. If we focus on her paradigm of the ascent of love in Diotima's speech in the *Symposium*, then four other projects immediately come to mind, utterly different from one another and from hers, not least because of the single-minded self-consistency that each displays. Iris Murdoch asks what is wrong with good old-fashioned Platonist aspirations to the good anyway (Chapter 4). Luce Irigaray ingeniously substitutes the supremacy of sexual difference for the sovereignty of the good (Chapter 5). But we will first look at the radical attempts to overcome the Platonic project of self-transcendence by two of the most dominant thinkers from the first half of the century: Martin Heidegger (Chapter 3) and Karl Barth.

## The curse of finitude

No Christian theologian has written about the finite conditions of human existence more often or at greater length than Karl Barth.[1] His starting point, as with Nussbaum, is that we are fatally tempted to regard our finitude as a constriction: 'We must divest ourselves of the idea (*Vorurteil*: prejudice) that limitation implies something derogatory or even a kind of curse or affliction'.[2] At a very deep level, Barth's work strives to liberate us from our inclination to regard our limitedness as an affliction. It is prejudice to think of our finitude as a curse.

Barth takes it for granted that, as a matter of fact, we have such an inclination, and that it needs to be exposed and eliminated. Long before Stanley Cavell, he would have endorsed his insistence that we have to work our way through to 'an acknowledgement of human limitation which does not leave us chafed by our own skin'. Oddly enough, the same metaphor is to be found in Barth: 'All our chafing against the limitations of our life must be irrelevant and superfluous'.[3] But the metaphor has been introduced by the translator. What Barth actually says, literally translated, is that 'the screaming and protesting against a barrier (Schranke) placed on our life' needs to be 'overcome' and would then become 'superfluous'.[4]

Why the translator, Professor R. H. Fuller for this stretch of the text, substituted the metaphor of our skin's being chafed for Barth's screaming protest is hard to explain. It seems a fairly dramatic transition, culturally as well as metaphorically, from regarding our finite condition as a barrier against which we scream defiantly to regarding it in terms of a harness rubbing our skin. What we have to do, in any case, so Barth says, is to move from a sense of our limitedness as threat and restriction, to perceiving it as 'a mighty, beneficent promise'.[5] The screaming and protesting have to give way to praise and thanksgiving, Loben und Danken.

Much of the rhetoric in Church Dogmatics is dedicated to converting us from feeling chafed by our human condition to celebrating our finitude.

## From the Cartesian self to Christ's humanity

The move that Barth always makes is well known: everything has to be referred back to the case of Jesus Christ, truly divine and truly human. The only satisfactory access to understanding human nature, and so of understanding how we might transcend our finite condition, lies through Christology. Human nature, although corrupted by sin, is neither destroyed nor transmuted into something different – Barth is as fearful as Nussbaum of any transcendence of our humanity which deprives us of our nature.[6]

There is no call to ignore non-theological and pre-theological understandings of what it is to be human – they have a certain access, indeed Barth will discuss them at length – but his characteristic move is always to take our bearings from the paradigm case of the man Jesus.

'Dieser Mensch ist der Mensch'.[7] This human being is the human being par excellence, we may say. The properly human, 'the true nature behind our corrupted nature', is revealed in the human being named Jesus of Nazareth, and 'in his nature we recognize our own, and that of every man'. This does not mean that we can deduce

24

Christian anthropology from Christology in any simple and straightforward way. On the contrary, it is an exegetical task of some delicacy, necessarily guided (Barth would think) by wider theological considerations. But what we find in Jesus as portrayed in the gospels is human nature as created by God, thus 'without the self-contradiction which afflicts us and without the self-deception by which we seek to escape from this our shame'.[8] In the case of Jesus, in effect, we are enabled to see 'human nature without human sin'.

None of this need have been the case. Early in *Church Dogmatics* Barth notes that 'recollection of God's enacted revelation' might have been equated with 'the actualisation of a revelation of God originally immanent in the existence of every man'[9]– the actualization, then, of 'man's own original awareness of God'. Thus, calling to mind God's enacted self-revelation would have been 'the discovery and fresh appropriation of a long hidden, forgotten and unused part, and indeed the most central and significant part, of the timeless essential constitution of man himself' – of our 'relation to the eternal or absolute'. Indeed, following Plato's doctrine of *anamnesis*, Barth goes on to maintain, Augustine ('the greatest Catholic theologian') understood *memoria* along such lines: knowledge of God for Christians would only confirm what human beings have known all along about God.[10] Recollection means inwardness, *Verinnerlichung* – 'man's return from the distractions of the outside world and reentry into himself to find God there'. God could indeed have been immanent as 'the foundation which was hidden for a time, but which steadily endured because it had been timelessly laid, so that standing on it need be only a matter of profound self-reflection'. But in fact, historically, 'it has pleased God to be [the Church's] God in another way than that of pure immanence'. The Church has to return to its own being, on the basis of which alone it may actually venture to preach – but the Church's own being is Jesus Christ himself: 'immanent in it only as he is transcendent to it'. The recollection of God's past revelation is, then, something totally different from reflection on the Church's own timeless ground of being – let alone on some reality immanent in ourselves.

But it is not easy for us, Barth thinks, to take the humanity of Christ seriously. He launches into an attack on whatever docetic inclinations we might have. If it is in the light of his resurrection from the dead that the New Testament witnesses look to Jesus as the one who will come again from the heaven where he is seated at

25

the right hand of the Father (as Barth assumes), they are (he insists) no less certain of his real humanity.[11] 'They seem never to have thought of a human being beyond history or prior to history, or hidden from and transcending history, when they thought of the real man Jesus'. Neither in his case nor *a fortiori* in ours, so the implication runs, is there any human nature which would be extra-historical – existing before its history, concealed behind its history or outlasting its history. Such a being is a phantom – although Barth clearly thinks that some Christians at some time might feel the charm of such a fantasy! But no Christian of the apostolic age ever doubted, Barth assures us, that Jesus was a real man and hence always to be identified with his history, his particularity, his finitude, his being in time.

On the other hand, Jesus was not exactly like other human beings. He was indeed soul and body like us.[12] He had a network of relationships with others.[13] Like all human beings, he had his time.[14] But, in accordance with the characteristically Barthian move, we are invited to think, not of how Jesus fitted into the conditions of our life and time, as we are readily inclined to do, but rather of how we are affected by having to share his life and time.

Jesus is the one in whose human nature we are all partakers. He participated in our history under specific conditions; but, instead of his having to share humanity – *our* humanity – with all the problems that traditionally arise about squeezing him into the limitations of our form of life (kenotic Christology and what all), it is rather that we human beings have to learn to understand ourselves as being allowed to partake in *his* humanity. Far from having to think of Jesus as conditioned and limited by specific determinants and characteristics of humanity as we are familiar with it, then, we have to remember rather that, in so far as humanity belongs to Jesus, it is he who 'limits and conditions these features and determinations'.[15] Our existence with its possibilities is to be explained in the light of his existence, not vice versa. Human nature with all its possibilities is not something presupposed to his humanity, as if it then just happened to apply in his case too. On the contrary, his being as a human being is what establishes and thus reveals human nature in all its possibilities in the first place.

If we were to ascribe a radical difference in constitution to human nature as it exists in us and as it exists in Jesus, we should be yielding either to Manichean or Marcionite tendencies or (much more likely in Barth's view! ) to that doceticism 'which the Church has failed to eliminate in spite of its formal rejection'.[16] In the end of the day, in Barth's judgement, resentment against our human finitude is inseparable from docetic temptations. Misconceptions in philosophical anthropology are interwoven with unsatisfactory and even heretical theology.

## Philosophies of self-transcendence

Barth's first move is to trace the history of various non-Christo-logically-centred versions of human transcendence. The traditional theological anthropology, which starts from the Aristotelian rational animal, produces a phantom, *ein Gespenst*.[17] There has never been any human being who has not been embedded in a history rooted in and shaped by God's attitude to him. Being related to God is not something fortuitous, contingent, supplementary and temporary. On the contrary, it is a necessary and constant constitutive determination of any man's being at all. For Barth, there could not be a truly godless human being.[18]

Moving into modern philosophy, Barth takes Fichte's book *Die Bestimmung des Menschen* (1800) as his text – partly, no doubt, because it has to do with 'the definition of man', but mainly because it deals first with the doubt allegedly felt by the human 'I' about its own reality in face of the external world, then with the claim that it is the 'I' itself which is, to the extent that it knows, the reality of the external world, and finally with believing, as the action in which the 'I' establishes and affirms itself as this one and only reality.

This brings us directly to the problem of limitation.[19] Fichte's doctrine of man as an absolutely autarchic self-standing subject rising above the merely natural order, springs (Barth argues) precisely from the lack of any limit (*Grenze*), the lack of any counterpart (*Gegenüber*). From the outset, Fichte was 'resolved to understand man in isolation, as a being who is not confronted by any outward reality which might call him in question, from which he must receive instruction, by which man is controlled, and at the disposal of which he must place himself'. Fichte's man, being free of all such constraints, is expandable in all directions. From the beginning, Barth says mockingly, Fichte's individual is 'the one and all'. Indeed, the only thing Fichte's man lacks, in *Die Bestimmung des Menschen*, is (ironically) *Bestimmung*, determinacy – 'er hat keine Grenze' (he has no limit').[20] Fichte's man can have no 'definition' precisely because he has no outside and thus no limit.

Fichte's man is supposedly self-determining. But how can the self be defined without the presence of some other? How can there be self-determination by a being for whom all determining from outside is excluded? How can there be a law, a command, duty, obligation, and so on, to which Fichte's man is supposed to conform, in the fulfilment of which he is supposed to proceed to action, and hence to constitute the world and himself together? Fichte's man has everything, but his creator has denied him the one thing which is a determining limit, the law, the source of the necessity and force for his action. 'From the very first he has total lack of the other in relation to which he himself can be.'

By excluding God in advance, methodologically, Fichte was left with nothing but another phantom: man as absolutely subjective with no other to limit him.[21] How can a human being exist without an other?

Thus Barth begins to work out a positive concept of what it is to be a being within limits.

Drawing next on Karl Jaspers, Barth examines existentialism, or what he identifies as Jaspers' doctrine of 'frontier situations'.[22] Instead of man as a 'self-contained and rounded reality' (as in Fichte) we now place emphasis on 'frontier situations', *Grenzsituationen* – 'the experience of [man's] disruption, and therefore the experience of his openness, his actual relatedness to this transcendent other, and therefore the experience of his real existence'.[23] This is of course much more promising. Jaspers's 'anthropology of the frontier', *dieser Anthropologie der Grenze*, as Barth calls it, comes near to a genuinely Christian understanding of human nature, as for example in Luther's account of election, vocation and temptation.[24] Above all, the situatedness of human beings in history, and their relatedness to each other emerge, in Jaspers's existentialism, albeit in privileged dramatic episodes.

Finally, reflecting on Emil Brunner, Barth concludes that, acceptable as much of what he says may be, he does not need the self-revealing God as the other. He places the emphasis on freedom of choice rather than on freedom of obedience, and thus fails to do justice to the priority of our relatedness over our autonomy.[25]

None of this will do. Traditional theology overlooks the way that human beings are rational creatures immersed in history. With Fichte we have the solipsism that is generated by excluding finitude. With Jaspers we have rediscovered the indispensability of 'frontier situations'. With Brunner we have discovered the historical dimension of human life. But none of these versions

of finitude answers the question of 'real man', *der wirkliche Mensch.*
These are all abstractions, with the focus on generic humanity. We
miss 'the one Archimedean point given us beyond humanity'[26] –
the only starting point for 'the ontological determination of man' –
which is, of course, 'the fact that one man among all others is the
man Jesus'.

## Real time

Barth's conception of time and the temporal conditions of human
life is there from very early in *Church Dogmatics.* It is part of his
tireless polemic against all forms (as he thinks) of doceticism. In his
eyes, at least, he is making a theological and indeed doctrinal point.
But he is also engaged in polemic against 'theologians with
Cartesian inclinations'.[27] Often implicitly, and sometimes explicitly, in debate with Augustine, Barth is striving to resist the
constant temptation towards a Platonic dissolution of time into
eternity. Over against that, what the doctrine of the incarnation
means is that God comes to us in time – fair enough, no one would
dispute that – but the Barthian thought is, as he puts it, that the
time of God for us is our only true time.[28] We have to let ourselves
be told what the concept of time means by attending to the data of
New Testament revelation itself.

This is always the Barthian move: reflection on the story of Jesus
Christ alone will teach us how to understand what it is for human
beings to be in time.

Barth begins his reflections with a couple of pages on Augustine
and Heidegger.[29] The conception of time which Barth is going to
develop originated, or at any rate became clearer, in his rejection of
the concept of time that he finds shared by Augustine and
Heidegger. Essentially, as Barth sees it, they both regard time as
a self-determination of man's existence as a creature. Human beings
have time by creating it, in effect. That our time may be the time
which God has for us, which God gives us, is quite an alien idea
both for Augustine and for Heidegger, so Barth holds.

Of course God and his revelation are not provided for in
Heidegger's system – time is just brought to a head in a preliminary
resolve by a future indistinguishable from existence – man himself.
But Augustine's idea of time is not a whit different from Heidegger's,
Barth holds. True, Augustine elsewhere speaks of God as *creator et
ordinator temporum;*[30] but in the 'great passage on time' in the

*Confessions* he never says that – on the contrary: past, present, and future are in the soul and nowhere else (*et alibi ea non video*).[31]

For Augustine, as for Heidegger, time originates in the act of the human spirit, and it never occurs to Augustine, so Barth says, that there might be difficulties about this notion of time. Time is just a *distentio* of my soul. It would be an intolerable anthropomorphism to attribute time to God on Augustine's view. But if we are to understand how God has time for us, in Barth's radically Christological perspective, then time cannot be understood merely as the product of human existence – time must be regarded as a proper reality, as accessible to God as is human existence.[32]

There are three times, Barth suggests: created time; fallen time, which is our present time; and revelation time, redeemed time, real time constituted by God's coming to us and to our time.[33] The time we think we know, and that with Augustine we have traditionally supposed to be our time, is by no means time as God created it. On the contrary, our time is 'lost' time, the time possessed by fallen creatures. God-created time has been 'lost' – if God has time for us now, in the time of the incarnation, then it must be a different time, a third time, created alongside of our time and the time originally created by God. This 'revelation time' is the time of the Lord of time and it is 'fulfilled time'. The time God has for us in the revelation which is the lifetime of the man Jesus Christ, a stretch of what we call historical time (and it is that, however much more it may be – it is not some sort of ideal but timeless content – 'It does not remain transcendent over time, it does not merely meet it at a point, but it enters time; nay, it assumes time; nay, it creates time for itself'), is the only 'real time'.[34]

In this revelation time we too have a present, a past, and a future as contemporaries of Jesus. The time of the incarnation as fulfilled time means that time is mastered; that all other time is exposed as resisting God's time; and that new time breaks into the old. To say that time is mastered is to say that there is no not yet or no longer – there is now only *eternal present*. The Word spoken from eternity raises the time into which it is uttered (without dissolving it as time) up into his own eternity as now his own time, giving it part in the existence of God, which is alone real, self-moved, self-dependent, self-sufficient. This new time – the time of God – is real time. It takes our 'fallen' time away from us, although, since this is as yet only intimated and not completed, our time remains until the fullness of redemption. The time God creates for himself in the incarnation – the genuine present, past and future – becomes our time. We become contemporary with this time of God's. His time 'replaces' the problematic improper time we know and have. It is only when we are transposed from our own fallen time into contemporaneousness with Christ as mediated by the witness of the prophets and apostles that we really have time.[35] We do not need any philosophical scepticism, any discovery of aporias in the concept of time, to know that we do not know what we mean by the word 'time'. Time as we think we know and have it is indeed merely an appearance. For Barth, it has taken divine revelation to unmask this semblance of time – to unveil it as an untruth. In that sense revelation takes our time away from us. Our time, this puzzling feature of our lives which we always merely suppose we know and possess, is limited and determined by revelation time.

## The Forty Days of Easter

The story of Easter is, for Barth, 'the Archimedean point'.[36] We have once again to get back to Jesus. To prepare ourselves to investigate our being in time we have to investigate the being of the man Jesus in his time. This means starting with the revelation of the being of the man Jesus in his resurrection from the dead. The absolutely decisive event on which Barth takes his stand, and from which he takes his bearings, is the bodily resurrection of Jesus Christ from the dead. In the time between the first Easter Sunday and the ascension, Jesus revealed himself as Lord of time.

This brings us to the amazing pages on the forty days from the resurrection to the ascension of Christ – the paradigm of our temporality[37]– by any standards one of the most remarkable disquisitions in modern theology.

We certainly have to remember that, like every human being, the man Jesus has his lifetime – a time bounded by birth and death, a fixed span. He is a man of his time. (We must resist all temptations to doceticism.) But the history of the man Jesus cannot be narrated except by keeping something else in mind, something further, which again is narrated as history (*Geschichte*). At the very point where the history of any other human being would stop unconditionally, he has a further history, beginning on the third day after his death.[38] Thus, after the plain conclusion of his first history, there is a second history – 'the fragments of a second history' – the Easter history – (*die Ostergeschichte*) – the story of the forty days between Jesus's resurrection and ascension.[39]

31

> That which was from the beginning, which we have heard, which we have seen with our eyes, which we have looked upon and touched with our hands, concerning the word of life – the life was made manifest, and we saw it, and testify to it, and proclaim to you the eternal life which was with the Father and was made manifest to us.[40]

Barth takes this passage absolutely literally. When the New Testament speaks of the Easter event, it means the Easter history, the Easter time. With these forty days we are just as much in history and time as we are with the accounts of Jesus's words and deeds – of his death. The Easter event is the prism through which the original community saw the man Jesus in his relationship to themselves – but this prism is no timeless idea – it actually happened. What created and shaped their faith and preaching was the memory of his being with them during these forty days. It was the particular memory of a particular time filled with particular history that constrained their conception henceforward of time. He was with them, in this time, beyond the time of his earthly life between his birth and death, in this *Offenbarungszeit* (revelation time). 'This is what really took place.'[41] The man Jesus, resurrected from the dead, came and went among the disciples, ate and drank with them, and so on – 'the man Jesus was manifested among them in the mode of God'.[42]

During these forty days the disciples came to see that Jesus had always been present among them in his deity, although hitherto veiled – now they actually beheld his glory. He was the concrete demonstration of the God who not only himself has a different time from ours but who wills to give us a share in his time – in his eternity.[43] The present time, with its limitation, is already illuminated, relativized, for now *all* time is *God's* time. That is: 'All other times have been placed in proximity to this time,' which 'means that even in them there may be discerned traces of this eternal time, of the true and proper time in which they necessarily have a share because, even though at a different level, they too are real times.'[44]

It would be docetic to deny that the risen Lord Jesus' being in time means what being in time means for us all[45] – but the time of Jesus is also the time of God. That means that the limitations, of the times of all other living creatures do not apply in his case.[46]

Of course the life of the man Jesus had a beginning, his time was once future – but that does not mean that it did not already exist. Of course the life of Jesus had a certain duration but that does not mean that it lasted just as long as the life of his exact contemporaries. Of course the life of Jesus ended – but that does not mean that it was no more. The distinctive thing about the time of the man Jesus is the removal of the limitations of its yesterday, today and tomorrow.[47] In Easter time God's time was revealed – eternal time.

## Against demythologization

For Barth, the Forty Days are presented in Scripture as the time during which the risen Lord Jesus was among the apostles. In an important excursus he defends the historicity of the Easter event, this Easter time, against Bultmann's demythologizing programme.[48] The importance of these Forty Days Barth then spells out. Jesus obviously moved among the disciples as true man; no less obviously he appeared in this time in the mode of God; it was this unveiled manifestation of his divinity that generated the Easter faith of the apostles, so that they had to call him Lord; in his real and physical resurrection from the dead Jesus thus manifested his eternal glory.[49]

True enough, Barth concedes, the resurrection narratives do not belong to the same genre as modern historical writing. Yet they are firmly committed to the historical reality of the appearances, the empty tomb and the ascension which marks the limits of the Easter happening.[50] Finally, for Barth, the Easter time reveals the mystery of the preceding time of the man Jesus, revealing it to be a time when God was man – showing it to be 'eternal time'.[51]

## Our allotted span

Turning from Jesus and his time to us and our time, Barth first views our time as *given*,[52] in pages that repay study, but it is when he gets on to our time as being *allotted*, as well, that what he says becomes most relevant to this exploration.

It is by no means evident in advance of reflection that human life requires an allotted span.[53] On the contrary, human life – to develop – seems to require duration, permanency. We resist the thought that one day it will cease. We protest against the barrier set by the allotting of time. Barth, however, is out to persuade us that, far from resenting it, we should welcome the allotment of our time with gratitude and joy. But we need first to listen to the protest, so he insists. Indeed it would simply be part of the disorder occasioned by the Fall if we were *not* to acknowledge these longings for duration – if we were *not* to feel the allotment of time as a threat – if we were just to resign ourselves to being allotted our time.

We should be troubled by the demand in ourselves for duration. We are not talking of an abstract craving for life. Rather, we are 'beating angrily against the barrier set up by the fact that [our] time is allotted'.[54] 'Man as he really is, as God created him, stands questioning before these frowning walls of rock which enclose him in the narrow gorge of being, and seem to fling at him the twofold taunt: Once you were not! and: One day you will be no more!'.[55] We simply cannot give up the desire that we should endure for ever and burst the limits of our temporality. Nor may we just shrug our shoulders – our discontent resides in our having been promised life with God, as gift and task.[56]

Would this demand for limitless duration, this irrepressible desire for perfection, be best served if we had infinite time at our disposal? Assuming that we are content to be creaturely and not to be God, assuming that we have no desire to leap over that boundary, a desire we could not have if we were really divine – if there is to be no allotted time then we have to have infinite time. So Barth's argument goes.

We should be worse off in an unrestricted life: 'Could there be any better picture of life in hell than enduring life in enduring time?'.[57] Once again we have to free the concept of limitation – now, of allotted time – from the character of a restriction and a threat. We have to break free of the picture of the narrow gorge and its enclosing walls. Where there was threat, repression, there has to be promise. Instead of being a threat, our span of days turns out to be the condition for God's being our neighbour and our being his: the rock walls have to become the protecting walls of a living room or workshop.[58]

How does this happen? How does Barth suggest that we overcome our prejudice against being finite? What we have to understand is that our lives are not abstractly limited – they are limited by God. The longing for an unlimited life in unallotted time begins to wither, so Barth maintains, once we realize that the limit and set span of our existence is the condition for the eternal God to be our counterpart and our neighbour. A being in unending time would be centrifugal. 'Limit in the creaturely dimension means a clear-cut outline and contour'.[59] I should not be *this* man, here and now, the concrete subject of *this* history, if my life did not have *this* outline and contour – if it did not have *these* limits and boundaries.

A being in unending time would be – like Fichte's self –

something other than a particular individual being to whom God can be an equally particular and concrete counterpart and neighbour, and with whom God can enjoy communication and intercourse. We are defined, delimited – but by God and for God, as those whom God encounters in *this* time with *this* particularity.[60]

Having an allotted span is a benefit. God cares for us by giving us an allotted span instead of unending time, Barth argues, for in so doing he sees to it that between him and us there can be a relationship: a singular unrepeatable unique bond. Thus it is wrong to rebel against this limitation, or merely to resign ourselves angrily or anxiously to its inevitability.[61] We should not exist in the first place unless we were *situated*. Gratitude is the only appropriate response to our having our allotted span.

The life of the man Jesus was a limited life in a restricted time.[62] Yet that life, with all its limitations, was the life of the eternal Son and Word of God. Once we reflect on that, Barth thinks, it becomes impossible to regard human nature in the light of the existence of this man Jesus without realizing that it is good for us to have a limited life in a restricted time – because there and then the grace of God is near and clear to us. But we cannot realize this except as we regard human nature in the light of the existence of this man Jesus – here again a certain conception of human life and its possibilities results from Christological considerations.

## Death as the wages of sin

The most negative thought we can have about finitude, at least in a Christian theological context, is that death is the wages of sin. Traditionally, Christians have believed that human beings were naturally immortal, and that mortality is the punishment of God imposed upon us as a result of the sin of our first parents. Since the introduction of the evolutionary perspective, in the nineteenth century, and perhaps particularly with the discovery of the laws of thermodynamics more recently, it has come to seem implausible that human beings were created never to die. Barth seeks to do justice to the traditional doctrine while opening the way to a view of death as the natural end of human life but again, of course, on Christological, not Darwinian or scientific grounds.

Is Barth here agreeing tacitly with Schleiermacher? Over against the traditional Catholic and Reformed view of death as 'the wages of sin' (Paul and Augustine), he was the first to break the connection between sin and death, arguing that in itself death is neither an evil nor a divine punishment but simply the temporal end of finite human beings.[63] Death would be regarded as evil and feared as a punishment only by those whose sense of God is disturbed by consciousness of sin. Those who have an awareness of God by divine grace would not fear death as punishment but regard it as a natural end.

Barth seems to have done his best to rework Schleiermacher's view but grounding it on Christology. Jesus died for sinners, he was himself 'without sin'. If sinners were the only mortals, then the man Jesus, being sinless, would have had to be immortal. He died a vicarious death for sinners but in itself it was the death of a sinless human being. In his case, at least, the connection between sin and death was broken. It must have been his own natural death. Finite human nature as such, exempt from sin, is thus always already mortal. In the New Testament death stands wholly under the sign of the divine judgement of sinful man fulfilled in it – but even more so under the sign of the setting aside of this judgement and thus the defeat of death.[64]

Barth now takes up the difficult question as to how far the finitude of our allotted time, and death as the end of our time, are a determination of the divinely created (and therefore good) nature of man. We rightly fear death, he maintains, seeing it as a sign of divine judgement.[65] Nevertheless, at the end of our allotted span, God awaits us as well as death – which might seem even more terrifying. But the Lord of death is the gracious God, who is for us even when we are against him, so that to fear him is to have the comfort of knowing that even when we die he will be for us.[66]

All this becomes concrete in Jesus Christ. In him God is the boundary of the death that binds us because he put death behind us when he bore our death in his. Even in and beyond death we may expect everything from him – our hope, victory, future, resurrection and life.[67]

Barth draws three simple conclusions. (1) The death of the sinner coincides with judgement – but in Jesus Christ even judgement is a freely accepted end. Then (2), because of the vicarious death of Jesus Christ the end of life no longer coincides with judgement – although it still serves as its sign. Thus (3), since death has been robbed of its sting by the death and resurrection of Jesus Christ we may still fear it as the sign of judgement but we need not fear it as real judgement. We cannot have been created to be sinners or in order to suffer God's condemnation. So if death is met as the sign of divine judgement on sinful man it cannot be a

36

divinely willed and created determination natural to our being – it must be an alien intrusion. Thus, we can see death again as the good and natural end of human life – human life which has a true beyond in God, in whom our being in time will be manifested in its glory and as eternal life in God.[68]

Finitude as such is not evil. In itself it is not unnatural but natural for human life to run its course towards this limit which is death. 'Man has no beyond' – we need no beyond. God is our beyond – already and always our covenant partner.[69] One day we shall have been, as once we did not yet exist. But the promise and hope is not liberation from this-sidedness, but glorification by God of our natural and lawful this-sided finite and mortal being.[70] It is not that our being in our time will be forgotten, extinguished, left behind, to be replaced by some new other-sided infinite and immortal being after our time. We are not redeemed from finitude; but as this being in the totality of my this-sided existence, above and beyond which there is no other, I am already claimed by and belong to the God who is my only beyond.[71]

## Finitude as freedom

The limitation which comes from God, far from being negative, has to be seen as radically positive – 'Limitation as divine decree means circumscription, definition, and therefore determination'.[72] It is characteristic of the void to be undetermined, and therefore unlimited. In differentiating creatures from himself, God of course limits them to be only his creatures; but in so doing he gives them precisely their specific genuine reality. In differentiating human beings from other creatures he limits them to be only human beings – and thus distinguishes them from all other creatures. In differentiating *this* human being from all others, God limits him or her, in relation to all others, to be only *this* particular human being. In so doing, he treats him or her as a soul, as a subject, as this unique and irreplaceable particular individual, as an 'I' to be addressed as 'Thou'.

By creating this particular human being with this or that uniqueness, singularity, and leading him or her to this hour in this or that way, God has of course once again limited him or her with regard to all the other possibilities necessarily passed over or left unfulfilled. In his life so far a man has had to be only this or that – but that is precisely how he finds himself fully affirmed and taken completely seriously by God.

What does the little word 'only' mean here? (it occurs twice as often in the original as in the translation), Barth asks himself. The regret, with which it seems to resonate, is certainly not appropriate here, he insists. On the contrary: 'When God wills and works "only" this or that, it means "precisely" this or that' – not 'only' but 'exactly'. When God differentiates, specifies and particularizes, and thus limits, there is no place for talk of curtailment or impoverishment, let alone of deprivation, of the being thus limited. On the contrary – God's limiting is precisely his wonderful giving: 'Precisely his limiting is his definite, concrete and specific affirmation.' In one of his characteristically pithy aphorisms, at the end of a lengthy disquisition, Barth says: 'The man who is *limited* by him is the man who is *loved* by him.'[73]

Instead of merely enduring our limitation with a sigh, we should take it seriously, affirm it, welcome it, praise God for it, that we are what we are precisely in our limitation by him – 'this and not something else'. In a properly theological perspective, that is to say, we are set free to celebrate our limitedness. We are no longer compelled to deplore and resent it. The sense of restriction built into the notion of 'only' gives way to the celebration of the uniqueness and particularity picked out by the adverb 'precisely'.

The whole discussion is designed to persuade us to understand our being human as a once-for-all 'occasion' – to be celebrated, rather than regarded as a restriction. In the first place, our relationship as creatures to God as creator rests on God's command calling us to obedience – an act and revelation of God's inscrutably free grace and power, but also an act and revelation of his wisdom and righteousness. It is not, then, Barth insists, an arbitrary act, as we might (he apparently thinks) be tempted to think – but, rather, 'a well-aimed arrow which hits its target'. Between the God who speaks and us who hear there is, however, a certain correlation, in which God makes his command recognizable as his command and in which it becomes recognizable by us as his command. It is never just the expression of some despot's mere will, which has to be accepted and respected (as again we might apparently be tempted to think). On the contrary, it is the expression of the will of the one who, as creator, has taken responsibility for the nature and existence of his creatures. On our side, we can and should count on it that the expression of that sovereign's will is in keeping with what we ourselves are – 'When God speaks to man in his command, he does not speak to one who is completely strange to him.' Whatever commentators have sometimes maintained about Barth's conception of the gulf between the creator and us creatures, he is clear that we are not *'von Haus aus fremd'* ('originally alien' or 'naturally foreign') to God – to the contrary, even our transgression can never alter the fact that God is our creator. Nor do we hear God's command as 'a completely alien demand'. Instead, the relationship within which God's command is spoken and heard is a relationship of mutual knowledge. The man with whom God has to do is not the weaker partner who has to accommodate himself to the alien power – on the contrary, we are already God's creation, handiwork, possession. God, with his demand for obedience, is not overwhelming, trampling down, driving us to the wall, as if the man upon whom this claim is made were to be pitied. Nor on the other hand is God in any way limited and determined by any counter-claim from our side. It is simply that we human beings already belong to God – we are 'predisposed and orientated by God as [our] creator and Lord to accept his command and to become obedient to it'.[74]

Putting it in ontological terms (and we may do so – *must* do so, Barth says – for this reciprocal knowledge is a real knowledge), we may say that the relationship between the God who commands and the human being who is called to obey is one of mutual co-ordination. Of course, lest we might be tempted to think that Barth is enunciating some general metaphysical truth, he hastens to stress that this is not something of which one can have a priori knowledge.[75] It is just that when God speaks and human beings hear, there is revealed, in and with the divine command that is laid on us, 'this objective co-ordination':

> Precisely in that which God wills of him and for which he has determined him, man finds himself exposed, understood and addressed in his innermost nature and being, and therefore not as an empty page upon which something has now to be written, not as a mere string upon which a note has to be sounded, but as a being which from the very first and as such, on the basis of the divine will and disposing, corresponds to this determination and is to fulfil it in freedom as summoned to obedience to the command of God.[76]

We have to recognize our own nature and existence in our correspondence to the divine will. We recognize that we are indebted for our being neither to ourselves nor to anything else but to God alone. We can no longer withdraw from the divine command by appealing to our own nature. On the contrary, we have to recognize ourselves and our own nature and existence as *Hinweis auf Gottes Gebot* (orientation or referral to God's command). We find ourselves called to bear witness to this command and to do so against our own disobedience. We find ourselves called to be living proof of the impossibility of such disobedience. We cannot but recognize that God's command addresses us.

Thus we best understand our relationship to God, as God's commanding and our recognizing his command, in terms of limitation – God's limiting and our being limited.

The only freedom there is for human beings lies precisely in our finitude.

## The sin against finitude

From the standpoint of our temporality, Barth tells us, *Sorge* (care) is *the* human sin.[77] Surprisingly, perhaps, the word 'care' has negative connotations in Barth's work. Once we have understood, by reflection on the divine mandate given in the resurrection of Jesus, who we really are, then we find ourselves reluctant to make use of our freedom, almost incorrigibly preferring to submit totally and from the bottom up to the power of our own stupidity, inhumanity, depravity and care.

The whole human situation has been transformed by the revelation of the resurrection of Jesus. We simply live in a wholly different world, now that Christ is raised from the dead and seated at the right hand of the Father. Whether we see it, like it or want it, we are already moved from the place where we should contentedly have remained at home if there had been no revelation of Jesus' resurrection. Because Jesus lives, we are no longer bound to our lowly condition, there is now no absolute impossibility of our being drawn into communion of life with God, we are no longer imprisoned, no longer unfree to let ourselves be exalted. We hear the words '*Sursum corda!*' –lift up your hearts! There is no human being (whatever he or she believes about all this, or about anything else) who does not live under the sign of this great '*Sursum!*'. Something has *happened*. Jesus is no isolated individual (*Privatperson*); on the contrary, as the firstborn and the head he is our brother and there is nothing anyone can do to escape being in this solidarity with him.[78]

In Jesus risen from the dead we are confronted with a human being who is with and for God as God is with him, at peace with God and therefore with others and himself. We are confronted with a human being in whom our nature is exalted to its truth, and completely fulfilled. In the light of the liberating presence of the risen Lord Jesus we are impelled towards – liberated for – an uncompromisingly sober assessment of the human situation.[79]

From the standpoint of the new possibility open to human beings since the revelation of the resurrection of Jesus, Barth maintains, the best description of sin – of all that holds us back from participating in the new life – is *Trägheit* (sloth). Barth spells this out as sluggishness, indolence, slowness, inertia. What is meant is a certain kind of inaction.

When Barth considered the doctrine of reconciliation from the standpoint of the Lord who humbled himself, he followed up with a study of sin as pride, thus in its Promethean form.[80] Now, having considered Jesus as the one who has been exalted, Barth wants to look at sin as resistance to the exaltation which has been opened as a gift from God in Jesus Christ.

In Protestantism, and perhaps in Western Christianity generally, Barth thinks, we are inclined to focus on Prometheus, Lucifer, the sinner as rebel and insurrectionary. But sin is not merely 'heroic in its perversion'; it is also 'ordinary, trivial and mediocre'. Sin is not always or even often very dramatic; on the contrary, it is mostly very mean and petty. As Barth says, the sinner is also 'a lazy-bones, a sluggard, a good-for-nothing, a slow-coach and a loafer'.[81] (The slow-coach appears in the translation.) With his characteristic habit of turning the conventional view upside down, Barth insists that inertly drifting is (if anything) a worse sin than shameless self-assertiveness.

The main point is that, in this sin of *Trägheit*,[82] we want, in various ways, simply to be left alone. We regard the renewal of human nature declared in the existence of Jesus as quite unnecessary. No doubt we see the limitation and imperfection of our present nature, but we are not so deeply affected by this that we cannot settle for it.[83] We know, or think we know, what is attainable within the limits of humanity. The limitedness with which we are content seems immutable and necessary; its transcendence in the man Jesus' freedom seems a work of fantasy, in which we wish to have no part.

Barth specifies four aspects to this life-endangering refusal of the freedom offered us in the man Jesus – a refusal in our relationship with God, with our fellow human beings, with our creaturely structure, and (the one that concerns us) with our timely historical limitedness.

41

Our allotted span becomes unendurable to us.[84] The revolt against this limitedness must be regarded as an irreducible form of human *Trägheit*. We find it hard to reconcile ourselves to the fact that all things, including ourselves, have their time and are thus limited. We resent death as the determination of human existence in virtue of which we are finite. The aim of our every desire is infinity. There is this unappeasable desire, which 'opens up magic casements with unlimited views which give us the thrill either of solemnity or of an arrogant rejoicing'.[85] At the heart of this thrill there is 'a terrible, irrepressible and irresistible longing in face of the infinity ... a thrill of horror at the actuality which consists in the fact that we are limited and not unlimited'. '*Carpe diem*', we may say; but this is just an expression of the panic in which we live. We are always too late, even in youth, certainly in 'dangerous middle-age'. For the dissipated man, who has broken loose from the unity and totality of soul and body in which God has created him for existence in the limit of his time, there cannot be anything but this fear of his own limitation and this attempt to escape it.

Finally, according to Barth here, our dissipation as well as our stupidity and inhumanity (all forms of *Trägheit*) are traceable to *Sorge*, care.[86] Indeed, 'the root of all evil is simply and powerfully human care'. All evil, Barth now declares, begins with our being unwilling thankfully to accept the limitedness of our existence. We fret at the inevitable realization that our existence is limited. All this fretting is empty, futile, not because of the inexorable fate that awaits us – it is right to struggle against nature – no: care is futile because 'our perishing, the terminating of our existence ... is the good order of God, one of the tokens of his gracious and merciful and invincible will as creator'. Barth speaks of 'the evil of [our] fear of this frontier, which is the good order of God'.[87]

## Christological ontology

Karl Barth offers us an extremely ingenious way of dealing with the aspiration to transcend our human condition which he takes to be natural to us. There is a way of transcending our existing humanity and it is the way of finding our humanity. It is not escaping or denying or disowning our humanity – just the opposite. The only truly human being there has ever been is the human being Jesus Christ, now raised from the dead and at the right hand of God the Father. It is possible for us to come to ourselves, to find our humanity, to receive our humanity as a gift, finding ourselves in our

42

absolutely unique particularity, freed into our finitude as creatures –
as creatures of the God who takes us in our singularity into the
plenitude of divine life, where we are not dissolved or evaporated or
fused, either into one another or into the sacred, but on the
contrary we are each preserved in our uniqueness.

Certainly, for Barth, we human beings deeply resent our finite
history-bound condition. But we should not, and need not, revolt
against our limitedness. More or less explicitly, Barth seeks, against
the temptations of Platonist-Cartesian ontologies of the self, to
reorientate our understanding of reality on the historical singularity
of the man Jesus Christ, risen from the dead. Against Fichte's
fantasy of the unbounded ego and Jaspers' anthropology of frontier
situations, Barth begins to work out his conception of human
boundedness. His ingenious proposal is simply to deny the traditional opposition between time and eternity.

If we redefine history as the event of differentiation we can say
that the inner life of the eternal God (as Trinity) is the only 'real
time'.[88] This 'real time' is precisely what has been revealed to those
with the eyes of Christian faith in the Forty Days during which the
resurrected Jesus moved among his original followers.

Far from resenting our finitude, then, we should celebrate our
allotted span: to that we owe our unique and singular identity. Even
death, traditionally regarded by Christians as punishment for the
sinfulness of supposedly originally immortal beings, turns out to be
natural. The only freedom for human beings lies in our finitude –
although, with Prometheanism on the one hand and sloth on the
other, sinfulness is indeed best regarded as resentment against our
limitedness.

All of this takes us well beyond anything that might count as the
philosophy of religion. But philosophy comes into it. Barth brings
great and deep knowledge of the history of philosophy to bear
throughout the *Church Dogmatics*. Yet philosophical approaches to
understanding what it is to be human will always prove inadequate
and wildly misleading, so he would think. Philosophical anthropologies never go far enough for Barth, as the theologian of the
humanity of God. We always have to go back to divine revelation.
God alone has taught us what it is to be a human being. The divine
Self-revelation in the particular history narrated in the New
Testament offers the only starting point for understanding what
it really is to be human. It is never a matter of proceeding step by
step through philosophical analyses trying to build up some
plausible discourse about ourselves and about the world which

might then open up towards the discourse of Christian faith. On the contrary, our understanding of the world has to come – can only come – from reflection on the history of Christian revelation. There is no need for us to try to work our way closer and closer to God, intellectually or in any other way – God has never been away from us in the first place.

What Barth offers, then, is a Christocentric anthropology – a theanthropology – an ontology of humanity, and thus of finitude, transcendence, and temporality, which is prompted, built up, at every step, by study of the narrated identity of the one human being at the centre of the gospels.

That goes for our nature as historical beings also. Indeed it is not we who are historical and God who adapts to our historical condition – on the contrary. 'The history of any being starts, is carried on, and is completed when something other than it ... encounters it ... and determines its being appropriately to this other, so that it is compelled and enabled to transcend itself in response.'[89] On that definition, history is self-transcendence – self-transcendence is always and already history. God's internal and eternal self-differentiation in the Trinity is the only real time – which has been revealed in the events of Easter to those who have been given eyes to see. Far from there being some gap to be bridged between time and eternity, the only real time is always already eternity, and the eternal life within the triune God is always already the most original history.

Thus Barth turns the old metaphysical picture inside out. Instead of moving step by step towards the ground of being, the eternal Other, as in Diotima's ascent of love, Barth rewrites metaphysics with the singular history of a certain human being taking the place traditionally occupied by the non-historical supra-temporal Form of the Good. If on Plato's story the ground of being, the Transcendent, is attainable only by abstraction from time and its particularities, then plainly no temporal entity can be at the centre of our attention – but why need we stick to this story? Why suppose it is a non-human non-historical abstract deity whose immortality we long for?

Barth's *Church Dogmatics*, as Robert W. Jenson says, is an immense metaphysical system – the first Western Christological metaphysics on an intellectual and spiritual level with the creations of Gregory of Nazianzus (329–89) or Maximus the Confessor (c.580–662) – 'a huge doctrine of being, which offends against the previous tradition of Western thought by putting an individual, the risen Jesus Christ, as the Ground of reality'.[90] Instead of trying to relate the historical event of Jesus' existence to the timeless realities such as goodness, truth and beauty, that transcend the limitations of time, we have to say, after Christian revelation, that God is in and of himself the event of history. History is self-transcendence – history happens when one moves towards what one is not yet. This movement of self-transcendence is possible only in relationship to some other – history is possible only in communion. For Barth, God is the paradigmatic historical being. Far from being timeless in the sense of being bereft of time he is the one who has time – all the time.

This is an awesome story, whether one is attracted or repelled. It certainly depends on an exegesis of the Forty Days of Eastertide, in the light of an already accepted thoroughly Chalcedonian Christology (Jesus Christ as having truly human nature as well as truly divine nature) and of a strong doctrine of God as Trinity (understood as eternal communion).

Objections are not difficult to see, even for Christian theologians. For example, do we really know anything like as much about the time of the risen Lord as Barth's exegesis makes out? Is his theological anthropology always well grounded in the narrated identity of the central figure in the gospels? Are the exegetical results not sometimes (even often) influenced (even determined) by a priori theological and metaphysical considerations?

In short: it is a brilliant, even 'inspired' thesis, this Barthian decision to ground a whole vision of what it is to be human precisely on the history of one particular human individual – on Jesus Christ raised from the dead. That our humanity, the world, should be understood in Christian terms is an attractive thought – but what about those who cannot accept the Easter history as the revelation of authentic humanity? And what about longings for immortality which, on the face of it, do not very obviously focus on the figure of Jesus Christ?

# CHAPTER THREE

# HEIDEGGER'S COSMOGONICAL MYTH

Martin Heidegger's work has a complicated relationship with Christianity, both Protestant and Catholic;[1] but our concern here is to explore his attempt to cure Western culture of the desire to transcend the finitude of human life. If Karl Barth replaces the abstract and eternal forms of the good, the true and the beautiful with the singular humanity of Jesus Christ risen from the dead, then Heidegger advances the world itself as the only proper site of human transcendence – the world conceived as the interplay of the non-human realities of earth, sky, death and the sacred: *das Geviert* (the fourfold), as he will say.

## The Christian invention of the worldless self

*Sein und Zeit* appeared in 1927.[2] The simplest way into it, as Gilbert Ryle noted, is to read it as an attempt (historically the first of many) to free modern philosophy from its 'Cartesian' inheritance – specifically by rooting out the remnants of Christian theology which, according to Heidegger, were still at work in the guise of the transcendental subject, the isolated worldless 'I', the self who has difficulty getting anything better than inferential knowledge of other minds, and so on.[3]

Heidegger writes as follows: 'What stands in the way of the basic question of *Dasein*'s being (or leads it off the track) is an orientation thoroughly coloured by the anthropology of Christianity and the ancient world'.[4] That is to say, Heidegger is as much out to deflate the conception of the self supposedly at work in Fichte and Descartes as we saw Barth was. For the early Heidegger, however, the appropriate way of dealing with the modern subject is certainly not by turning to the figure of Jesus Christ as the one human being

46

in whom all others may find authentic humanity. He sought, rather, to embed the subject properly in the world.

When the subject of consciousness is redescribed as *Dasein*, a way of being *there*, a way of being *situated*, then the a priori of human subjectivity turns out to be the familiar facts of human life. Far from capturing the a priori transcendental conditions of subjectivity, as philosophers in the 1920s hoped, notions such as 'pure I' and 'consciousness' only obscure the realities in which the human way of being is immersed. It does not secure the distinctive character of human subjectivity to remove it from the ordinary everyday world. On the contrary, we have to rediscover the transcendental conditions of being human in facts of life, such as Heidegger has already been describing in his phenomenology of *Dasein* – in the hermeneutic of the everydayness of being with one another.

Heidegger repeatedly mocks the notion of the Cartesian self in such terms that it gradually becomes clear that his implication is that only a god would fit the picture. The 'knowing subject', whose way of being is left unexamined, is plainly *'das Geistding'* ('mental thing'), the 'isolated subject', *'das Ichding'* ('ego thing') and above all the 'bare subject without a world' – for short, the 'worldless subject'.[5]

Heidegger wants to show that our human way of being is a way of being in time – at least that. He starts from the conviction that, in traditional philosophy, we set aside, or simply forget, the historical and temporal nature of the cognitive subject. The subject of consciousness, who dominates modern philosophy (epistemology, external world scepticism, etc.), is the mirror image of the only being who supposedly exists outside the world and time, free of history and independent of all other beings: none other than God, as conceived in the tradition of theology with which Heidegger is obviously operating – a version of theism, or deism, in which no allowance is made either for the doctrine of the immanence of God in creation or for the doctrine of the incarnation of the Word of God in history.

But there is something strange about all this. Heidegger's attitude to Christian theology, hostile at one level, overtly and explicitly so, attributing the monstrous invention of the transcendental subject to Christian theology, is also proprietorial, indeed exploitative of and even parasitical upon Christian theology. Time and again, at crucial points, he appropriates and transmutes some Christian topos. It may even be said, without much exaggeration, that almost every philosophical innovation in *Sein und Zeit* may easily be traced to a theological source.

## Appropriating New Testament themes

Heidegger does not conceal his indebtedness to these Christian sources. The phenomenon of *Angst*, for example, of which he makes so much, while it may never have been properly acknowledged by traditional philosophers, has received plenty of attention in Christian theology.[6] Secondly, the even more important notion of 'care' (*Sorge*), is related to the Stoic notion of *merimna* but also, more particularly, to the New Testament notion:

> The way in which 'care' is viewed in the foregoing existential analytic of Dasein is one which has grown upon the author in connection with his attempts to interpret the Augustinian (i.e. Helleno-Christian) anthropology with regard to the foundational principles reached in the ontology of Aristotle.[7]

Thirdly, and most significantly of all for Heidegger, it is in Christian theology 'from Paul right up Calvin's *meditatio futurae vitae*' that the phenomenon of mortality has been brought to bear upon (philosophical) anthropology.[8] Nor do these exhaust the list of key Heideggerian notions which owe a great deal to the inspiration of Christian theology.

These three do, however, obviously characterize human beings in a way that undermines and eliminates the Cartesian conception of the self as a centre of rational consciousness. To insist on affectivity (*Angst* as a mood), on the human way of being as always already a way of being concerned (*Dasein* as *Sorge*), and on what we might as well call finitude (being-towards-death) – on human beings, then, as in (or out of) tune with their situation, as inescapably involved with others (even if taking flight), and as living under the shadow of death (albeit denying it) – is clearly to dissolve the fantasy of the self as a purely rational, disengaged and timeless entity. The notion of the 'transcendental ego' collapses, in *Sein und Zeit*, but under pressure from New Testament themes.

Above all, however, it is the idea of 'world', and thus of 'being-in-the-world', which Heidegger develops from theological sources. His indebtedness is barely visible in *Sein und Zeit*, but other writings about then make it abundantly clear. In effect, it is the Christian notion of being 'in this world but not of it' that enables Heidegger's anti-Cartesian project to get going. If it is the biblical-patristic anthropology that generates the misconception of the human way of being which is the myth of the isolated worldless subject (as Heidegger claims), then it turns out, paradoxically, that reflection on primitive Christian language and experience supplies the notion of 'being-in-the-world' which seems so decisively and easily to deflate that myth. The theologically generated fantasy of the worldless subject is thus subverted by the theologically rooted notion of the moral agent as always already being in the world. Basically: a deistically conceived god generates the Cartesian self, and an incarnational theology gets the Cartesian self back into the world.

In *Vom Wesen des Grundes* Heidegger tells the following story about the notion of 'world' as he wants us to understand it. Invoking the work of the classical scholar Karl Reinhardt, he first tells us that, in ancient philosophy, the word for 'world' – *kosmos* – means neither some particular entity nor the sum of all entities. His airy allusion to pre-Socratic fragments to support this carry little conviction. His relief is perceptible when he turns to the New Testament:

> It is no accident that in connection with the new ontical understanding of existence that appeared in Christianity the relationship of *kosmos* to human *Dasein*, and so even the concept of world, was focused and clarified. This relationship was experienced so profoundly that *kosmos* thereafter came to signify a basic type of human existence. In Paul (cf. 1 Corinthians and Galatians), *kosmos houtos* ['this world'] means not merely, or even primarily, the condition of the 'cosmic', but the condition and the situation of man, the character of his stance with regard to the cosmos and of his evaluation of what is good.[9]

In other words, when Paul refers to 'this world', he means the human condition as such, rather than the world as the topic of cosmology, geography and so on. With New Testament Christianity, so Heidegger is claiming, a new sense emerged of the place of the subject in the world – a new sense, rather, of how the things of this world impinge upon human beings – of how things come to *matter*.

In a nutshell, the Heideggerian case here is that the neglect of the phenomenon of world leaves a vacuum which has been filled by 'a privileged domain of something eternally existent'. The world gives way to something else beyond itself, the really real is imagined to be elsewhere – or the world disappears into our minds, absorbed in some kind of unmediated intuition. In effect, the lack of attention to the phenomenon of becoming, to history, to the passage of time, and so on, means that we relate ourselves far too early to a certain transcendental reality, without ever attending to the world in which we are involved. The other side of this is that we think we can have knowledge of the world without mediation – knowledge, then, without signs, and thus without language.

We have our being 'in the world'. That is 'transcendence' for Heidegger at this point. In effect, for Heidegger at this stage, being human is a matter of being together with others in the ordinary everyday 'life-world'.

## Dwelling poetically on this earth

In his later meditations (if that is the right word) Heidegger tries to bring out how this world, in which we belong, is the self-sustaining 'event' of the interplay of certain non-human realities. The pragmatistic anthropology of *Sein und Zeit* gives way to a mytho-poeic cosmogony of playfulness in which human beings come into their own as participants. Instead of allowing ourselves to be drawn away in search of significance in some 'other world', behind or beyond or above this world in which we live, Heidegger invites us to live poetically on this earth, quoting a phrase from Hölderlin.[10]

One way into what Heidegger is up to is by considering what he has to say about things. The Greeks had a good word for 'things', so Heidegger thinks:[11] *pragmata*, connected with practice, meaning that with which one has to do, that with which one has to deal and to cope, in everyday practical reaction to and intervention in one's natural and cultural environment. It is this 'pragmatic' aspect of the things with which we have to do that has dropped out of our awareness, in the metaphysical tradition (already among the ancient Greeks, Heidegger thinks), in favour of seeing things as objects of observation. Things have been uprooted from their natural context in the ongoing relationships which at least partly constitute their significance. Heidegger tries to recreate a sense of things in terms of the notion of tool (*das Zeug*): any sort of gear or equipment. Things are never mere objects, as we are tempted to think, or so Heidegger would say. Things are certainly never mere objects upon which we subsequently and arbitrarily confer significance. On the contrary: such objects are always already tools, things with which we have dealings, in countless ways. The world is full of things with which we find ourselves collaborating all the time, shaping them, being shaped by them, and so on.

After abandoning *Sein und Zeit*, Heidegger moved from this affirmation of objects as always already *pragmata* and thus as related to us as the gear which *homo faber* relies upon, to a radically different, poetic, artistic, aesthetic, perception of things. In effect, the poet and the artist have to take precedence over the engineer and the craftsman. If the early Heidegger's reminder is that the bare particulars which the metaphysician discusses, the objects which the scientist investigates, all perfectly legitimately, are always already *pragmata*, things with which we first of all have dealings in everyday practical existence – and the misperception, the impoverishment, is that metaphysics and science have been so successful that we are inclined to see ourselves as neutral disengaged observers only – the later Heidegger's story is that it is 'poetically' that we 'dwell on this earth'.

## Misconceptions of things

In 'The Origin of the Work of Art', lectures originally given to an art appreciation society, an audience with no special interest or training in philosophy, Heidegger sketches a history of the three taken-for-granted conceptions of what a thing is that have prevailed in our culture.[12]

First of all there is the common-sense notion of a thing as a bearer of properties:

> This block of granite, for example, is a mere thing. It is hard, heavy, extended, bulky, shapeless, rough, coloured, partly dull, partly shiny. We can take note of all these features in the stone. Thus we acknowledge its characteristics. But still, the traits signify something proper to the stone itself. They are its properties. The thing has them. The thing? What are we thinking of when we now have the thing in mind? Obviously a thing is not merely an aggregate of traits, nor an accumulation of properties by which that aggregate arises. A thing, as everyone thinks he knows, is that around which the properties have assembled. We speak in this connection of the core of a thing.[13]

This common-sense conception of a thing is, in other words, the age-old assumption of dualistic metaphysics that a thing is a substance with accidents. The difficulty about regarding things as hidden cores with surfaces is that the thing itself disappears. On this view, we never see anything; we see only the shell within which we deduce or infer that the thing is concealed.

There is a second view of things. Here, the thing is conceived as the unity of a manifold of sensations. If the first perception 'keeps the thing at arm's length from us', by concealing the inner essence within a shell of external properties, this second account is 'an inordinate attempt to bring it into the greatest possible proximity to us'. The thing becomes 'the *aistheton*, that which is perceptible by sensations in the senses belonging to sensibility'. This is clearly radical empiricism, laying stress on the primitive character of sense data. 'Everything that might interpose itself between the thing and us in apprehending and talking about it must first be set aside'. But, as Heidegger points out,

> we never really first perceive a throng of sensations, e.g. tones and noises ... rather we hear the storm whistling in the chimney, we hear the three-motored plane, we hear the Mercedes in immediate distinction from the Volkswagen. Much closer to us than all sensations are the things themselves. We hear the door shut in the house and never hear acoustical sensations or even mere sounds. In order to hear a bare sound we have to listen away from things, divert our ear from them, i.e. listen abstractly.[14]

So if the thing itself becomes the hidden essence underneath the surface properties on the first story – on this second story the thing is the construction of my allegedly pure, atomized and immediate sensations.

The third story is the neo-Scholastic hylemorphism with which Heidegger was familiar as a student – the thing as formed matter or enmattered form – a conception ramifying into the much more pervasive conception of a thing as being a compound of stuff and shape, form and content:

> That which gives things their constancy and pith but is also at the same time the source of their particular mode of sensuous pressure – coloured, resonant, hard, massive – is the matter in things. In this analysis of the thing as matter (*hule*), form (*morphe*) is already co-posited. What is constant in a thing, its consistency, lies in the fact that matter stands together with a form. The thing is formed matter. This interpretation appeals to the immediate view with which the thing solicits us by its look (*eidos*).[15]

This way of perceiving things has a certain validity, Heidegger says, unlike the first two accounts; but only with things which have been *made*, when the raw material can be distinguished from the idea in the craftsman's or the sculptor's mind, and the shape of the finished product displays the creator's plan.

This approach to all things in terms of one very particular kind of things – crafted or manufactured things, works of art – becomes intertwined with biblical faith, Heidegger thinks, in which 'the totality of all beings is represented in advance as something created, which here means made'. The hylemorphic conception of things smuggles in a certain amount of theology, then, to extend itself beyond a certain range of things.

Each of the three prevailing conceptions of what we mean by a thing blinds us to the thingly character of things. If Husserl's famous slogan at the outset of phenomenology was that we should get 'back to the things themselves', then Heidegger is now radicalizing that invitation. In our culture, so he maintains, a thing is something like the hidden core of which we see the surface (metaphysical realism); a thing is the product of my private sense data (phenomenalism, logical empiricism); a thing is matter informed (crypto-theology, doctrine of creation) – but on all three views things as they really are to the innocent eye of the ordinary inhabitant of the world disappear. A thing vanishes into hiding within its outward appearance; a thing comes into existence as the product of my sensations; or every thing gets forced into the category of things that are *made*. How are we to unlearn these ways of treating things so that we allow things to be what they are?

## A pair of old boots

Heidegger invites us to question these conceptions of what a thing is by invoking a Van Gogh painting of an old peasant woman's boots. If we can learn from the artist to see what he sees in the old woman's boots, then perhaps we can begin to look at various things around us in a different way – in ways that allow things to work on us so as to disclose and establish the only world in which our nature as human beings will have a chance of flourishing.

It has to be admitted that it all sounds a bit rich in translation, even rather comic, but it is actually a very sensitive and subtle piece of analysis – exploratory meditation, rather. Heidegger invites us to see what the old woman's boots in the picture disclose:

> From the dark opening of the worn insides of the shoes the toilsome tread of the worker stares forth. In the stiffly rugged heaviness of the shoes there is the accumulated tenacity of her slow trudge through the far-spreading and ever-uniform furrows of the field swept by a raw wind. On the leather lie the

dampness and richness of the soil. Under the sole slides the loneliness of the field-path as evening falls. In the shoes vibrates the silent call of the earth, its quiet gift of the ripening grain and its unexplained self-refusal in the fallow desolation of the wintry field. This piece of equipment is pervaded by uncomplaining anxiety as to the certainty of bread, the wordless joy of having once more withstood want, the trembling before the impending child bed and shivering at the surrounding menace of death.[16]

The peasant herself (of course) would simply live, unselfconsciously, in her world – in the world that Van Gogh catches, conjures up, embodies, reveals for us, in his concentrated painting of her worn shoes. The idea is that, as we look at the boots in the painting, we begin to recognize the context – the context begins to impinge upon us – latent in the boots, not behind or beyond or above the boots, but right in the boots. The whole world of the woman to whom they belong emerges, reveals itself, becomes visible, perceptible, manifest – opens up to include us. It is as if the picture opens out a space for us to enter, instead of remaining an object on the wall in front of us at which we stand and stare. We cease to confront the object and are instead drawn into the ambit of the world that it instantiates.

Of course, the language works against what Heidegger is trying to show us. In our culture at least we are accustomed to think of ourselves as centres of consciousness projecting significance on things in the world around us, whereas Heidegger wants us to picture the world much more as a clearing in a forest into which we are drawn. We cast light on things, certainly, but only to the extent that we are always already in a patch of light. We come into the light and things begin to reveal themselves. They would not be revealed if we did not come on the scene; but the encounter between us and things is instigated neither by us nor by things themselves but by the clearing in which we meet.[17] This particular thing, these worn old boots as painted by Van Gogh, gather the whole world – draw us into her world. The boots begin to display the dimensions of her life – trudging over the fields, in winter, at harvest, with anxiety in the background about birth and death and so forth. The peasant's boots, as Van Gogh enables us to see them, become a microcosm of her world.

Heidegger regards himself as practising a kind of phenomenological description here. As he says, his study of the peasant's boots in the Van Gogh picture explores something about the nature and reality of the thing itself –

> not by a description and explanation of a pair of shoes actually present; not by a report about the process of making shoes; and also not by the observation of the actual use of shoes occurring here and there; but only by bringing ourselves before Van Gogh's painting. ... In the vicinity of the work we were suddenly somewhere else than we usually tend to be.[18]

That is to say, a whole world opens up in a thing such as these old boots, as they are seen by the painter's eye and as we too can see if we can learn to see with the painter's eye. It is not that the boots exist 'in themselves', as bare objects, and that the painter, Heidegger himself, or we ourselves for that matter, 'work up', afterwards and in retrospect, the pathetic story of how the boots 'symbolize' the peasant woman's way of life – for us then only to project all this upon the boots. That is, of course, a very tempting account of what Heidegger is doing here – so tempting (he would say) that it only proves how strong the grip of metaphysical avoidance of the thingliness of things actually is on our minds. What Heidegger means, rather, is that the relations that are displayed in the boots as perceived by the artist – relations to the earth, to the passing of time, to the seasons, to birth and death and so on – are constitutive elements of the very existence of these particular boots. The peasant's world is gathered and communicated – shared with us in her old boots as Van Gogh enables us to see them.

## The Greek temple

Another example of what Heidegger means is when he turns to reflect on a Greek temple:

> A building, a Greek temple, portrays nothing. It simply stands there in the middle of the rock-cleft valley. The building encloses the figure of the god, and in this concealment lets it stand out into the holy precinct through the open portico. By means of the temple, the god is present in the temple. The presence of the god is in itself the extension and delimitation of the precinct as a holy precinct. The temple and its precinct, however, do not fade away into the indefinite. It is the temple-work that first fits together and at the same time gathers around

itself the unity of those paths and relations in which birth and death, disaster and blessing, victory and disgrace, endurance and decline acquire the shape of destiny for human being. The all-governing expanse of this open relational context is the world of this historical people.[19]

This brings us back to Heidegger's concept of 'world' – to the 'poetic' conception of the world which appears in his writings from the 1930s onwards, a much richer concept than the pragmatistic-anthropological one. The temple, like the work of art, is the surfacing, the upheaving, of a world – but what is meant then by such a world?
Heidegger writes:

The world is not the mere collection of the countable or uncountable, familiar and unfamiliar things that are just there. But neither is it the merely imagined framework added by our representation to the sum of such given things . . . . World is no longer here an object that stands before us and can be seen. World is the ever-nonobjective to which we are subject as long as the paths of birth and death, blessing and curse, keep us transported into being. Wherever those decisions of our history that relate to our very being are made, are taken up and abandoned by us, go unrecognized and are rediscovered by new inquiry, there the world worlds.[20]

When Heidegger writes of the world, then, he does not mean the sum total of everything – everything that is the case; nor on the other hand does he mean some conceptual framework that we impose upon everything to give it unity. The world can never be regarded as 'a great big object', as if we could look at it from outside, nor can it be reduced to the product of our imagination. But now, for the later Heidegger, the conception of the world that he drew earlier from the New Testament has been greatly expanded. The world is a whole way of being, it is ongoing, it is self-sustaining, so to speak – which is why he prefers to speak of the world as 'worlding'. A world 'worlds' (not that he uses quotation marks) wherever the constitutive decisions of our history fall, and are either appropriated or neglected by us, misunderstood or freshly interrogated – and such decisions, clearly, are not primarily our decisions. On the contrary – they are the paths of birth and death, of blessing and curse, which force or call us into being. By the phenomenon 'world' Heidegger means that always unobjectifiable space in which we live as long as we remain cast into being. Stones have no world in this sense. Plants and animals likewise have no world. The peasant woman, by contrast, has a world because she dwells in the open, in the space of what there is. Her stay is in the interplay of the relationships of birth and death, earth and time, and so on.

What Heidegger wants us to realize about the peasant's boots is that they do not 'represent' anything in the sense that they might stand for or symbolize something behind or beyond themselves, so that you could then forget them and go on thinking about the values and virtues of peasant life or whatever. That would be using the thought of the boots to go beyond, to transcend, this gross material world to some ideal and spiritual realm elsewhere. What Heidegger wants us to see is that the whole world of the peasant woman is in her boots – the boots lead out from themselves, unfold a world – but the boots are the thing where this whole world gathers. Gradually or suddenly, the world of the peasant displays itself in all its complexity, unfolds in all its dimensions, in this pair of old boots. A thing such as her boots displays, in microcosm, the structure of significances, the pattern of relationships, which is her world – the world to which we too belong, if we allow the artist to let us see it.

Far from being a world of bare objects, of mere things, upon which the human mind must then confer or project some pattern and significance, our world always already discloses itself as a whole – not perhaps in everything, but certainly in Heidegger's view in a fair variety of things. And now not even as a space of pragmatic opportunity, an anthropocentric world, a craftsman's world, a world where things are at hand, handy, hand sized (think of all the games we play with our hands) – but now a world which is itself play (*Spiel*), as Heidegger can say.

The Greek temple he chooses, as he says, because nobody could be tempted to think of it in terms of representation, i.e., as something which merely stands in for something else, in the sense of something that is merely a copy or a sign of something else which would be what really matters – the really real which might perfectly well be represented in some other way. What Heidegger means is that the world which the Greek temple gathers and unfolds is in such things as itself and nowhere else. You cannot throw away the temple once you have taken in what it discloses. (That would be what a tourist might do, taking a snap and getting back into the coach.) On the contrary, the message is in the medium – the world which the Greek temple reveals is the world to which it belongs and there is no other way of entering that world.

In 1950, once again to a largely non-philosophical audience, Heidegger gave a lecture entitled simply 'The Thing'.[21] If one text more than another provides access into the later Heidegger's way of thinking this is surely the one.

## The quaternity in a jug

Consider a jug. Once again Heidegger begins by challenging the assumption that he supposes most of us would make to get at the nature of an object such as a jug. We would turn either to metaphysics or to physics, he thinks, in search of some metaphysical proposition or some scientific formula. But the thing the jug is simply disappears when we think in those terms. In one way or the other this is to make the jug abstract – to replace the jug by something else. The results of physics are correct and certainly valuable, Heidegger says here explicitly. It is simply that we must resist the temptation to think that what is really real is never what we are actually looking at here and now but always something which it takes special techniques to discover, whether metaphysical or scientific. What things are, he thinks, is always already obvious – if only we let them be. The more elaborate and technical our attempt to get at what things really are the more easily and completely we lose sight of them, the further they withdraw from the light.

The destruction that nuclear warfare would bring would only be the most eloquent verification of an annihilation of things that has already been going on for a long time, in our culture.[22] Indeed, for Heidegger, the tradition of metaphysical thought has generated just this obliviousness towards things. Hence the life-and-death significance of getting your philosophy right, he would think – although he never suggests that the merciless blindness to the humanity, say, of Middle European Jews, gypsies and so on, might be a consequence of this obliteration of the intrinsic character of the things that constitute our sacred space. The Holocaust might surely be described as *das Entsetzliche*, something so terrible as to deprive us of our bearings, and ascribed at least partly, or in some deep sense, to a failure of perception, to obliviousness to reality (*Seinsvergessenheit*), an obliviousness to the context that provides our nature with its humanity, or something of this kind – but he seems never to have made any such connection.

The point of a jug is that it holds (say) wine, so that the wine may then be poured: 'To pour from the jug is to give ... The giving can be a drink. The outpouring gives water, it gives wine to drink'. Thus the point about a jug comes out in its being a vessel from which wine or water is poured – but then:

> The spring stays on in the water of the gift. In the spring the rock dwells, and in the rock dwells the dark slumber of the earth, which receives the rain and dew of the sky. In the water of the spring dwells the marriage of sky and earth. It stays in the wine given by the fruit of the vine, the fruit in which the earth's nourishment and the sky's sun are betrothed to one another. In the gift of the water, in the gift of the wine, sky and earth dwell. But the gift of outpouring is what makes the jug a jug. In the jugness of the jug, sky and earth dwell.[23]

Thus it is in the gift of water, or of wine, in the actual outpouring, that the nature of the jug is to be found – which is certainly to place the jug as a piece of equipment, gear (*Zeug*), within the familiar human world of ordinary everyday activities and relationships. But much more deeply, nearer to us than that, Heidegger wants to articulate the tacit reference in the outpouring of wine or water to the impersonal dimensions of earth and sky which ultimately condition the outpouring of wine or water. As soon as the jug of wine is placed in the only context in which it has its proper being and function – a context of outpouring, of giving and receiving, and so on – then this context itself turns out to be in a much wider context, in the sense that earth and sky come together in the act of pouring.

Yet this is only half the story:

> The gift of the pouring out is drink for mortals. It quenches their thirst. It refreshes their leisure. It enlivens their conviviality. The jug's gift is at times also given for consecration. If the outpouring is for consecration, then it does not still a thirst. It stills and elevates the celebration of the feast. The gift of the pouring now is neither given in a pub, nor is the poured gift a drink for mortals. The outpouring is the libation poured out for the immortal gods. The gift of the outpouring as libation is the authentic gift. In giving the consecrated libation, the pouring jug occurs as the giving gift (*Im Schenken des geweihten Trankes west der giessende Krug als das schenkende Geschenk*).[24]

The translation is valiant but makes it all sound a good deal more exotic than it is. Pouring (*giessen*), is not just filling up and emptying out. In fact Heidegger wants to highlight something very familiar and ordinary. After all, it is not difficult to think of times when a jug is just filled up or emptied out, and other times when it might be handled with care, with a certain ceremony, offered carefully to some sick or elderly person, offered as loving cup at some college feast, or brought to the altar.

The wine (we may say) which refreshes us when we are weary, creates a friendship among human beings, who thus become implicitly aware of their bonds, the passing of time, their mortality, and so on, and is also the wine which marks certain moments of passage such as funerals, births, weddings and anniversaries, when it becomes a kind of libation and the presence of that which never dies is invoked and recollected.

## The dance of the quaternity

Heidegger notes that we may be suspicious that he is trying to produce a new meaning for the word 'thing' out of etymology:

> This reference to the history of language could easily tempt us to misunderstand the way in which we are now thinking of the nature of the thing. It might look as though the nature of the thing as we are now thinking of it had been, so to speak, thoughtlessly poked out of the accidentally encountered meaning of the Old High German thing. The suspicion arises that the understanding of the nature of the thingness that we are here trying to reach may be based on the accidents of the etymological game. The notion becomes established and is already current that, instead of giving thought to essential matters, we are here merely using the dictionary.[25]

He concedes that it was a pleasure for him to find that the word 'thing' did once mean 'gathering' but he insists that he is trying to think 'something altogether different, to which no thought whatever has hitherto been given'. By trying to let the thing be, with a new innocence – by taking up Husserl's slogan 'To the things themselves!', thus by practising a certain kind of phenomenological description – Heidegger hopes to bring us to see how, in a thing such as a jug of wine, the entire life-world in which the thing has its place is tacitly present – the life-world of which the dimensions are, as he discerns them, earth, sky, mortality and divinity:

> Earth is the building bearer, nourishing with its fruits, tending water and rock, plant and animal ... The sky is the sun's path,

the course of the moon, the glitter of the stars, the year's seasons, the light and dusk of day, the gloom and glow of night, the clemency and inclemency of the weather ... The divinities are the beckoning messengers of the godhead. Out of the hidden sway of the divinities the god emerges as what he is, which removes him from any comparison with beings that are present ... The mortals are human beings. They are called mortals because they can die. To die means to be capable of death as death. Only man dies.[26]

And Heidegger insists that each of these four dimensions implies the other three – 'Earth and sky, divinities and mortals – being at one with one another of their own accord belong together by way of the simpleness of the united fourfold' – *das Geviert*, the quaternity.[27]

This takes us to the centre of Heidegger's way of thinking. Our life-world is established and sustained, establishes itself and sustains itself over and over again and all the time – by this quadrilateral structure of non-human non-subjective dimensions, these four 'quarters' of our world: the sky above, with all that the sky and heaven have meant and mean in the experience and imagination of the human race; the earth beneath our feet, mother earth, the soil, the land, bedrock, the dust from which we come and to which we return, and so on; death, the shadow under which we are born and always have to live, our transience, vulnerability, mortality; and fourthly and finally the sacred, the holy, intimations of something divine, something gracious.

Our collective human existence is thus, for Heidegger, the interplay of this quaternity of objective forces – this play, this game (*das Spiel*), in which each of the four refers to and reflects all the others – this mirror-game (*Spiegel-Spiel*). Heidegger thus equates 'the permanently happening mirror-play of the unity of earth and sky, divinities and mortals' with the world.

This, he is saying, is all that there is – nothing more, nothing less. The cosmos which is the human world and the human tradition – our whole life-world – is the effect of the interplay of the quaternity. Our world is constituted by the impact upon one another of the four dimensions – the four world-regions as he will call them. This world is sustained in being by such play – and the importance of this for Heidegger comes out immediately:

That means, the world's worlding cannot be explained by anything else nor can it be fathomed through anything else. This impossibility does not lie in the inability of our human thinking to explain and fathom in this way. Rather, the inexplicable and unfathomable character of the world's worlding lies in this, that causes and grounds remain unsuitable for the world's worlding.[28]

That is to say, we have been led to what is ultimate and irreducible. It makes no sense to ask for any cause or grounds or explanation for the world's being beyond or in addition to its being, its worlding. That is what there is, no more, no less, mysteriously, gratuitously, inexplicably.

The being of the world, the cosmogony celebrated as the interplay of the fourfold, requires no explanation outside itself – 'it is neither explainable by means of anything else nor justifiable on the basis of anything else'. The phenomenon of the world needs no explanation in terms of something else nor does it require to be grounded upon something else. It is not that we wretched human beings with our limited mental powers are incapable of explaining and grounding the world in something else – in some elusive and hard to establish conception of God, let us say. On the contrary, we are trying to do that all the time, that is the history of metaphysics Heidegger would say. That is exactly what he wants to bring to a stop. In the case of the world itself 'such things as causes and grounds remain inappropriate'. Indeed, as soon as we yield to the temptation to look for some kind of explanation of the world in terms of causes and grounds, that means, not that we are thereby transcending the world (taking a god's-eye point of view) but rather that we are falling short of what the world is – 'the human will to explain just does not reach the simpleness of the unity of the world'. Clearly, Heidegger continues to react vehemently against his early memories of a kind of natural theology that is bent on quasi-scientific explanation of the world's existence.

Heidegger's lecture culminates in a dithyrambic chant in praise of the world. One would need to hear his voice (many recordings exist), as his incantatory rhetoric works on the listeners to think of things differently – poetically. The paronomasia and interplay of assonance make the text radically untranslatable, but this is Albert Hofstadter's brave effort:

> The human will to explain just does not reach to the simpleness of the simple onefold of worlding (*in das Einfache der Einfalt des Weltens*). The united four are already strangled in their essential nature when we think of them only as separate entities, which are to be grounded in and explained by one another.

The unity of the fourfold is the fouring (*die Vierung*). But the fouring does not come about in such a way that it encompasses the four and only afterwards is added to them as that compass. Nor does the fouring exhaust itself in this, that the four, once they are there, stand side by side singly.

The fouring, the unity of the four, presences as the appropriating mirror-play (*das ereignende Spiegel-Spiel*) of the betrothed (*Zugetrauten*), each to the other in simple oneness. The fouring presences as the worlding of the world. The mirror-play of world is the round dance of appropriating (*der Reigen des Ereignens*). Therefore, the round dance does not encompass the four like a hoop (*nicht erst wie ein Reif*). The round dance is the ring that joins while it plays as mirroring (*der Ring, der ringt, indem er als das Spiegeln spielt*). Appropriating, it lightens the four into the radiance of their simple oneness. Radiantly, the ring joins the four, everywhere open to the riddle of their presence. The gathered presence of the mirror-play of the world, joining in this way, is the ringing (*das Gering*). In the ringing of the mirror-play ring (*im Gering des spiegelnd-spielenden Rings*), the four nestle (*schmiegen sich*) into their unifying presence, in which each one retains its own nature. So nestling, they join together, worlding, the world.[29]

Only to the extent that we yield to Heidegger's incantatory language are we enabled to allow 'the thing in its thinging' (*das Ding in seinem Dingen*) come forth from 'the worlding world' (*aus der weltenden Welt*). Thinking in this kind of way, we allow ourselves to be approached by 'the worlding being of the thing' (*lassen wir uns vom weltenden Wesen des Dinges angehen*). This means that 'we are called by the thing as the thing' (*vom Ding als Ding gerufen*). To let every thing *be* – to allow everything to gather and unfold the four dimensions of our world – is to let us see how conditioned we are. For here Heidegger's cosmogonical myth plays a joke on Kantian philosophy: 'We are the be-thinged, the conditioned ones. We have left behind us the presumption of all unconditionedness.'[30] Taking up the characteristically Kantian word for our being conditioned, *bedingt*, Heidegger hyphenates it. We human beings are situated – 'in the world' in the earlier Heidegger's jargon; but we are '*die be-Dingten*' – 'the be-thinged, the conditioned ones'.

'We have left behind us the presumption of all unconditionedness' – the assumption, the arrogance, the pretentiousness, the presumption in that sense, of ever being unconditioned. We are always, and always already, surrounded and supported by things. Thus, we leave behind any sense of the human subject as transcendentally independent of finitude or as creator of significance, projecting meaning and value upon the world around us. We do not exist without conditions – our being is not unconditioned and unlimited, such as a god's existence is traditionally supposed to be. Once and for all, Heidegger has relieved us of the temptation, the illusion, of regarding ourselves as beings capable of transcending the limits of our finite condition in some godlike way.

All this poetry is in aid of the prose of ordinary life. It is only as we let the world be what it is – the interplay of the fourfold – that each thing 'fits into its own being' so that

> inconspicuously compliant is the thing (*ring ist das Ding*): the jug and the bench, the footbridge and the plough. But tree and pond, too, brook and hill, are things, each in its own way. Things, each thinging from time to time in its own way, are heron and roe, deer, horse and bull . . . mirror and clasp, book and picture, crown and cross.[31]

As we learn to let such things exert their power over us, then we shall be retrieving the world itself. Poetic and mythopoeic as Heidegger's language certainly is, he is only insisting that things such as he names at least are what they are, not because of any meaning imposed upon them by us – rather it is in such things that our whole existence as human beings establishes itself in the first place. It is by such things that our way of being, our communion in being, is established and sustained. Such things are gatherings, moments, events, in which and by which all we mean by sky and earth, by the prospect of death and by the pressure of the sacred, assembles – in simple everyday things. Their being is already significant, their being as things already unfolds our world.

By bringing the phenomenon of world as play of the fourfold into the centre of his thinking Heidegger dislodges the notion of the human being as subject and origin of meaning and value. At the same time he eliminates any conception of some transcendent being as cause and origin of everything. A certain conception of the human being and a certain conception of God thus disappear together. The space left by the departure of the isolated worldless subject and the world-founding supreme being, in this double cancellation of humanism and theology, is now occupied by the world itself or anyway by the round-dance of the quaternity.

The move out of explanation to recollection is not so easy. It is certainly not just a shift of attitude. Attitudes are always committed, together with the ways they change, in the domain of representational thinking:

> A mere shift of attitude is powerless to bring about the advent of the thing as thing ... Nor do things as things ever come about if we merely avoid objects and recollect former objects which perhaps were once on the way to becoming things and even to actually presencing as things ... Whatever becomes a thing occurs out of the ringing of the world's mirror-play. Only when – all of a sudden, presumably – world worlds as a world.[32]

We do not have the power to compel things to give themselves to us, Heidegger insists. They do not come through our doing – nor however do they appear without 'the vigilance of mortals'. And the first move towards such vigilance is breaking free, in a sudden moment of unexpected illumination, from 'the thinking that merely represents ... to the thinking that responds and recalls'.[33]

## From subject of consciousness to gift of the fourfold

Heidegger never repudiated the amazing remark in the lecture course of 1935, published in 1953, without even a footnote of explanation, condemning the books peddled about as Nazi philosophy and insisting that they 'have nothing whatever to do with the inner truth and greatness of this movement', which is, Heidegger explains, 'the encounter between global technology and modern man'.

The Nazi movement offered a way for modern man to come to terms with what we might call instrumental reason, scientism:

> What is at stake is nothing less than a humanity, a being-human determined by the essence of being (*physis*) ... the definition of the essence of man required here cannot be the product of an arbitrary anthropology that considers man in basically the same way as zoology considers animals ... In accordance with the hidden message of the beginning, man should be understood ... as the site which being requires in order to disclose itself. Man is the site of openness, the there. The essent juts into this there and is fulfilled.[34]

What I am, what characterizes me as a human being, is not my being a centre of consciousness opening up towards what surrounds me – on the contrary: I am always already this site, an intrinsically open locus, ready to be invaded by what exists.

This whole project of replacing subjectivism, positivism, and so forth, by a version of metaphysical and epistemological realism which pictures us as intrinsically open sites invaded by the sublime and overwhelming power of Nature is certainly very different from Karl Barth's rewriting of Western metaphysical antihistorical realism in terms of the historical figure of Jesus Christ. Barth's way and Heidegger's way of overcoming the desire of the subject to unite with a world-transcending nonhuman reality might have been composed in mutual opposition. One is not surprised to know that Barth was an eloquent opponent of the Nazi movement from the beginning, indeed he left his job in Germany in 1935; one is not surprised to find that, in Heidegger, the repudiation of the picture of the self as the will that imposes whatever sense and value there is on everything, leads to a radical anti-humanism: one is simply a place-holder – the site where Nature discloses herself. This is perhaps not very different from Karl Barth's picture of the Christian community as no more than a void in which the gospel reveals itself[35] – except that in Barth's story it is a particular historical human being who is revealed (raised from the dead, admittedly), whereas in Heidegger's story it is the dance, the game of the nonhuman elements – sky, earth, death, the sacred – that takes centre stage.

For Heidegger we transcend our finite historical condition precisely by taking part in the cosmic game that locates us in finitude – we are, each of us, *ein Aufenthalt*, a stay, a sojourn, a pause, within the quaternity, the square dance, of earth sky death and divinity.

Thus, while his old friend Bultmann and many of his theological disciples sought to demythologize the world, Heidegger strove, in a series of mythopoeic studies, to remythologize the world. What for modern theologians is the mythological shell that needs to be removed becomes for Heidegger the experience of the worlding of the world. To the God of metaphysical theology – the offspring of Platonism and Christianity – he opposes the play of the cosmos: 'Man can neither pray nor sacrifice to this god [of ontotheology]. Before the *causa sui* man can neither fall to his knees in awe nor can he play music and dance before this god.'[36] In place of the god of the metaphysical tradition Heidegger invokes the truly divine god, the god whom human beings would worship with song and ceremony. But whose god is the god to whom one can neither sacrifice nor pray? Presumably this was the god, the *ens supremum*, of a certain neo-

Scholastic natural theology about whom the young Heidegger argued in his student years (1909–15). Such a god never had anything to do with the triune God revealed in the Christian dispensation, and the only God with whom Heidegger, as the sexton's son, could have had to do in the local Catholic church. For a philosopher who believed (rightly) that a certain kind of theorizing about things often only occludes the reality of what is at issue, it is sad that he seems to have allowed his acquaintance with a rationalistic natural theology to block any deeper understanding of Christian revelation.[37] It would be an exaggeration, perhaps, to say that Heidegger's work from beginning to end is built on his rejection of a thoroughly deistic notion of God; but his lifelong attempt to create a religious, even a sacramental, view of the world, quite independently of the Catholicism of his youth or the Lutheran sympathies of the Marburg years, surely owes much of its fervour and inspiration to disillusionment with his understanding – or misunderstanding – of God as *causa sui*. Once again, a certain theology exerts a fateful influence in a major philosophical project.

The mythopoeticized world of the quaternity is the interplay of the sky, the earth, the gods and us mortals. The sky, instead of being the outer space into which we fire our rockets, is the sky that measures our days and seasons. The earth is our shelter, the source of our food and the womb to which we return at death. We are mortals as we live gratefully on the earth, looking always to the horizon that opens up before us and yet always gives us perspective – under the sovereignty of the heavens and settled on the solidity of the earth. And the gods? 'The gods are the beckoning messengers of the godhead. Out of the hidden sway of the divinities the god emerges as what he is, which removes him from any comparison with beings that are present' – which reiterates Heidegger's concern with theology, though, as in all his writing from beginning to end, the god remains occluded in ambiguity.[38]

# CHAPTER FOUR

# BACK TO PLATO WITH
# IRIS MURDOCH

Iris Murdoch[1] speaks of Heidegger's later work as 'demonic'. For one thing, she thinks that he has got Plato all wrong – partly, indeed mainly, because 'Plato continually makes jokes. Heidegger has no sense of humour, and this is one of the reasons why he misunderstands Plato. Funniness mocks totality.'[2] Wherever that line of thought may take us, the point in looking at her work is that, far from seeking to neutralize the inheritance of Plato, as Nussbaum, Barth and Heidegger try to do, in of course very different ways, Plato is the philosopher – the religious thinker, she will say – to whom we must turn, so Murdoch wants to persuade us. She offers the most sustained and eloquent attempt by any philosopher, in the Anglo-American analytical tradition at least, to open up a way of conceiving ourselves as finite beings, who are nevertheless capable of a certain self-transcendence which fulfils and does not negate our humanity. In effect, we have to go back to Plato and the sovereignty of the form of the good to save ourselves, morally, ethically – indeed to save Western civilization from anarchy.

It is to Plato that Murdoch wants us to return – certainly not to Aristotle. In her novel *The Book and the Brotherhood* (1987), the protagonist Crimond is writing a massive work of philosophy – the book – financed by a club of his old university friends – the brotherhood. At a certain point in the novel he is asked what his projected book is about; he replies that it is about 'everything'. 'Everything?' his interlocutor says, incredulously, 'Everything – except Aristotle: I regard him as an unfortunate interlude, now happily over', Crimond insists. Murdoch must be mocking herself: her own massive philosophical book (500 pages) was being written and rewritten during the years when she was also writing this massive novel (400 pages) about someone writing a massive philosophical book – hers, if not exactly about 'everything', then certainly excluding Aristotle.

## Reviving ethical intuitionism

In 'The Idea of Perfection', the earliest of her philosophical essays, Murdoch starts by noting that, in the moral philosophy of the 1950s, among the facts of life that interest her but which 'seem to have been forgotten or "theorized away"' are the fact that 'an unexamined life can be virtuous' and that 'love is a central concept in morals'.[3] Philosophers talk a great deal about the connection between consciousness and virtue but we have to be able to do justice to both Socrates and 'the virtuous peasant'. Many people are virtuous, even saintly, without always being particularly reflective and self-aware, let alone in the habit of making choices with great deliberation. Philosophers write frequently of freedom but seldom enough of love, and yet, in the experience of ordinary life, freedom of choice often seems limited by bonds of love. More generally, as Murdoch will argue, our freedom to choose this or that course of action presupposes that one or other is *attractive*. We are perhaps drawn towards some desirable objective before the possibility of making this or that choice arises.

Before she investigates the lacunas in philosophy of mind which underlie what she finds so unsatisfactory in contemporary moral philosophy, Murdoch directs us to the work of G. E. Moore (1873–1958). From his *Principia Ethica* (1903) onwards he set the agenda well into the 1930s. By the 1960s, however, it was startling to see how many of his beliefs were 'philosophically unstatable'. He believed, for example, 'that good was a supersensible reality, that it was a mysterious quality, unrepresentable and indefinable, that it was an object of knowledge and (implicitly) that to be able to see it was in some sense to have it'. In effect, he thought of the good on analogy with the beautiful; he regarded goodness as 'a real constituent of the world'. This did not mean that he thought that knowledge of values could be derived from knowledge of facts; on the contrary, the objective reality of the goodness of certain states of affairs, such as beauty, pleasure, friendship and knowledge, was indeed a matter of knowledge but only by a certain kind of intuition.

By the 1950s, however, at least wherever Oxford philosophy held sway, such ethical intuitionism was discredited. Moore was no doubt right to say that good was indefinable but wrong to say that it existed independently – on the contrary, it was now thought that 'judgments of value depend upon the will and choice of the individual'. On the modern view: 'Goodness is not an object of insight or knowledge, it is a function of the will.'

Murdoch tells us that, 'on almost every point', she agrees with Moore, against the philosophers of her own generation who seemed so delighted that 'metaphysical entities were removed, and moral judgments were seen to be, not weird statements, but something much more comprehensible, such as persuasions or commands or rules'. Her rehabilitation of Moore's beliefs, or at least her retrieval of his agenda, played a decisive part in the history of modern moral philosophy. Since the 1980s, while many continue to believe that we live in a world where there are no objective values or moral truths, but that, since we are beings with certain needs and desires, we react favourably to certain actions and unfavourably to others (it may have to do with evolution, the survival of the fittest, or our genetic make-up), and the source of value is thus in ourselves, many philosophers would hold that, on the contrary, what is morally right or wrong does not depend on how we feel about it but that there are values to be found and moral truths which we can discover. Few would be happy to call themselves intuitionists; in the current jargon they would prefer to be moral realists. Many of the current exponents of moral realism are more likely to appeal to Aristotle than to Plato or G. E. Moore, but they quite often refer with respect to Murdoch's decisive influence on the renewal of the case for objectivity in ethics.[4]

The moral philosophers against whom Murdoch was writing would now be labelled non-cognitivists. They believe that 'value terminology' is 'the prerogative of the will', and since on this view will is 'pure choice', independently of thought, let alone vision, they regard 'sincerity' as 'the fundamental and perhaps the only virtue'. No doubt simplifying and caricaturing somewhat, Murdoch gives us a portrait of the moral agent as she finds him in the moral philosophy of the day, in both Sartre with his existentialism and such Oxford philosophers as Stuart Hampshire, R. M. Hare, and A. J. Ayer with their variations on utilitarianism, emotivism, prescriptivism, etc.: 'Characteristic of both [traditions] is the identification of the true person with the empty choosing will ... There is no point in talking of "moral seeing" since there is nothing morally to see.'[5] Over against this, however, Murdoch believes that she has the testimony of ordinary people on her side:

For I would suggest that at the level of serious common sense and of an ordinary non-philosophical reflection about the nature of morals it is perfectly obvious that goodness is connected with knowledge: not with impersonal quasi-scientific knowledge of the ordinary world, whatever that may be, but with a refined and honest perception of what is really the case, a patient and just discernment and exploration of what confronts one, which is the result not simply of opening one's eyes but of a certainly perfectly familiar kind of moral discipline.[6]

## Against voluntarism in ethics

From the beginning, then, Murdoch has attacked Oxford moral philosophy as having the same faults as Sartrian existentialism. Both (she thinks) oppose, in much too simple a fashion, an innocent self to a guilty society – something they inherit from Romanticism. For her, French existentialism and Anglo-Saxon linguistic philosophy share a certain voluntarism – a Romantic emphasis on The Will. Both separate the moral agent from all that surrounds him and, in speaking of The Will as if it were or could easily be 'free', they wholly ignore the power of the hidden, always opaque and frequently obsessive 'inner life'. They have an image of the moral agent as 'a highly conscious self-contained being', called to make choices dramatically in a kind of void. She wants to argue as follows:

> [I]f we consider what the work of attention is like, how con-
> tinuously it goes on, and how imperceptibly it builds up structures
> of value around us, we shall not be surprised that at crucial
> moments of choice most of the business of choosing is already
> over. This does not imply that we are not free, certainly not. But
> it implies that the exercise of our freedom is a small piecemeal
> business which goes on all the time and not a grandiose leaping
> about unimpeded at important moments. The moral life, on this
> view, is something that goes on continually, not something that is
> switched off in between the occurrence of explicit moral choices.[7]

Her moral psychology comes down to rejection of the idea of sudden or rapid moral change – 'conversion' – which seems to her a romantic and false idea. In contrast, she defends slow moral change as something difficult, piecemeal and always incomplete.

In an early essay Murdoch plays off the existentialist heroes in Hemingway, D. H. Lawrence, Sartre, Camus, Kingsley Amis, and others, against the characters in 'mystical' novels, where freedom and virtue are obedience to the Good – as in Graham Greene, Patrick White, Saul Bellow, Muriel Spark, William Golding and by implication herself: 'the new version of the man of faith, believing in goodness without religious guarantees, guilty, muddled, yet not without hope ... man as frail, godless, and yet possessed of genuine intuitions of an authoritative good'.[8]

At least since *The Time of the Angels* (1966), the novel which opens with the West Indian maidservant stumbling over a copy of Heidegger's *Sein und Zeit* on the study floor and centres on a memorably squalid and malignant priest (Anglican as it happens), Murdoch's fictions have explored what morality might mean in a world without God. What needs to be rediscovered is the possibility of having 'intuitions of an authoritative good'. Finally, in *Metaphysics as a Guide to Morals*, she sets out a vision of the sovereignty of the form of the good as offering the only salvation for a society as sick as ours – if we could learn to practise a certain self-discipline and spiritual asceticism. Far from fearing Diotima's ascent of love on the grounds that it requires gradual abandonment of our human particularity (Nussbaum's fear), Murdoch regards it as a paradigm, or anyway a parable, of the only way of moral growth that will bring us to full humanity. On her view, 'perception of beauty as unselfish attachment can bring about spiritual change':

'Falling in love', a violent process which Plato more than once vividly describes (love is abnegation, abjection, slavery) is for many people the most extraordinary and revealing experience of their lives, whereby the centre of significance is suddenly ripped out of the self, and the dreamy ego is shocked into awareness of an entirely separate reality.[9]

Plato, in the *Symposium* and elsewhere, is perfectly clear about the ambiguity of love, Murdoch thinks, but (unlike Nussbaum) she has no fears of Diotima's programme for the 'unselfing' by which one learns to see what is not oneself – by learning to see 'the authoritative good'.

## Fear of the fact/value dichotomy

'It is always a significant question to ask about any philosopher', Iris Murdoch once noted, 'what is he afraid of?'[10] Her own fear over the years has plainly been that the fact/value dichotomy which has dominated philosophy at least since Hume and Kant has had immensely destructive effects throughout our culture, in aesthetics and especially in the realm of ethics.

The idea that getting the facts right is an entirely separate enterprise from evaluating them means, at its best, that we can train ourselves to resist passing moral judgement on a situation until we have an objective and impartial account of what happened – not from some mythical neutral spectator's totally disinterested and indeed uninterested viewpoint – but as objective and impartial an account as is humanly attainable. When it turns out that the God's-eye viewpoint is unattainable, there is no call to rush to the other extreme, into the belief that objectivity and impartiality are *never* available for human beings – that it is *always* an illusion to think that such objectivity and impartiality have been attained, either because our minds are radically corrupt (on some theological story) or because we are always held in thrall by the ideology of our place in the class system or struggle (on some Marxist story).

It is fatally easy to slide into supposing that what is judged to be right or wrong can never be one of the facts but must always be nothing more than the arbitrary and optional projection of our subjective feelings about the situation. What Murdoch fears is that, with the loss of faith in traditional religion, people have no way of seeing that certain actions are transparently wrong or absolutely right – whatever the consequences and however one may feel. The results of an action may be painful or pleasurable, injurious or beneficial, for a large number of people in the vicinity, but that would not determine the rightness or wrongness of the action, so Murdoch would think. That is utilitarianism. We may feel good or otherwise about this or that action, and may even all have the same feelings about it, but for Murdoch the goodness or wickedness of an action is determinable independently of how we feel about it. That would be emotivism.

## Demythologized Christianity

Religion is inescapable, Murdoch clearly believes, and Platonist metaphysics is the only viable form it can now take – Christianity we can have only in a radically demythologized form. She refers with respect to Paul Tillich but Don Cupitt is the theologian for whom she has the greatest admiration: 'a very brave and valuable pioneer and a learned and accessible thinker'. 'We need a theology', she says, 'which can continue without God'.[11]

Murdoch is attracted by von Hügel's insistence on 'the actual practice and experience of specifically religious souls' – morality as a code of action but religion as deep spiritual sensibility.[12] His terms may 'now seem somewhat old-fashioned'; but his defence of the 'mystical element in religion' over against morality as a code of action 'may at least provide some useful alternative to philosophical attempts to discuss morality in terms of conflicts between (for instance) relativists, consequentialists, absolutists, etc'. Her obvious impatience with these currently flourishing debates has to do with the fact that in these debates religion is usually ignored – 'being regarded as something personal, perhaps aesthetic, a more colourful way of looking at morals, or as the last repository of a genuine belief in absolutes'.

As with Nussbaum and Heidegger, not to mention Barth, the unavoidability of religion is a theme that pervades Murdoch's work, both her fiction and her philosophy. The place of Christianity, however, among the great ancient religions, she finds very difficult. Judaism and Islam, 'partly because of a stricter avoidance of picturesque anthropomorphism and image-making', seem more acceptable. The difficulty with Christianity lies in God's being mediated into humanity by the figure of Jesus – 'a semblance of empirical being' (she takes it for granted that Christianity is irretrievably docetic). This illusion cannot be removed from believers' minds 'without removing the whole substance of belief'.[13]

The 'scandal of particularity', as theologians call it, the rootedness of Christianity in a set of determinate historical events, is the problem for Murdoch. She could not be more remote from Barth's Christocentric ontology – or from his conception of God as Trinity. She finds Plato's Trinity (Forms, Demiurge, World Soul as in the *Timaeus*) 'more morally radiant than that of the Church'. But then she thinks of the Christian Trinity as 'a mutually adoring set of thous'.[14] On the other hand, she regards Heidegger's renewal of the sacred as 'a piece of poetic metaphysical drama', in which the substitute for 'God' is 'a sinister historicised Fate'.[15]

Religion has to be demythologized. Murdoch invokes the institutionalized dichotomies of intellect/will, reason/faith, and fact/value and notes that they have been employed in 'recent theology' as 'an instrument of demythologization'. She mentions Ian Ramsey's *Religious Language* and John Robinson's *Honest to God*, but neither offers 'a programme for a totally new religious outlook' – that 'more ruthlessly radical position occupied by Don Cupitt'.[16]

'Modern man cannot accept the old religious story as, literally, descriptive.' Applying 'the fact–value fork', Cupitt insists that when the descriptive element in religious myth is separated out it proves to be false – but the value element may be preserved 'for its own sake'. Religious language is not descriptive but expressive. This means that 'the relation to God has to be enacted in spirituality because it can in no way be articulated in knowledge'. Murdoch finds the following remarks 'lucid and moving':

> [T]he religious imperative that commands us to become free spirit is ... an autonomously authoritative principle which has to be freely and autonomously adopted and self-imposed ... We choose to be religious because it is better so to be ... We must strive with all our might to become spirit, and what God is appears in the striving to answer this call ... God is, quite simply, what the religious requirement comes to mean as we respond to it ... A religion is a cluster of spiritual values.[17]

Cupitt 'stirs up thought where it is most needed. He speaks directly, as few do, about the necessity of new thinking about God and religion as something which concerns us all.' Murdoch likes his frequent references to 'Buddha and Void', and so on. Specifically, 'We have to learn to think of God in a new way, not as an object, not as a person.' 'That there is no God is also God.'

Murdoch's generous appreciation of Cupitt's demythologized Christianity does not rule out some 'contentious matters' – above all, his completely misguided conception of Plato. Before turning to that, however, it is worth noting that, as a philosopher in the analytical school, she regards a remark such as the one last quoted as making sense! As we shall see, she has great respect for Anselm's ontological argument, but her knowledge of medieval theology evidently does not include the standard thesis that God is not to be regarded as an object in any kind.[18] Christian theologians who are orthodox enough to believe in God as Trinity would have caveats about referring to God as 'a person'.[19] Above all, Cupitt's version of Christianity depends so totally on the fact/value dichotomy that it is surprising to find Murdoch treating his remarks so sympathetically.

## Against voluntarism in theology

Deeply attracted as she plainly is by it, Murdoch has certain worries about the doctrine that the reality of the deity is equatable with our personal striving toward the ultimate goal of free spirit. Such a 'subjectivist non-cognitive philosophy separates spirituality from knowledge'. In religion, as in ethics, it turns out, as we should expect from her early opposition to voluntaristic individualism, Murdoch is committed to metaphysical realism. In religion, as in ethics, some at least of the judgements that we make bear on what is the case, objectively, in the real world. If religion is 'separated from the world of fact and science', affording a certain personal spirituality no doubt, Murdoch admits that ' the programme may remind us ... of Feuerbach and Sartre'.[20]

It turns out that she wants to retain something at least of 'the spiritually informed understanding of "all the world" which traditional theism has implied'. The language of expressivism, non-cognitivism, etc. pictures religion as 'a matter of private (existentialist) choice': 'The idea of choosing the spiritual or religious as (an item among others but better) seems oddly abstract.' What is required, Murdoch says, apparently thinking she is supplementing or even correcting Cupitt, is 'an enlargement of our concept of religion through our greater tolerance and knowledge of other religions'. His emphasis on 'spirituality' apparently is not such an 'enlargement'.

But Murdoch shows little interest in other religions. If she uses Cupitt's demythologizing against the scandal of particularity in traditional Christianity, she also uses Platonist realism to discredit his voluntaristic non-realism. In 'Above the Gods', a dialogue in the manner of Plato,[21] she has Antagoras ('a sophist') vigorously attacking traditional religion ('essentially magic, a desire for power over hostile forces', etc.), insisting that 'We are the source of morality and rational judgment ... Now we can separate fact from value ... We are the lords of meaning ... There's nothing high, there's nothing deep, there's nothing hidden', etc. – very much in Cupitt's wake. Against this, Acastos ('a serious questing youth') argues that we are drawn to the idea of a sort of central Good: 'after all morality feels more like discovering something than just inventing it' ... 'religion is having an intense attitude and no time off' – it is 'about those awful deep things'. Morality is not just what we happen to think. Religion is a perpetual effort to take up a humble, unselfish vision of the world as a whole – much like Murdoch's own view, as we shall see in more detail. The Servant is called on to say what he thinks and he turns out to *know* there is a god – indeed he cannot even understand the problem – he is thus a (somewhat embarrassingly portrayed) representative of the many millions of unsophisticated believers in the various religions of the world. He might even be cast in the part that the 'virtuous peasant' plays in Murdoch's moral philosophy.

Finally the young Plato is compelled to speak. He argues that religion is not just a feeling or a hypothesis or something we happen not to know:

> [I]t's got to be the magnetic centre of everything ... it's beyond us, more real than us, we have to come to it and let it change us ... we're not volunteers, we're conscripts ... it's about what's absolute, what can't not be there ... it's happening all the time. If it's not everywhere, in the air we breathe, it isn't what I mean ... It's to do with life being a whole and not a lot of random choices ... If it's anything it must be everything ... It's not retiring from the world, it's knowing the world, the real world, this world as it really is, in all its details ... everybody knows this ... People know that good is real and absolute, not optional and relative, all their life proves it. And when they choose false goods they really know they're false. We can think everything else away out of life, but not value, that's in the very ground of things ... Religion is the love and worship of the good ... Nowadays people think of religion as something exotic and formal, and a bit aside from life, whereas what I mean is everywhere, like breathing ... it's about what ordinary people can believe ...

And so on.

'Expressivist voluntarism' is 'anti-Platonic' – 'segregating intellectual factual language [it] forces itself to discover a pure non-factual expressive language appropriate to religion.' This reminds Murdoch of Derrida, who 'makes a somewhat similar distinction between old ordinary prose and the ecstatic poeticized rhetoric of post-philosophical reflection'. True, the crisis in which theology and religion find themselves at present, in 'our' culture, poses problems of language – but 'these problems can be dealt with by all the vast resources of our ordinary reflective procedures and our ordinary metaphorical evaluative language'. Moreover: 'We are not cut off from St Paul.'

With these remarks Murdoch moves on to the attack. 'A division of language itself between fact and value not only isolates and diminishes value, it may damage the concept of truth. (As it is damaged by Derrida.)' Cupitt's picture of religion as a 'cluster of values' suggests 'a corner, a place among places, a thing among things'. That is not her sense of how things are: 'We have not been driven out of a brightly coloured mythical world which now belongs to a false illusioned past, leaving us with many facts, an imageless striving will and an expressive language' – rightly or wrongly the impression she gets from Cupitt's writing. On the contrary: 'We still live in the old familiar mysterious world and explain and clarify and celebrate it in the old endlessly fertile and inventive modes of speech' – a beautiful avowal of her faith: 'We enjoy the freedom of an imagination.' The picture of the world as 'full of images of God and hierarchies pointing to God', a picture we are supposed to want to demythologize and abandon, is – rather – 'fundamental in religion'. 'I think this is what (if we put Good for God) the world is full of.' That is to say, far from settling for nothing but the negative way, Murdoch speaks up for the affirmative way, 'which can find the divine everywhere in all the desire-driven burrowings of cognition' – which thus 'relates spirituality to the whole of our being'.[22]

Desire-driven, certainly – burrowings only, if you like – but *cognitive*. Plainly, for Murdoch, the world remains a site for the revelation and discovery of the Good. Religion has always been, she now says, passionate love of the Good. Now that there is no God for most of us to love (as she believes), the only way forward is back to Plato.

Far from having to reconstruct personal spirituality on the basis of the culturally institutionalized dichotomy between facts and values, we must – and can – return to Plato and recover a sense that the good is what we naturally love. It is what prompts us to look for the truth (the facts) as well as what gives our lives meaning (values). The good is there, whether or not we perceive or pursue it. It is not impossible to get from what 'is' to what 'ought' to be.

Murdoch cannot be happy with Cupitt's attitude to Plato, or his attitude to metaphysics in general. He accepts the metanarrative that has been with us at least since Nietzsche – that Western philosophy simply is Platonism – and, furthermore, that Platonism is 'a wholly unjustified and superstitious supernaturalism of thought, a supernaturalism of our intellectual standards, a supernaturalism of meanings (essentialism) and of knowledge, and finally a super-naturalism of philosophy itself . . . all of which has suddenly come to seem utterly absurd and unendurable'.[23]

Plainly this is our theme again. Cupitt – so Murdoch thinks – recognizes the absurdity and unendurableness of these possibilities of knowledge, meaning, truth, etc., always regarded as beyond our merely human attaining – always revealing us, then, as powerless and impotent beings who are trapped in an incurably defective cognitive plight, incapable of transcending our finitude in the way that we desire.

But to charge Plato with 'superstitious supernaturalism of thought' is too much for Murdoch. Rather, as we shall see, it is only by retrieving something of Plato's 'supernaturalism', his ontology of transcendence, that we shall be able to save humanity from the illusions of solipsism and the will to power.

## A mother-in-law's change of heart

Looking for an example with which to mount her attack, Murdoch chooses the story of the state of mind of a mother towards her daughter-in-law.[24] The mother has always felt hostile, thinking her a good-hearted girl, not exactly common but certainly unpolished and lacking in refinement – inclined to be pert and familiar, sometimes positively rude, always tiresomely juvenile, not good enough for her son. But the mother is very correct, behaves beautifully, manages never to let her real views appear. Suppose now that the young couple have emigrated or even that the daughter-in-law is now dead. Murdoch wants us to focus on what is happening, morally and spiritually, as something that happens entirely in the mother's mind. Time passes and of course the mother might settle into her picture of the daughter-in-law – never thinking of her but with regret that her son married such a person. But the mother might also be capable of self-criticism – capable (as Murdoch insists) of asking herself whether she was prejudiced, old-fashioned, narrow-minded, snobbish, perhaps even jealous. She might think again about her daughter-in-law. It may be too late to change her behaviour to her, but she can change her mind about her. She might come to see that the daughter-in-law had her good points – not so much vulgar as just down to earth or a bit unconventional, and so forth. The whole point, for Murdoch, is that the mother's view of her daughter-in-law changes – and it would all happen 'inside'.

One gloss would be that saying her attitude to her daughter-in-law had changed simply means that, if she now has to say something about her, she would say different things from the things she used to say. Then of course a change of mind often takes the form of coming out with a new view without anything in the way of introspection having occurred – you might not have realized your view had changed until you heard yourself saying something you would never have said a few months previously. But Murdoch works hard here to clear away the power of behaviourist/existentialist theorizings to let us see what she believes we all know perfectly well – which is that what the mother is trying to do is to see her daughter-in-law *justly*. She is learning to see her more *objectively*.

In this case, which Murdoch elaborates at much greater length than is quoted here, the mother is doing something with which we are very familiar. It is a struggle of the sort that innumerable novels describe: 'Freedom is not the sudden jumping of the isolated will in and out of an impersonal logical complex, it is a function of the progressive attempt to see a particular object clearly.'

The liberal-individualist conception of the will propagated by the behaviourist moral philosophers trades on the Humean picture of an impersonal world of facts – 'the hard objective world out of which the will leaps into a position of isolation'. More than that, 'Hume and Kant, the two patron saints of modern philosophy, abhor history, each in his own way, and abhor the particular notion of privacy which history implies'. They think they have to accept 'the fearful solitude of the individual marooned upon a tiny island in the middle of a sea of scientific facts'.[25] But all of that, Murdoch thinks, is the imposition of a false philosophy – the grid of the fact/value dichotomy above all – on perfectly ordinary everyday experience.

Murdoch's view is not new, she insists. On the contrary, it is commonplace in the Christian ethic, but most satisfactorily of all in the Platonic tradition:

> We ordinarily conceive of and apprehend goodness in terms of virtues which belong to a continuous fabric of being ... Where virtue is concerned we often apprehend more than we clearly understand and grow by looking ... This conclusion is feared and avoided by many moralists because it seems inimical to the operation of reason and because reason is construed on a scientific model ...26

But reality is *there*: 'There exists a moral reality, a real though infinitely distant standard ... Where virtue is concerned we often apprehend more than we clearly understand and grow by looking.' Murdoch spells this out. There is a process of learning, a progress, with which we are all familiar, which need not but often does take place in moral concepts in the dimension they possess in virtue of their relation to an ideal limit.

## Obedience, not resolution

What Murdoch wants is to remind us of the metaphysical background to morals – goodness is 'a magnetic but inexhaustible reality'. As moral agents, she thinks, we are *drawn*. 'Will is obedience not resolution.'[27] We do not so much leap into a void as allow ourselves to be led by a sense of the whole, however ambiguous and obscure.

Again and again, Murdoch refers us to the artist's eye – 'Any artist would appreciate the notion of will as obedience to reality, an obedience which ideally reaches a position where there is no choice.'[28] Indeed, the great merit of the moral psychology Murdoch proposes is that it does not contrast art and morals. It shows them to be two aspects of a single struggle – the struggle of the human subject to see whatever it may be *justly*. On the existentialist/behaviourist view art has to be for its own sake, gratuitous play, 'a sort of byproduct of our failure to be entirely rational'. But, in one of those important movements of return from philosophical theory to simple things which we are certain of, we come back to what we have always known about great art and about the moral insight it contains and the moral achievement it represents – 'Goodness and beauty are not to be contrasted ... Plato, who tells us that beauty is the only spiritual thing which we love immediately by nature, treats the beautiful as an introductory section of the good.' That is to say: aesthetic situations are not so much analogies of morals as actually cases of morals. 'Virtue is *au fond* the same in the artist as in the good man in that it is a selfless attention to nature: something which is easy to name but very hard to achieve'.[29]

## Anselm without theology

Murdoch is deeply attracted by the ontological argument for the existence of God – often treated as an absurdity, she says, but since its ancestry is congenially Platonic, she has no difficulty in rehabilitating it, in a demythologized form.

As a formal argument, set out by Anselm of Canterbury, it emerged from a context of deep belief and disciplined spirituality.[30] It has to be understood as an intellectual clarification of something that is already known and taken for granted. It is not an argument that might be put to an outsider. At best it is an argument to give oneself. But the main thrust of Murdoch's discussion is to lead us away from the famous objections to the ontological argument (God must exist in reality since he is something than which nothing greater can be thought, for otherwise he would not be something than which nothing greater can be thought) towards something that we know perfectly well empirically, which is that there are degrees of goodness which we see in ourselves and in the world. She speaks of 'our most general perceptions and experience of the fundamental and omnipresent (uniquely necessary) nature of moral value'[31] – 'thought of in a Christian context as God' – but some (like herself) would think that this has nothing to do with any God, Christian or otherwise. They would return to Plato and claim some uniquely necessary status for moral value (goodness) as something that (perhaps uniquely) defies ever being thought away from human experience – as something that, if once conceived of, is known henceforth as irrecusably real. This claim might go with concepts of religion which reject a personal God.

Anselm quotes Paul (Romans 1.20) in the course of arguing to the effect that we can conceive of God, seeing the invisible in the visible, the uncreated in the created, and the sovereign good in the lesser good. The context in Paul, 'interestingly enough', is the conduct of those who can or could see God but turn away. As Murdoch notes, there is no evidence Paul had ever read Plato – but 'Paul was certainly breathing Greek air and his intense mystical religiosity, which has so long and variously fed and disturbed the church, might find a home in Platonism'. She even quotes Karl Barth in support of this view![32] She appeals, however, not to esoteric or supernatural experience but to our ordinary perceptions of what is valuable. A vast array of different everyday situations suggests this internal connection between the good and the real. True, Anselm's argument comes from his sense of personal communion with God; but it has a background, through Augustine and Plotinus, in Plato, at least in Neoplatonic transformations of Plato's form of the good into a personified being. But we can demythologize that. We can return to Plato's insight into the fundamental connection between epistemology and ethics. The supremely good is the supremely real. Plato pictures objects of thought at different levels of insight as possessing different degrees of reality. The idea of the good cannot be compromised or tainted by its inclusion in actual human proceedings – just the opposite: its magnetism is omnipresent at the lowest levels. 'Good is unique, it is above being, it fosters our sense of reality as the sun fosters life on earth.'[33]

More than the ascent of love in Diotima's discourse we need to focus on the paradigm of the Cave in the *Republic*. What philosophers call the theory of forms is presented as a pilgrimage where different realities exist for individual thinkers at different levels, appearing at lower levels as shadows cast by objects at the next higher level – 'an endlessly instructive image'. 'The pilgrimage is inspired by intimations of realities which lie just beyond what can easily be seen.'[34]

Plato is much less 'democratic' than Anselm, Murdoch concedes. As a Christian, he believed that anyone could conceive of God – admittedly because he also believed that the Christian God gives the individual pilgrim direct supernatural help, a kind of help not offered by the form of the good.[35] The form of the good 'exerts a magnetic force' – but it is also 'impersonal and very distant' – which is not a very serious objection, in Murdoch's view. On the contrary: the favourite Christian theme about how near God is to us, and how personal the Christian God is, seems a banal story of how God ingratiates himself in a way that diminishes him. Far from finding the traditional Christian story of the God who becomes one of us attractive, she plainly finds it distasteful. She does not share Nussbaum's fears that identification with transcendent goodness must be alienating and dehumanizing. Murdoch clearly prefers the form of the good to be something remote – *semper major*, so to speak. Throughout her work she has insisted that our besetting vice is self-centred delusions of love, egoistic fantasies, that prevent our ascent to an objective vision of what is absolutely and intrinsically good. The more alienated we become towards the selfish ego the more human we become, Murdoch would think.

The best commentary on the Platonic ideas comes, Murdoch holds, in the myth of *anamnesis* in the *Meno*.[36] The slave boy, solving the geometrical problem, lets his attention focus on something dark and mysterious upon which light then falls and which he is then able to make his own – he 'sees' an object, invisible but grasped as 'there'. He is able to concentrate, to attend – and to attend is to wait. These metaphors are indispensable, Murdoch insists. It is as if the boy always knew the solution and were simply remembering it: 'The process of discovery is to be thought of as accompanied or motivated by a passion or desire which is increased and purified in the process' – and we are referred to Dante, *Paradiso* I, 7–9:

> approaching the object of its desires,
> Our intellect is so deeply absorbed
> That memory cannot follow it all the way

Again, this is something which we can all recognize, there is nothing special about it, it can be illustrated in many different kinds of human activity. In learning, in loving, in creatively imagining, in all such activities we are familiar with the experience of being overcome at a certain point by a sense of certainty: 'The importance and value of this disturbing experience is not dimin-ished by the fact that "certainties" or "recollections" are not solitary revelations, but take place in a general world where they can also be judged by results.' Moreover, 'you can only see at your own level and a little above'. Plato means that there is nothing esoteric or wildly metaphysical about any of this, Murdoch insists – it happens all the time: 'Truth and progress (or some truth and some progress) are the reward of some exercise of virtue, courage, humility, patience'. 'The creative artist is like the slave [in the Meno], he attends to the dark something out of which he feels certain he can, if he concentrates and waits, elicit his poem, picture, music: it is as if he remembered it or found it waiting for him, veiled but present.'

In other words, Murdoch is totally opposed to all those theories in ethics and aesthetics which may be classified as non-realist, anti-realist or projectivist. She rejects any philosophical story according to which we should accept that we project moral properties on to a world, and situations and entities within it, which in themselves have no moral properties. She believes that the non-cognitivist tradition in moral philosophy is just wildly untrue to what every-body knows perfectly well. The achieving of goodness is endlessly difficult, but everybody knows that too. Murdoch keeps returning to what she finds in familiar ordinary life: this belief in the existence of standards of goodness and truth which we never manage to attain – but which we certainly do not project or invent.

'It is of course a part of Anselm's faith that an omnipotent God can save any creature, that all, however benighted, may receive grace, distinguish right and wrong, have intimations of light, pray to God and experience his presence'[37] – that, for Murdoch, is illusory. Anselm, however, like Plato, appeals to our sense of goodness discoverable everywhere in life : 'The Forms are pure, separate and alone, the Form of the Good is above being' but 'we are saved by Eros and techne, by love and toil, by justice, by good desires and by the search for truth' – 'by the magnetism which draws us to innumerable forms of what is good; whether we are philosophers or mathematicians or politicians or lovers, or craftsmen'. In ordinary everyday life, 'we are continually shown the reality of what is better and the illusory nature of what is worse'. 'We learn of perfection and imperfection through our ability to understand what we see as an image or shadow of something better which we cannot yet see.'

Murdoch wants to strip away the supernatural aspects or

accidents of the traditional Christian God, especially his claim to be a person, in order to recapture Platonic or neo-Platonic realism. She wants religion to continue, in a way not unconnected with its past, as an assertion of an absolute (necessary) moral claim upon humanity. All our experience, as human beings, parents, lovers, artists, mechanics, etc., reveals and verifies how the unique and special and all-important knowledge of good and evil is learnt and relearnt in every kind of human activity: 'The question of truth, which we are indeed forced to attend to in all our doings, appears here as an aspect of the unavoidable nature of morality.'

To speak of 'religious language' as something specialized, supposedly expressive rather than referential, is to separate religion from the truth-seeking struggle of life as a whole: 'religion is not a special subject or one activity among others'. What is required is *attentiveness* – a learning, often with immense difficulty, to wait for something to be revealed, to wait for illumination from something other than oneself.

## Desire for perfection

We know of perfection as we look upon what is imperfect ... The human scene is one of moral failure combined with the remarkable continued return to an idea of goodness as unique and absolute ...The idea of perfection haunts all our activity, and we are well aware of how we try to blot it out ... This 'Good' is not the old God in disguise, but rather what the old God symbolized.[38]

Kant, who took the duty of truth-telling to be absolute, also said that 'the beautiful was a symbol of the morally good'. 'The good artist is a sort of image of the good man, the great artist is a sort of image of the saint' – and just as one jibs at this assertion and thinks that one has found the weakness in Murdoch's picture of the moral life, she at once says – 'he is only a sort of image, since in his whole person he may be a dreadful egoist'. 'Artists have their own specialized temptations to egoism and illusions of omnipotence' – 'Art is power' – but inside his work, and 'in so far as he is an artist', the artist can be 'humble and truthful and brave and inspired by a love of perfection'.[39]

There is always work to do:

We can always work at something, somehow, for someone, for some truth or some good ... Art and craft are formal images of all our busy activities wherein we do well or badly ... good art can figure, not only as an image, but as a kind of evidence, a sort of Ontological Proof, since here we may see more clearly on display how when we connect what is real with what is good we find out what truth means, and how in seeking truth (the right formulation, the better work) we also understand virtue and the 'feel' of reality.[40]

Murdoch quotes Rilke, about Cézanne: 'The consuming of love in anonymous work'.[41] The egoism of the good artist or craftsman is 'burnt up' in the work – just as in the quiet unpretentious life of some selfless person egoism disappears unobtrusively into care of others. 'Some saintly figures are self-evidently "religious", others may be invisible, buried deep in families or offices or silent religious houses.' 'At the highest level this is practical mysticism, where the certainty and the absolute appear incarnate and immediate in the needs of others.'[42]

The proof, the evidence, of the necessity of good runs through the grasp of an idea of perfection which comes to us in innumerable ordinary everyday situations, where we are trying to do something well or are aware of failure. Without this grasp we should lose our grip on our humanity. Those who are not grasped by the necessity (non-contingency) of goodness have a very inadequate understanding of our situation. 'What is perfect must exist, that is, what we think of as goodness and perfection, the "object" of our best thoughts, must be something real, indeed especially and most real, not as contingent accidental reality but as something fundamental, essential and necessary.'[43] 'What is experienced as most real in our lives is connected with a value which points further on' ... 'Our consciousness of failure is a source of knowledge' ... 'We are constantly in process of recognizing the falseness of our "goods", and the unimportance of what we deem important' ... 'Great art teaches a sense of reality, so does ordinary living and loving' ...'We find out in the most minute details of our lives that the good is the real'.

## Back to Plato

Murdoch insists that Plato is a deeply religious thinker – not that he believed in a personal god or gods – he did not, which is precisely why he speaks to our age. A thinker is religious, in Murdoch's sense, when he finds there is no gap, ultimately, between the facts and our values. On the contrary: we live in a world that makes claims on us, morally, ethically – claims we can ignore, claims to which we may be blind, but we are not the ones who invent them or project them – we find them, discover them. And, far from being haunted by standards of perfection according to which we shall always be diminished and dehumanized (Nussbaum's fear), it is precisely because we constantly recognize our imperfections, our failures, that we have access to knowledge of reality and knowledge of ourselves. That is Murdoch's version of aspiring to transcend ourselves.

In her rich account of his attack on artists – in which she insists on 'the fundamentally religious nature of Plato's objections to art' – Murdoch offers an account of Diotima's discourse on love which is fascinatingly different in emphasis from Nussbaum's, albeit plainly a reading of the same text:

> Plato's Eros is a principle which connects the commonest human desire to the highest morality and to the pattern of divine creativity in the universe ... In spite of Plato's repeated declaration that philosophers should stay chaste and his require-ment that the soul must try to escape from the body, it is the whole Eros that concerns him, and not just some passionless distillation.[44]

In fact sexual love, and sexual energy in its many transformations, are central to Murdoch's conception of Plato's philosophy:

> The Eros described to Socrates by Diotima in the *Symposium* is not a god but a daemon, a mediating spirit of need and desire, the mixed-up child of Poverty and Plenty.... This Eros, who is lover not beloved, is the ambiguous spiritual mediator and moving spirit of mankind.

Specifically:

> Carnal love teaches that what we want is always 'beyond', and it gives us an energy which can be transformed into creative virtue. When a man has thus directed his thoughts and desires towards beauty of the mind and spirit he will suddenly receive the vision, which comes by grace, *theia moira*, of the Form of Beauty itself, absolute and untainted and pure.

Murdoch quotes F. M. Cornford's remark that 'the best commen-tary on the *Symposium* is to be found in the *Divine Comedy*', where as Dante parts from Virgil he feels the magnetic pull of divine wisdom in the person of his beloved Beatrice (*Purgatorio* XXVII):

> I have brought you here with intelligence and art;
> Now you must take your pleasure for your guide

But we need to prolong the quotation: Virgil leaves Dante sitting in the sun, in a field of flowers:

> While those beautiful eyes, happy and beautiful,
> Which, in their tears, moved me to come to you,
> Are coming ...

It is to be the face, and in particular the eyes, of his beloved, that will take Dante beyond where Virgil's intelligence and art have brought him. The metaphysical intention that is so passionately woven into Plato's erotic myth is to the effect, Murdoch insists, 'that a sense of beauty diminishes greed and directs the energy of the soul in the direction of the real and the good'. To see the real is to see its independence and hence to recognize its claims – and 'to overcome egoism in its protean forms of fantasy and illusion ... is automatically to become more moral'. As we respond to the authority of the good and the beautiful our desire is transfigured and 'we experience the transcendence of the real and the personal ego fades' – just as Plato says: we 'escape from the mean petty slavery of the particular case and turn towards the open sea of beauty'.[45]

Far from dehumanizing us, Diotima's project releases us from our naturally self-centred state. We are inspired to 'activities which increase our grasp of the real, and because they diminish our fantasy-ridden egoism are self-evidently good'. The difference from Nussbaum's interpretation lies in Murdoch's starting point – her conviction that we are by nature selfish and egocentric beings who need the authority of independent non-human absolutes such as truth, goodness and beauty, to draw us away from the desire 'to de-realize the other, devour and absorb him, subject him to the mechanism of our own fantasy'.[46]

# CHAPTER FIVE

# IRIGARAY AND THE SENSIBLE TRANSCENDENTAL

Luce Irigaray[1] offers a reading of Diotima's speech in Plato's *Symposium* which is interestingly different from those by both Nussbaum and Murdoch. Neither Nussbaum nor Murdoch, let alone Barth and Heidegger, would be expected to have much interest in feminist theory.[2] In *An Ethics of Sexual Difference*, in conjunction with the rest of her substantial body of writing, Irigaray deals with the metaphysics of self-transcendence in another way, utterly unlike any of the four that we have examined so far, but worth attention.

## *Hegel on sexual difference*

One of the problems for readers of Irigaray's work who are sympathetic to the case for feminism is whether or not her project is not so utopian and eschatological – so religious, in a sense – that she only perpetuates the ideology of sexual difference in our culture which reflects and corroborates discrimination against women in all sorts of ways.

Consider first one of the standard texts on the difference between men and women – Hegel:

> Women are capable of education, but they are not made for the higher sciences, philosophy and certain forms of artistic production, which demand something universal. Women may have happy ideas, taste, and elegance, but they do not possess the ideal. The difference between man and woman is like that between animals and plants. Men correspond more to the character of an animal, while women correspond more to a plant because it is a more placid unfolding, the principle underlying it being the more indeterminate unity of feeling. When women are at the helm of

government, the state is at once in jeopardy, because women regulate their actions not by the demands of universality, but by arbitrary inclinations and opinions. Women are educated – who knows how? – as it were by breathing in ideas, by living rather than acquiring knowledge. A man, on the other hand, attains his position only by they stress of thought and much technical exertion.[3]

Every metaphor there calls for analysis. Women are like plants, placidly unfolding, absorbing knowledge by breathing it in, governed by contingency, inspiration and taste; men are like animals, developing by struggle and effort, attaining the order of generality, universals and ideas.

The physical difference between men and women generates a difference at the level of intellectual and ethical significance, so Hegel says. That is to say, one sex is mind, *das Geistige*, intellectuality or perhaps spirituality, where the self divides into self-directed personal autonomy and into knowing and willing of free universality – the self-consciousness of conceptual thinking and the willing of objective final end. The other sex is also mind, *das Geistige*, certainly, but maintains itself in unity as knowledge and willing of the substantive in the form of concrete individuality and feeling. Men have their real substantive life in the state, in science and suchlike, in struggling and labouring with the outside world and with themselves: they fight their way out of their *Entzweiung* (splitness) to self-subsistent unity with themselves. Women, on the other hand, have their substantive destiny in the family, and have their ethical *Gesinnung*, inwardness, in family piety.

For Hegel a community cannot, as contract theorists imply, consist of individuals who, constantly reflective in their thoughts and deeds, maintain themselves in unity by deliberate acts of choice. On the contrary: there has to be a background, a matrix, of unreflective relationships and activities, in which people do not stand out as individual subjects. This background is the ethical substance. Reflective self-aware subjects emerge from a substantial life in which people are at one in unreflective ties of feeling – above all, then, in family piety as particularly sustained and preserved by women.

Of course, Hegel's picture of the difference between men and women is absurd, at one level. Surely men also sometimes have bright ideas, taste, etc? (But perhaps these would be artistic men, ballet dancers and the like, hence displaying femininity, not to say effeminacy?) Do men in charge not often rule according to arbitrary inclinations and opinions? (But perhaps that would only mean that they had fallen away from the highest standards of rational deliberation, impartiality, etc., and become in effect as irrational as women?) There again, is not all education dependent on an atmosphere? Is not the stress of reflective thinking always dependent on the substantive life of the community, if by that we mean the background of unchallengeable practices, pre-theoretical reactions and convictions, emotional stability, etc.? Has not a great deal of recent philosophical work been out to remind us of just how dependent any intellectual life always is on the tacit and unexamined, indeed unexaminable and untheorizable practices of the tradition-borne and tradition-bearing cultural-linguistic environment, and so forth?

The deepest motivation of *The Fragility of Goodness*, it might be said, is Nussbaum's desire to relate the Platonic conception of the life of reason and the ideal of rational self-sufficiency to 'a kind of human worth that is inseparable from vulnerability, an excellence that is in its nature other-related and social, a rationality whose nature is *not* to attempt to seize, hold, trap, and control, in whose values openness, receptivity, and wonder play an important part'. She finds an interplay of images in these two distinctive conceptions of practical rationality, aligning the agent as hunter, trapper, male, with a soul that is hard and impenetrable, over against an image of the agent as plant, child, female, with the soul soft and porous though with a definite structure. Put simply, the thesis in her book is that Plato feared the image of the moral agent as a plant, elaborated an extremely attractive version of rational self-sufficiency, the story in the *Symposium*, and came himself to think it lacking in some indispensable human values (hence the *Phaedrus*); but that it fell to his student Aristotle to work out an account of rationality that incorporates both sets of imagery.[4]

Heidegger's work is motivated by a desire to remind us of the obvious (though often forgotten and 'theorized away') fact that we have a more basic relationship to the world than that of a self-sufficient subject directing himself at the world by means of his mental content. For the Heidegger of *Sein und Zeit*, the background to all intelligent activity is our everyday skill at coping with things in the world and with one another. For the Heidegger of the later essays, the human being is a player in the game of the fourfold. Either way, Heidegger is trying to replace rationality in the network of practices – intelligent and intelligible practices – that exhibit what we *are*. He calls into question the Platonic assumption that intelligent activity is essentially a display of theorizing and the Cartesian conception of the self-conscious subject – both of which are easily detectable in Hegel's account of the difference between women and men.

Neither Nussbaum nor Heidegger places much emphasis on Hegel's concept of the divided self (*die Entzweiung*), which characterizes men. Women develop their sense of self-identity more harmoniously, in the family (the realm of caring). Men, on the other hand, have to struggle to construct their self-identity, in effect because they are out in the streets, in the market, the legal profession, the police force, or whatever (the realm of competition). What Murdoch brings to the discussion, perhaps in her novels more than in her philosophical writings, is a deep sense, not only of the rich background of everyday skills and practices which allows us occasionally to have moments of illumination and crises of decision, and so on, but also of the inner turbulence of *any* human being, man or woman. Perhaps this is due to her interest in the legacy of Freud. 'The background to morals', Murdoch says, 'is properly some sort of mysticism, if by this is meant a non-dogmatic essentially unformulated faith in the reality of the Good, occasionally connected with experience'. 'The virtuous peasant', she goes on to say (certainly one of Heidegger's familiars!), 'knows, and I believe he will go on knowing, in spite of the removal or modification of the theological apparatus, although what he knows he might be at a loss to say.'[5] But there are few peasants, virtuous or otherwise, in Murdoch's fictional world, which is, rather, a world of (mostly) southern English professional people – 'vain bookish civil servants, morally squeamish men whose sheer egoism is driving them mad, emotionally greedy women, precocious adolescents, isolated and awkward good characters' – 'all involved in the great, lonely hunt for love and consolation and power'. The assumption is always that 'people are secretly much odder, less rational, more often powered by obsession and passion than they outwardly pretend or know'.[6] To that extent, Hegel's placid housewives have surely overtaken his inwardly divided men, and all have become vastly more troubled beings.

## Sexual difference

Sexual difference, according to Irigaray, is *the* philosophical issue in Western culture at the present time, which could be our salvation if we were to think it through. In this respect at least, like Barth,

Heidegger and Murdoch, Irigaray is out to save our society from impending doom by offering a systematic account of what we must do in order to retrieve or, rather, in her case, to discover for the first time what the authentic human way of being is. Her proposal is every bit as single minded and all-encompassing and just as unique and idiosyncratic as, and therefore incommensurable with, any of those we have looked at. Where Barth centres on the singular humanity of Jesus Christ raised from the dead, Heidegger on the playfulness of the quaternity, and Murdoch on the sovereignty of the form of the good, Irigarary invites us to focus on the ultimacy of sexual difference.

Whether she turns to philosophy, science or religion – and, significantly, Irigaray never doubts the inescapability of religion[7] – she finds that sexual difference as an issue remains undiscussed and neglected. If we were to explore it, however, the implications would be immense:

> Think of it as an approach that would allow us to check the many forms that destruction takes in our world, to counteract a nihilism that merely affirms the reversal or the repetitive proliferation of status quo values – whether you call them the consumer society, the circularity of discourse, the more or less cancerous diseases of our age, the unreliability of words, the end of philosophy, religious despair or regression to religiosity, scientistic or technical imperialism that fails to consider the living subject.[8]

Whatever the changes that have occurred in recent decades, with respect to the liberation of women in Western society, the revolution that Irigaray seeks has not yet begun.

She is not simply drawing attention to the fact that sexual difference is a topic that has been neglected in philosophy as if it could now be added to the agenda without affecting the subject as a whole. It is only now that women, and men, have noticed that women have never contributed much to philosophy that the issue of sexual difference has become visible. Philosophy has been such a man's subject, Irigaray thinks, that its androcentric assumptions have always been invisible until recently. She argues that the categories in which the nature of women has been conceived derive from the imagination and experience of men. Thus women do not, and cannot, appear as themselves. They are incorporated in philosophical and religious constructions which effectively render them invisible. What Irigarary urges is that women learn to break into this symbolic order, with claims about their sexuality and spirituality, which may eventually unsettle assumptions about their 'difference' from men. Women have to learn to assert the feminine from the side of their own bodies – from the site of their own bodies.

We may be inclined to think that the alternative to men, in the Western understanding of human life with its associated practices, must be women. Irigaray maintains, however, that the alternative to men, and thus the other kind of beings over against whom men have identified and defined themselves, have always been, not women, but gods. To get her version of self -transcendence going, that is to say, she has to get deep into religion. Quite explicitly, there is no way of doing philosophy now which does not involve doing a good deal of theology. That does not just mean clearing theology out of the way, as Heidegger once thought it was necessary to do. It means, as he too evidently found, that existing religion, whether properly understood or not, needs to be challenged by new forms of religious discourse – his cosmological myth of the mirror-game of the fourfold. But we need to get some other pieces of Irigaray's argument in place before we come to her interest in religion.

## Diotima's speech

One of her central notions is that of what she calls 'the sensible transcendental'. This apparently paradoxical expression is a heuristic device, something of a metaphysical conceit, a yoking of contraries, bringing the sense-perceptible together with the transcendental in the hope of subverting or avoiding or simply outflanking the traditional metaphysical duality of the physical-empirical versus the spiritual-intelligible orders – Plato's two worlds. By the time of Kant, in modern philosophical jargon, there is a distinction between the material or sense-perceptible and the transcendental or intelligible domains. That is to say, there is a distinction between knowledge of time-bound entities and situations, for which evidence may be acquired directly through experience, and knowledge of temporally unconditioned structures and conditions of possibility, which do not themselves appear, but make the appearance of these direct evidences possible. Knowledge of these temporally unconditioned structures is available only to beings that are also temporally unconditioned. For Kant, that is to say, there is no knowledge for human beings of transcendental conditions of possibility.

In *An Ethics of Sexual Difference* Irigaray suggests that in order to make sense of this Kant has to construe the relation between the unlimited and the finite on the model of the relation claimed in Christianity between God and Christ. She then suggests that such dependency on a Christian model subverts the conceptuality of Kant's argument. Irigaray notes that what usually happens is that men appropriate to themselves the nontemporal standpoint from which it is supposed to be possible to acquire unconditional knowledge while women are assigned the position that makes such knowledge impossible.

According to Irigaray, there are two different possibilities within ancient Greek philosophy. In the pre-Socratic fragments, and in the work of Plato and Aristotle, but of course obscured, there are insights opposed to the surface tenor of the text. In Diotima's speech in particular, Plato both glimpsed love as some kind of 'intermediary' and lost sight of it.

The intermediary position that love occupies between a series of oppositions is its defining characteristic, so Irigaray maintains. Diotima's doctrine is dialectical – but not in the usual way – not using opposition to make one term pass into another in order to produce a synthesis of the two but rather, from the outset, Diotima uncovers an intermediary that will never be left behind merely as a means. She does not have to destroy two terms in order to achieve a third, a synthesis, that is neither one nor the other. Rather: Diotima reveals a third term that is always already there – permitting movement from poverty to wealth, from ignorance to wisdom, from mortality to immortality.

What can love – eros – be, Socrates asks Diotima, when they have agreed that eros is not a god?[9] Can eros be a mortal? Anything but that, she replies – eros is 'something between a mortal and an immortal'. Eros is 'a great *daimon*, for the whole of the daimonic is between the divine and the mortal'. Diotima goes on to speak of love as 'that which possesses the power to interpret and transport human things to the gods and divine things to human beings, entreaties and sacrifices from below, ordinances and requitals from above' – 'being midway between, it makes each supplement the other, so that the whole is combined in one.' 'Gods and human beings do not mingle; but *to daimonion* is how all the intercourse and conversation of humans with gods and gods with humans takes place.'

What is the method (*tropos*) of those who pursue love, Diotima asks Socrates – what is the behaviour (*praxis*) whose eagerness and straining are to be termed love? What is this work (*ergon*)? 'Can you tell me?' To this Socrates has nothing to say: 'Ah, Diotima, in that case I should hardly be admiring you and your wisdom, and sitting at your feet to be enlightened on just these questions!' That is to say, the philosopher whose mission was to enlighten as many of the young men of Athens as would allow their ideas to be submitted to his critique finds that he needs to be enlightened by Diotima's wisdom about matters erotic. 'Well, I will tell you', she says: 'it is a begetting on a beautiful thing by means of both the body and the soul.' But Socrates confesses that he does not understand this. 'Let me put it more clearly', Diotima says: 'The union of a man and a woman is a generation, a thing divine; in the living creature that is mortal it is something immortal.'

This remark, Irigaray claims, 'never seems to have been heard'.[10] Indeed it is not clear that Diotima pauses long enough for it to be grasped. For she immediately accentuates the procreative aspect of love. What the text means, however, according to Irigaray, is that the action of love is always already fecund, prior to any procreation. Diotima speaks, almost at once, of 'something eternal and immortal in our mortal life'.[11]

Misconceived perhaps, and thus misreported by Socrates, anyway by Plato, Diotima proceeds to discuss mortal and immortal love separately, as if they were different in kind and as if she had forgotten her claim about the 'divine thing' that lovers confer on one another. She talks of lovers in body and lovers in soul. Could this be the effect of 'the foundational act of meta-physics', Irigaray asks. Diotima seems to betray her insight that falling in love is a becoming of the lovers themselves, of love in each lover, or between the lovers. Instead, she allows it to become 'the teleological quest for what is deemed a higher reality and often situated in a transcendence inaccessible to our mortal condition'. That is to say: 'Immortality has already been put off until death and does not figure as one of our constant tasks as mortals, a transmutation that is endlessly incumbent upon us here, now – its possibility having been inscribed in the body, which is capable of becoming divine.'

For Socrates, beauty of body and beauty of soul have been split. The love of a woman becomes the lot of a man who, being incapable of creativity in his soul, can do no better than perpetuate his name by fathering a son. 'By getting children they acquire an immortality, a memorial, and a state of bliss, which in their imagining they for all succeeding time procure.' But that means that 'the lovers disappear'. Their relationship now has a teleology, a goal, a duty, an end beyond itself. We have even been taught to believe, Irigaray says, that it is forbidden or futile to be lovers unless we have procreation as our goal. Yet, if we look more attentively, we see that Diotima's claim is rather that the union of man and woman is itself already always a divine affair – 'an immanent efflorescence of the divine of and in the flesh' – 'an irreducible mediator, at once physical and spiritual, between the lovers' – 'not already codified duty, will, desire'.[12]

Diotima understands love as 'the intermediary state that inhabits lovers and transports them from the condition of mortals to that of immortals'. Socrates understands this, but, so Irigaray claims, the more teleological love becomes, the more of an objective it has, the farther away it gets – the more marginalized and suppressed it is. Having children is regarded as better than being in love: 'carnal procreation is subordinated to the engendering of beautiful and good things'. For Socrates, having adopted sons is better than having your own – sons found in the elective affinity of philosophical exchange rather than sons born by merely impregnating a woman. Love between men, not surprisingly, becomes superior to love between man and woman. According to the ascent of love – after pursuing beauty in a body one passes to pursuing beauty in someone's soul and eventually one has a vision of a beauty 'which is eternal, not growing up or perishing, increasing or decreasing'. One attains this sublime beauty starting with loving the natural beauty of young men and passing step by step from beautiful male bodies to beautiful occupations, sciences, and so on, until one reaches that sublime science which is supernatural beauty itself. Having contemplative vision of the divine one becomes immortal – 'It will not appear to you to be according to the measure of gold and raiment, or of lovely boys and striplings' – what Irigaray calls 'a sensible transcendental', 'the material texture of beauty'. One will have 'seen' the real which precedes all reality, all forms, all truth of particular sensations or constructed idealities. 'Neither the good nor the true nor justice nor government of the city would occur without beauty.' 'Beauty itself ... confounds the opposition between immanence and transcendence ... as an always already sensible horizon on the basis of which everything would appear.' 'But one would have to go back over everything to discover it in its enchantment.'

A birth into a transcendence, that of the other, still in the world of the senses ('sensible'), still physical and carnal, and already spiritual ... This would be possible only when we are faithful to the perpetual newness of the self, the other, the world. Faithful to becoming, to its virginity, its impulsion, without letting go the support of bodily inscription.[13]

Here, Irigaray appeals to Descartes: 'Wonder would be the passion of the encounter between the most material and the most metaphysical, of their possible conception and fecundation one by the other.' She picks up his notion of 'admiration'. Wonder, she claims, refers to the surprise of a first encounter. Instead of the ignorance of, or hostility to, the otherness of the woman, the notion of women's alterity that prevails in a patriarchal culture, we have to return to the first of all 'passions'. 'When the first encounter with some object surprises us and we judge it to be new, or very different from what we supposed that it ought to be, that causes us to wonder and be surprised.'[14] When an object exceeds one's expectations – particularly with its self-contained unpredicted autonomy, its otherness – this causes surprise and wonder. It is encountered for the first time, without preconceptions, without being fitted into some teleological scheme. One is simply awe-struck by its uniqueness, its originality.

What would happen, Irigaray asks, if a man and a woman were to experience this wonder, in the recognition of the sexual difference one from the other:

What the other is, who the other is, I never know ... But the other who is forever unknowable to me is the other who is sexually different from me. This astonishment, marvelling, wonder in the face of the unknowable should return to its place: that of sexual difference. The passions have been either repressed, stifled, reduced or reserved for God. Sometimes a space of wonder is reserved for the art object. But never is it situated nor dwells in this place: between man and woman. In this place, attraction, avidity, possession, consumption, disgust, etc. emerge. Not this wonder which looks at what it looks at forever, always for the first time, and which never seizes the other as its object. To whom this object remains unable to be taken (in), unable to be possessed, irreducible.[15]

When two sexually different beings encounter one another, in acceptance and respect of their own and their partner's specificities, their meeting will be marked with astonishment, wonder, endless wonder. When two such autonomous sexual beings meet, each marvels at and is surprised by the other's difference. This wonder is based on the recognition that 'the two sexes are unable to be substituted, one for the other, in the status of their difference'. Each is awed by the other – only then can each give to and take what the other has to offer:

> Wonder keeps the two sexes non-interchangeable regarding the status of their difference. It maintains between them a free and attracting space, a possibility of separation and union ... There would never be an overstepping of the interval. There would never be an accomplishment of consummation. This accomplishment being a deception. One sex is not entirely consumable by the other. There is always a remainder.[16]

An erotic encounter must leave something of a remainder of each partner untapped by the other, a residue that is irreducible to their relationship. This untapped reservoir is what guarantees the radical alterity of each to the other, and yet explains their attractions and the fruitfulness of their encounter. Neither seen as identities, opposites nor complements, the two sexes occupy their own spaces, create their own ideals – man and woman is a most mysterious and creative couple. This is not to say that other couples may not have a lot in them, but that man and woman is the most mysterious and creative.

The meeting of the two sexually different beings is generative, productive – not just, then, in terms of the 'product' which is a child. On the contrary, and this is the whole point, as Irigaray sees it, the remainder left over by the couple, that unconsumable residue within each sex, has to be reserved 'for God'.

In the appropriate kind of erotic encounter, then, the opposition between immanence and transcendence would be confounded; there would be *extase instante*, in another of Irigaray's phrases: an outward going which is always an inward going, immanent transcendence, sensibility transcending itself.

Summing all that up, then, we may say that, for Irigaray, sexual difference is inescapable and that we are only at the beginning of freeing femininity from masculine images of it so that at last women's sexual specificity and autonomy can be fulfilled, or rather discovered for the first time. How this is to happen, primarily and in practice, is by way of erotic exchanges between two beings who are in awe and wonder of each other's otherness – marriages – in which at last the male subject's encounter is not with his own reflection but with an autonomous other, in which the female becomes a subject in her own right, not just the fulfilment of the male's patriarchal-phallocentric needs.

It is a good story – why does it have to be supported by the claim that eros, in Diotima's speech, the *daimon* between mortals and the divine, this 'divine affair', this 'immortality in the mortal', means a non-teleological and non-procreative sexual encounter? In her detailed analysis of the *Symposium* Nussbaum never mentions this section of the text, though there need be little doubt that she would endorse Irigaray's conception of the 'transcendent immanence' of sexual intercourse independently of any child-making purpose. Murdoch is happy to speak of eros as 'the high translated form of sexual energy, a daemon not a god', and count it (him) as 'our guide into the realm of spirit'. She also thinks that Schopenhauer's conception of sex as ensuring the continuation of the species is a good deal less than Plato's eros. In her most substantial analysis of the text she too makes no reference to the phrases of which Irigaray makes so much. She insists, rather, on Diotima's reference to Eros as a terrible magician, an alchemist, a sorcerer: 'This creature, appearing amid the funny confused *joie de vivre* of the *Symposium*, is one of the most enlightening images in the mythology of morals'. (She lets him loose in many of her novels.) But her interest lies in eros as an 'energy' that can be 'obsessive, destructive and selfish, as well as spiritual, unselfish, a source of the good life'. It does not occur to her to invoke this text in support of a conception of sexual union as the possibility of 'something eternal and immortal in our mortal life', independently of its leading to the conception of a child or a work of art.[17]

## No androgynous utopia

Irigaray is totally opposed to 'gender neutralization' in some future utopia of androgynous beings. She is quite apocalyptic about this: 'to wish to suppress sexual difference is to call for genocide more radical than any previous destruction in history'. The ultimate aim of the 'liberation of women' is not 'equality with men', which would only be deeper assimilation into masculinity as traditionally represented and imagining itself. Indeed she regards a certain egalitarianism as the ultimate ruse of masculine supremacy. For Irigaray, the incontestable fact – simultaneously biological and cultural, sensible and transcendental – is the division of the human species into two kinds, feminine and masculine, which is not the primitive residue of humanity's animal origins or a trivial difference exalted out of all proportion by phallocentric mythologies out to subjugate women, or whatever. Quite literally, the fate of the world lies in this difference: either a totalitarian neutralization or a culture in which the drama of sexual alterity will bring about unprecedented and unimagined creativity.

'Unimagined', of course, because 'the liberation of women goes well beyond the frame of feminist struggles which nowadays too often go no further than critique of patriarchy, separatism, or the claim to equality with men, without putting forward new values to live sexual difference with justice, civility and spiritual fertility.'[18] In fact we need a more profound understanding of what distinctively feminine identity is, or might be. And it is happening – a new kind of relationship between women and men is emerging, in certain marriages. What is now at issue, Irigaray sums up, is a kind of politics of the couple: 'The most intimate and universal, the most everyday and divine locus of this is situated between woman and man.'

## The unavoidability of theology

But, finally, this discovery of the divinity in sexual encounter cannot be separated from revaluation – rediscovery – of the divine. 'Religion as a social phenomenon cannot be ignored.' 'God' must be 'not simply neutered in the current pseudoliberal way' but 'questioned' – more than 'questioned':

It seems we are unable to eliminate or suppress the phenomenon of religion. It re-emerges in different forms, some of them perverse: sectarianism, theoretical or political dogmatism, religiosity ... Therefore, it is crucial that we rethink religion, and especially religious structures, categories, initiations, rules and utopias, all of which have been masculine for centuries. Keeping in mind that today these religious structures often appear under the name of science and technology.[19]

According to Irigaray, then, women have to rediscover their relation to the divine – to discover a relation to the divine which would be *theirs*, and not just men's. Man – that is to say, *men* – have defined themselves by reference to a God who serves as the horizon of their identity, as the free and autonomous subject of whom they are the images. Women have no such divine mirror, and thus are alienated: 'deprived of God, they are forced to comply with models that do not match them, that exile, double, mask them, cut them off from themselves and from one another, stripping away their ability to move forward into love, art,

101

thought, toward their ideal and divine fulfilment'.[20] The role which women are accorded within men's religion is a 'vocation for collaborating in the redemption of the world through suffering and chastity'.

Religion, in one way or another, often involves sacrifice. Irigaray notes René Girard's story about how any and every human community survives by periodical cathartic immolation of some scapegoat. The function of religion is supposedly to keep violence out of the community by means of scapegoating or by some ritual that substitutes for it.[21] But she sees a more fundamental sacrifice that Girard never mentions: the exclusion of women. And this leads her to a series of questions about the necessity of sacrifice in the first place:

> How does it come about that men cease to regulate their meetings, their communities, their prayers exclusively in accordance with natural cycles: morning, noon, and night; the different seasons; the solar and lunar periods; the various positions of the earth, or the other planets, etc?[22]

Is it impossible for a community to gather together without needing a sacrifice? Irigaray reminds us that there are many different traditions with non-sacrificial ways of religious expression. Certain (Eastern) religious traditions have ritual and prayer consisting in bodily exercise such as yoga, tai chi, karate, song, dance, the tea ceremony and flower arranging – without any sacrifice of the other – and they often have a 'much richer spirituality' as well as a 'more fertile eroticism'. Certainly these traditions have been affected by 'modern life', Irigaray allows, but they still 'show greater respect for sexual difference in their concern with bodily positions, in the images of their gods (who are often shown coupling), in their calendars, horaries, etc.'.

'The organs of the body', Irigaray concludes, in these non-Christian religions, 'are considered and situated according to their masculine or feminine energy circuits, according to the seasons, the hour of the day, etc.'. In short: 'The sacred consists in *honouring* nature, not *immolating* it' (my emphasis). So the question to Girard remains: 'Can a society live without sacrifices, without aggression?' Is his theory built on a false premiss? True enough, she allows, destruction itself is an inescapable element of the biological cycle; it 'ends to signal growth and a new beginning'. Yet we can surely achieve 'ethical, social, and religious being', not by sacrificing anything in the living order but by honouring it. This we should do by attending to the physiological, cosmic and social metabolisms which can all work together. 'The sacrificial order overlays the natural rhythms with a different ... temporality that dispenses and prevents us from attending to ... the moment of cosmic temporality.' The richness of some religious traditions at least, she thinks, has been lost by elevating the sacrificial element.

This is peculiarly the case with Christianity, Irigaray argues. These reminders of the existence of non-sacrificial religious activities release us from what she regards as an unduly narrow conception of the Christian religion. 'Christ is usually represented on the cross in places of worship' – Irigaray always has Roman Catholic churches in mind – 'Festivals, miracles, mystery, play little part in our churches', she laments. It might well have been different, say in the Middle Ages, but during the years in which Irigaray had her early experience of Catholicism (she was brought up in Belgium), the focus in worship was no doubt upon the crucifix, and the central act was the 'holy sacrifice of the Mass'. She is never explicit about this, but it is not difficult to see the kind of Christian experience with which she was familiar and against which she reacts. (What she would make of happy-clappy Eucharists that are regarded primarily as meals?)

But the crucifixion, she thinks, was an 'accident', not 'an essential part of Christianity'. It just shows how 'certain powers' – in effect the sacerdotal-military-patriarchal institutions of the day – refused to accept the message that Jesus proclaimed. But the message is what remains, independently of the contingent circumstances of that refusal. The message is that 'the flesh has been divinely redeemed by the son of Mary'.[23]

There, clearly, Irigaray touches on a number of very sensitive theological issues. How far may we separate the message from the history of the messenger? Luther famously spoke of authentic Christian theology as *theologia crucis*, meaning that our knowledge of God must be derived from reflection on the sufferings that Jesus underwent on the cross, as opposed to the Scholastic theologians of the day whom he regarded as practising *theologia gloriae*, in the sense that they thought they could obtain knowledge of God from the study of nature. Irigaray certainly wants to relativize a Calvary-centred Christology, and doctrines of atonement through the sacrificial death of Jesus, and suchlike. Equally, she wants to celebrate the cosmic and natural world. But the theology of glory which she repeatedly enunciates (no other phrase fits) derives essentially from the love revealed in the incarnation of Christ.

Irigaray's explorations of the Christian religion are quite complicated. Her attitude is just as ambivalent as Heidegger's: she neither endorses in wholesale terms nor does she reject outright the claims and discourse. Instead, like him, she selects many of the deepest and most characteristic themes and metaphors and puts them to work in her remythologization of everyday life.

## Roman Catholicism

Irigaray is often very harsh about the Roman Catholic Church, the only form of institutionalized Christianity with which she ever shows much concern. In her psychoanalytical terms, it remains central to the maintenance of the phallocratic economy of Western culture.

Many people go around repeating that God is dead, that religion in Western society is irreversibly declining, and so on. But, for Irigaray, that kind of self-styled secular humanism leaves the deep and pervasive power of theology intact, 'because even though many people go around saying God is dead, few would question the fact that the Phallus is alive and well'. Indeed, 'many of the bearers of the said phallus walk around today claiming to be gods no less'. On any view of religion that treats it as a phenomenon separate from the surrounding culture, containable within definable boundaries, and describable in terms only of very overtly 'religious' activities (rituals, creeds and the like), the real power of age-long identification of the supreme being with all that functions with supreme authority in our culture (rationality, logic, and logos assumed to be male privileges; creativity, dominance, initiative, and so on, metaphorically allied with the generative powers of the male, and suchlike) simply remains out of sight. Where monotheistic religions have been interwoven for many centuries with the social, political and ideological economies of society, the fact that few educated people go to church, that Christian discourse becomes increasingly unintelligible in the public realm, and so on, as commentators frequently claim, has very little bearing on the disappearance of what philosophers in Derrida's wake would label *phallogocentrisme*.[24]

It is one thing to say that the God, the proofs of whose existence have been refuted, is dead; or to say the same of the God whose self-revelation in Scripture or in church dogma has become unbelievable. It is another matter altogether to begin the work of uncovering the privileges of men in societies in which they have always been the mirror image of the deity they have discovered or projected.

The phallocratic assumptions of the obviously ecclesiastical institutions are relatively easy to see, Irigaray would think. The bearers of the god Phallus are everywhere: 'even in the holy Roman Catholic church where the Holy Father the Pope believes it right to forbid us once again: contraception, abortion, extramarital relations, homosexuality, etc.'. On the other hand, precisely in the central rite of that most blatantly patriarchal institution, Irigaray sees the possibility of a further revelation:

> And yet, when the minister of that one and only God, that God-Father, pronounces the words of the Eucharist: 'This is my body, this is my blood', according to the rite that celebrates the sharing of food and that has been ours for centuries, perhaps we might remind him that he would not be there if our body and our blood had not given him life, love, spirit. And that he is also serving us up, we women-mothers, on his communion plate.[25]

Notice that Irigaray claims the rite as 'ours' – 'ours for centuries' – claiming the Catholic Eucharist for herself and for women down through history. Her point is to remind the man presiding at the rite that he owes his existence to the body and blood of a woman. 'But this is something that must not be known', Irigaray goes on to say – 'That is why women cannot celebrate the Eucharist ... If they were to do so, something of the truth that is hidden in the communion rite would be brutally unmasked.'

This unmasking of the truth hidden in the Eucharist would have significance far beyond the merely ecclesiastical arena. If a woman was to preside at the Eucharist, Irigaray says, 'the human race would be absolved of a great offence':

> If a woman were to celebrate the Eucharist with her mother, giving her a share of the fruits of the earth blessed by them both, she might be freed from all hatred or ingratitude toward her maternal genealogy, and be hallowed in her identity as a woman.[26]

The power of the traditional Catholic liturgy is so great, evidently, that it needs to be broken, or disseminated, by a women's liturgy. It cannot just be ignored; on the contrary, transforming it in this way would inaugurate or instantiate an absolution of the human race (not just men, then) of a great offence (the denial of the sexuality of women in the framework of a phallocratic economy).

Irigaray has made several attempts to retrieve neglected or distorted elements in the Christian religion. 'Despite the message of the New Testament (which is clearly a complex one as far as the absent heavenly father is concerned), Christianity makes a one-way demand that women give up their family rights and their female genealogy in favour of the right of the father, of his wealth, his genealogy.' The New Testament, however, 'hints at quite a different method and path'. This is occluded: 'The force of patriarchal rights, already felt at the time of Christ, continues to distort his words and his actions and to propose a sacrificial purpose that is quite at odds with Christ's message.'[27]

One of Irigaray's most substantial essays in theology – conducted in terms of reflections on themes in Hegel, Heidegger and Merleau-Ponty – concludes as follows:

> The cultural functions that women might have performed have been judged asocial ... They were accused of being *witches*, or *mystics*, because of the potency of the relations they maintained with the cosmos and the divine ... Useful in the elaboration of the Other of the masculine world, women could have only a forbidden Other of their own. Which was often called demonic possession whereas in fact it involves an ability to perceive the divine (*daimon*) to which man in his shell, his various shells, remains a stranger. In so far as he is alien to a sensible transcendental – the dimension of the divine *par excellence* – and of its grace – man would remain a little outside the religious world, unless he is initiated into it by women.[28]

But in certain religious traditions, 'even in our own' (once again unembarrassed to own it) – 'if one knows how to read certain texts: from the New Testament, from the Song of Songs, from the mystics, and so on', since 'our "tradition" is in fact a sedimentation laid down in its time by earlier traditions' – Irigaray clearly believes we can find elements that would contribute to the creation of a theology beyond that of the transcendental signifier/signified of a discourse owned by a single gender, of what she calls 'a monosexed truth'.[29] The death of that God, far from leading to the end of religion, allows rather for 'the return of the divine'. Neither Nietzsche nor Heidegger, when they proclaim the death of God, is talking about the disappearance of religion, Irigaray says. On the contrary, they are issuing a 'summons for the divine to return as festival, grace, love, thought'. This would be 'the approach or the annunciation of another parousia of the divine'. It has great social and political implications, since 'it involves the remoulding of the world, of discourse: another morning, a new era in history, in the universe'.

## Another parousia of the divine

How is this to come about, seriously? Irigaray has this proposal:

> In a West that seems to have lost its regulating questions: about the transcendental, about God, about the aporias we experience in regard to the problem of the infinite ... Who or what can move us ... except a return to the bodily-fleshly values that have never yet come to full flower?

How this might begin, in practice, in our culture, would be by men's desisting from assigning the female to reproduction, as a 'maternal machine designed to have babies, populate the home, but also keep it clean, supplied with food, etc.'. Secondly, men might stop assigning women to 'guardianship of the dead', as if a woman was a 'mute tomb for the sign-body, keeper of the hearth, "vestal" of the desire and the mind of man (especially as fetish)'. Thirdly, men need to stop treating women as 'a kind of *mechanical doll* for lovemaking'. Finally, men must desist from treating women as the incarnation of their fantasies: 'Perhaps man might then discover that something of another world persists in the female. Something that lives. That is, neither plant nor animal, neither mother nor child simply. Something or someone other. So very different that he can have no idea of it?'[30]

On the whole, these proposals would fit comfortably on any feminist or equal rights agenda in Western culture. But Irigaray has a much more lyrical eschatology: 'I shall return at the end of time', says Christ – 'an era when the spirit will come to the bride to seal the alliance of heaven and earth'. Irigaray bursts into hymnodic passages like this, one after the other:

> Waiting for parousia would require keeping all one's senses alert. ... Keeping the senses alert means being attentive in flesh and in spirit. The third era of the West might, at last, be the era of the *couple*: of the spirit and the bride. After the coming of the Father that is inscribed in the Old Testament, after the coming of the Son in the New Testament, we would see the beginning of the era of the spirit and the bride.[31]

This may sound, and is no doubt meant to sound, like a retrieval or rather a revision of the apocalyptic mysticism of Joachim of Fiore (c.1132–1202), the monk whose sanctity is unquestioned (Dante describes him as *di spirito profetico dotato*), but some of whose theological views were denounced at the Lateran Council in 1215. His central doctrine is a Trinitarian conception of the whole of history. The age of the Father, lasting until the end of the Old Testament dispensation, in Joachim's terminology, was character- ized by the 'order of married men' (the patriarchs and kings). The age of the Son, characterized by the 'order of clerics', covers the New Testament dispensation. And the age of the Spirit, which Joachim expected to begin about 1260, would be characterized by the 'order of contemplative monks'. Many movements, such as the Spiritual Franciscans and Fratricelli, were sometimes inclined to believe themselves Joachim's new order of men living in the freedom of the Spirit. Irigaray turns the whole story on its head, calling for a new age, not of spiritual men, but of incarnately ecstatic couples.

Time and again, Irigaray takes hold of some well known Christian theological theme and shakes it into a different pattern. She is not simply evoking Christian images. They are constitutive for the remythologization of the world which she regards as essential if women are ever to escape from subjection to men's image of them. In *Marine Lover*, her most substantial theological work so far, she gives an account, from the viewpoint of the forgotten woman, of the gods who figure so prominently in Nietzsche's work: Dionysos, Apollo, and Christ. She sees the ancient Greek myths as a trace of the time when a matriarchy was giving way to patriarchy. Her interpretation notes first the marks of the struggle and then the period of 'oblivion' that has obliterated and continues to obliterate the traces of a maternal genealogy. In the myth of Dionysos, she suggests, we can still see the signs of the deadly struggle between the two conceptions of the world: 'He participates in both, and clearly shows he is torn apart by that double allegiance.' His mother was reduced to ashes by Zeus's thunderbolt before his birth, and he is implanted in Zeus's thigh, from which he is actually born. In the case of Apollo the maternal genealogy will be supplanted by the patriarchal order. Apollo signifies the moment when allegiance to both parents, so painfully experienced by Dionysos, is resolved by the triumph of a single genealogy: 'One kinship line submits to the other.' The split between men and gods, the material-sensible body and the immaterial disembodied spirit, is consolidated and has marked Western civilization ever since.

Finally, however, comes Christ. Throughout her *Epistle to the Last Christians* Irigaray rewrites the Nietzschean revulsion against Christianity, but she also appropriates and develops some central Christian themes, the doctrine of the incarnation in particular:

> The word made flesh in Mary might mean – might it not? – the advent of a divine one who does not burst in violently, like the god of Greek desire, does not simply rule the world from a heaven of dreams, and does not remain closed in a text of law either ... The god does not brutally enter a body, only to throw it off at once ... He does not hide behind an unending series of appearances that ease the pain of living by giving mortals a chance to gaze upon an alien perfection. He is not made known only through writing. He is made flesh.[32]

Once again we find a text interwoven with theological assumptions that are not always explicit or uncontroversial. The main point of interest for us is no doubt her allusion to the 'alien perfection' – the repeated glimpse of a non-human kind of fulfilment which would help us to endure our mortality. Irigaray, on the positive side, likes to recall that this god is revealed, not in a text but in a body – not in 'a love that is carried over after death' but in 'some incredible nearness in life':

> A nearness revealed by the effect it has, read in certain gestures or words. Eluding a single way of speaking or showing? Always and still prophetic. Was he really untouchable? His miracles are usually based on touch. Even his words aim to touch rather than to prove or convince. His teaching is almost always contradictory, and converts or heals by touching. A touch that is not a violent attack, like that of Dionysos. That does not strike from afar – like Zeus or Apollo, or even Dionysos. That is respectful of bodily space, of sensual space, of openings in the skin. Each one remains himself, these and those get close, meet, touch one another. Sometimes by a miracle in the moment, sometimes by a parable.[33]

In such texts Irigaray begins to explore the connections between her notion of a 'sensible transcendental' and what Jesus Christ might be as a privileged instance of incarnate transcendence. Could there be an integration of the spiritual and the bodily in his way of touching?

Mainly, so far at least, Irigaray believes that 'this aspect of Christ is still to be discovered'. What distinguishes her project from those of Heidegger or Murdoch is, however, that she clearly sees the necessity of reconstructing Christianity. On the other hand, Irigaray's appropriation of Christian themes generates a remythologization of human existence which is no less exotic than Heidegger's. It is also not entirely clear whether her celebration of the figure of Jesus requires that he need ever have existed in any more substantial a fashion than Dionysos or Apollo. In that respect, Irigaray's insistence on the unavoidability of Christ may not be very different from Murdoch's incredulity that God might have become one of us, historically.

## Feuerbachian theism

There is no doubt that, for Irigaray, the discourse of religion cannot be ignored. It works against women, in innumerable ways; but there is no point in their pretending that it has come to an end or has lost its power, in our symbol systems and hence in culture and society. The only course is for women to join in – as women – and insist on having their own forms of religion.

Here, to a great extent, Irigaray follows the analysis of religion classically expounded by Ludwig Feuerbach (1804–72) in his famous book *Das Wesen des Christentums* (1841), translated by George Eliot as *The Essence of Christianity* (1854). Rejecting all belief in God, he held that theology is a form of anthropology, in the sense that the supreme being supposedly discussed in theology is an idealization of the man (certainly the man) with whom philosophical discussions of human nature are concerned. In his Hegelian language, theistic religion is the 'dominance of subjectivity', a projection of the autonomous self that allows him to see himself at his most powerful, at least with a good deal of idealization. Those who accept Feuerbach's analysis generally conclude that religion is an illusion, and that we can forget about it. Irigarary, however, believes that religion is not so easy to get rid of, as we have seen. But she interprets Feuerbach as meaning that a divine principle was necessary in order to establish mankind as a species over against other animals. Man – or rather, of course, men – exist as a kind (*genre*) precisely because a divine other has been posited as a limit, an ideal, and a guarantee of human (male) distinctiveness. The male self-image is in crisis, in Western societies, which means that the male projection of God is in some difficulty, though it still retains its power in our political and social symbol systems, so Irigaray would think. But for women to discover themselves, it is necessary for them to have their own divine horizon. When we speak of 'God', Irigaray says, we are not referring to 'a transcendent entity which is not subject to becoming', but designating 'the horizon of the accomplishment of a *genre*'.[34] 'Only a God can constitute a place where we can meet, which will leave us free.'

Under the existing theological regime, women alone represent the body, the sensible, and are excluded from the ideal or transcendent, as we saw Hegel saying. Here again, with the notion of the sensible transcendental, Irigaray hopes that the body should be identified and symbolized in such a way that women would no longer be aligned with the corporeal and deprived of the mental-spiritual. What has to be imagined, by women, is 'the perfection of our subjectivity': women need a mirror too, a mirror which will reflect them in their autonomous subjectivity, in what they are, and not just in how they have always looked, to men – and hence to themselves, as men's image of them.

Much of Irigaray's most recent writing is a kind of chant – not unlike the incantatory prose with which Heidegger tries to cajole his readers, or rather listeners. His German is, of course, very different from her French. But just as he tries to sing us into re-entering the everyday world with our minds and imaginations alert and receptive enough to perceive it as a cosmogonical game, so she ruptures conventional academic discourse, writing in a sequence of questions, exclamations, and ruminative musings, with the intention of provoking an epiphany, or a theophany, of the divine horizon that would bring women, and consequently men, out of the shadow of the phallogocentric god. In the case of Heidegger's cosmogonical myth there is a real world which he is trying to get us to see differently.

The chief problem with Irigaray's Feuerbachian projection of a divine horizon for women is to see how she thinks it could come about. The divine, for women, has to be the projection of ideals that will create the space, imaginatively and symbolically, within the cosmic as well as the terrestrial order, for a perfected self-representation of women as autonomous sexual beings, subjects as well as objects of desire. How are women deliberately to project this idealization of themselves? If the God of the existing male-dominated regime may be unmasked as a projection of men collectively defining themselves over against other animals, it has surely to be conceded that the projection was unconsciously generated and that it was always interwoven with, and supported by, countless practices and beliefs that favoured patriarchy and male dominance in all recent societies. Even with Irigaray's incantatory prose, it is difficult to see how a divine self-image can be conjured up deliberately and to order. In addition, of course, some might question the morality of worshipping something that has no reality but what we have projected – which would open lines of discussion, clearly, both with Don Cupitt's voluntarist expressivism and Iris Murdoch's critique of such non-realism.

Irigaray's work is thus shot through with religious considerations. In the end, as in the beginning, her project is an exploration of the implications of trying to live at last under the sovereignty of the difference between men and women. She sometimes alludes to Hegel's story; but her whole point is that, in our culture, we are only on the brink of a massive shift in sensibility which will enable women to see themselves in their otherness from men, really for the first time. It is not clear how this will go. In the meantime, however, we can discover the intrinsic value of sexual intercourse independently of procreation – it is already the event of something 'divine'. (Whether Diotima knows anything about it is another matter.) Really to open the possibility of women's discovering their identity we need, not only to continue Nietzsche's brutal critique of Christianity, but also to invent the divinities in whose image women may find themselves.

# CHAPTER SIX

# STANLEY CAVELL AND THE TRUTH OF SCEPTICISM

In his classic essay 'The availability of Wittgenstein's later philosophy', Stanley Cavell suggests that, for the later Wittgenstein, traditional philosophy (the metaphysical tradition from Plato, we might say) 'comes to grief not in denying what we all know to be true, but in its effort to escape those human forms of life which alone provide the coherence of our expression'.[1] That is to say, the metaphysical tradition does not go astray by arguing that tables are not real, one has no knowledge of other people's minds, and suchlike, standard fare in first-year philosophy classes.[2] Wittgenstein, on Cavell's account, would not be interested in refuting philosophical doctrines that are flagrantly in conflict with common sense. His interest, rather, would concentrate one step farther back, so to speak, in the desire to transcend language altogether. What Wittgenstein wanted to bring about by his later philosophical work was 'an acknowledgement of human limitation which does not leave us chafed by our own skin' – chafed, in particular, 'by a sense of powerlessness to penetrate beyond the human conditions of knowledge'. (Epistemology, theory of knowledge, was at the centre of Anglo-American philosophy in the early 1960s; perhaps it still is.)

'We' – we who have done some reading in traditional philosophy, certainly, but Cavell means anybody and everybody, potentially, in 'our' culture – have a sense of the limitedness of our intellectual powers, which makes us feel 'chafed by our own skin'. It is a fascinating metaphor. Cavell's initial move, in philosophy, was this thought that, just by being brought up in this culture with its deep-seated aspiration to a certain transcendence of our finitude, we have from the outset some sense of our epistemic status as an *affliction*. Traditional philosophy is understood to be constituted by the desire – the compulsive drive – to transgress the limitedness of human existence, rather than (for example) settling for thinking mortal thoughts, which would be one possibility.

## Cavell's Wittgenstein

Of course, as Cavell at once notes, the connections with Kant are obvious. The true purpose of philosophy, as Kant insisted, is to 'expose the illusions of a reason that forgets its limits, and by sufficiently clarifying our concepts to recall it from its presumptuous speculative pursuits to modest but thorough self-knowledge'.[3] Substitute language for reason and that remark might go straight into Wittgenstein's *Investigations*. 'The greatest and perhaps the sole use of all philosophy of pure reason is therefore only negative; since it serves not as an organon for the extension but as a discipline for the limitation of pure reason, and, instead of discovering truth, has only the modest merit of guarding against error.'[4] 'There must', as Kant goes on to note, 'be some source of positive modes of knowledge which ... give occasion to error'. 'How else can we account for our inextinguishable desire to find a firm footing somewhere beyond the limits of experience?'[5]

What is new, according to Cavell, is the method by which Wittgenstein tries to bring us to this 'acknowledgement of limitation' which will not be felt like a chafing of our skin. 'What *we* do [Wittgenstein's emphasis] is to bring words back from their metaphysical to their everyday use.'[6] Actually, to bring '*the* words' back (my italics) – the words that he has in fact just listed: knowledge, being, object, I, proposition, and name – the sort of words that '*the* philosophers' (my italics) are accustomed to employ – when they are striving to apprehend the *essence* (*Wesen*) of whatever is under discussion (Wittgenstein's emphasis). The original source of this remark is dated to 1930–31.[7] It certainly marks the turn in his thinking which generated Wittgenstein's later philosophy.

One may ask, of course, who 'the philosophers' were, over against whom he was distinguishing himself. Over sixty years later, one may wonder whether any such philosophers are to be found. But no doubt the sort of thing Wittgenstein had in mind[8] was, for example, the notion of knowledge as something radically unachievable because we only really 'know' something if all possibility (even) of doubt is excluded. That is surely still a very tempting thought. Again, we know that although Wittgenstein was familiar with Heidegger's writing about 'Being', it is more likely that he had in mind the early Russell's discussion of being as a property of anything thinkable. The metaphysical fertility of the first-person pronoun needs no demonstration – Wittgenstein certainly had that as a target. Words such as object, proposition and name, support a great deal of work in philosophical logic – in Wittgenstein's own early work, for example, and in a fair amount of analytic philosophy since.

It is only when the philosophers have sought to grasp the essence of knowledge, being, objects, the self, and so on, by metaphysical extension – *alienation* – of these words, that (Wittgenstein suggests) we should ask ourselves the question 'But is this word ever actually used in this way in the language in which it is at home?'

Whether Cavell's reading of Wittgenstein's later work is entirely defensible is not our concern here. His own work, and that of many recent writers, Nussbaum, Barth, Heidegger, Murdoch and others, suggests that there is indeed nothing more human than this desire to escape our limited human condition – nothing more central, philosophically, then, than working out strategies either to express this desire in some reasonable way, to give relief to it in some way that respects our human nature, that neither demeans nor distorts our epistemic condition – or to deliver us altogether from it. 'Nothing is more human', however, as Cavell says, 'than the wish to deny one's humanity'.[9]

## Ordinary-language philosophy

Cavell has always had a very high regard for the work of J. L. Austin as well as for that of the later Wittgenstein. (It was Austin's William James Lectures at Harvard in 1955 that stopped Cavell from giving up philosophy.) In their work, he suggests, we find concepts of the ordinary and of the everyday entering into (very different) attempts to 'turn aside scepticism', or rather, to 'lay out what it is that scepticism threatens'. In their work, 'perhaps for the first time in recognizable philosophy', we have 'this threat of world-consuming doubt' interpreted 'in all its uncanny homeliness'.[10]

Cavell regards J. L. Austin's 'Other Minds' as of permanent importance. It exemplifies all that many philosophers have found offensive – oppressive, even – in ordinary-language philosophy – in the sense that ordinary-language philosophy 'claims mind–reading powers for itself'.[11] When Austin claims that, when I say 'I know', I am not claiming to penetrate more deeply or certainly into reality than when I say 'I believe', that I am (rather) taking a different stance to what I communicate – I give my word differently – the greater penetration is if anything into my trustworthiness. Such illuminating insights Austin derives from studying the ordinary ways in which we speak of knowing and believing. In this instance, he questions, perhaps repudiates, the conception that has been with us since Plato, in his allegory of the Divided Line, gave us the idea of belief as moving into knowledge, an idea we surely find very attractive.[12] But for Austin, attending to how we ordinarily speak, the decisive difference lies not in some having knowledge and most having nothing better than belief (opinion) – as if there were a certain class of persons who possess a special degree of knowledge. The difference is rather, Cavell suggests, in 'their intellectual scrupulousness, their sense of what one is or could be in a position to say, to claim authority for imparting, in our common finitude, to a fellow human being'.[13]

Cavell started out offering a defence of – an apologia for – 'ordinary-language' philosophy and particularly for the work of J. L. Austin. He begins from the idea which many philosophers at the time, in the 1950s, indeed found very 'oppressive': 'that what we ordinarily say and mean may have a direct and deep control over what we can philosophically say and mean'. At the time, many philosophers resisted, as many still do resist, the idea that what can be said and meant in philosophy might have to be controlled by what we ordinarily say and mean. On the contrary, it seems that the whole point of doing philosophy is to get beyond what people ordinarily say and mean – to transcend and transgress the bounds of ordinary everyday language.

One response to this suspicion of ordinary-language philosophy would be a conciliatory one: calming such fears by saying that the (then) new philosophy at Oxford which treated what we *ordinarily* say as some kind of control over what one might want to say *metaphysically*, is just another way of dealing with the traditional problems. Indeed, as was often maintained at the time, previous philosophers such as Locke, Hume, even Aristotle, were drafted as ordinary-language philosophers. With this 'revolution' in philosophy, it turned out that many of the greatest philosophers in the Oxford canon were actually ordinary-language philosophers already. Thus there was no need to feel so oppressed.

Cavell rejects that sort of response, not that he thinks there is nothing in it; but he wants us to feel the oppressiveness, not to conjure it away so facilely. After all, he insists, there surely *is* something oppressive about a way of doing philosophy in which it is

116

claimed that we already have all the information we need to solve our philosophical problems. Philosophical problems, such as one's knowledge of other minds, or of the existence of the external world, or about distinctions between the descriptive and the normative, fact and value, and so on, seem too deep to be dealt with by attending to what we ordinarily say. If philosophy 'leaves everything as it is', in Wittgenstein's famous phrase,[14] are we not depriving ourselves of some of the greatest speculative achievements of the human mind – contenting ourselves to ' sit quietly in a room'?[15]

## A Pascalian theme

Cavell is alluding there to Pascal's remark about the human condition as an unhappiness caused by, and causing, an incessant need for distraction or diversion: 'I have discovered that all the unhappiness of men arises from one single fact, that they cannot stay quietly in their own chamber.'[16] According to Pascal, if human beings were happy they would be all the happier having no *divertissement*. They would be like the saints or like God, with nothing, and needing nothing, to distract them – to divert their attention.

Yes, Pascal says, but is not a man happy who is able to find delight in *divertissement*? You might think so, but Pascal thinks not: *divertissement* comes from somewhere else, from outside. That means that one is *dependent* – always and everywhere liable to be disturbed by a thousand and one accidents, which inevitably cause distress.

*Divertissement* comes in, and is badly needed, when we discover that we are unable to cure death, wretchedness and ignorance. We decide not to think about such things but to toy with something else. Despite these afflictions we want to be happy. The best thing would be to make ourselves immortal, but as we cannot do that, we are well advised to stop ourselves thinking about our mortality, vulnerability, contingency, and, in short, our finitude.

These Pascalian thoughts inform Cavell's whole project:

> I feel that it is possible that I might never have existed, for my self consists in my thoughts; therefore I who think would never have been if my mother had been killed before I had come to life; therefore I am not a necessary being. I am not eternal or infinite either, but I can see that there is in nature a being who is necessary, eternal, and infinite.[17]

Then the remark comes: thinking about the various activities, the dangers and troubles people face at Court, in war, and so on, giving rise to so many quarrels and passions, daring and often wicked enterprises. Can't you see that '*tout le malheur des hommes vient d'une seule chose*'? – which is that we do not know how to 'stay quietly at home'.

If you had everything you need you would never leave home – if you knew how to enjoy being at home. If you enjoyed living in town you would never join the army. If you enjoyed staying at home you would never go in for the diversion of gambling. And so on. To be *chez soi avec plaisir* – that would be ideal. But it is not possible. And the reason for our discontent lies in the natural unhappiness of our condition – our feeble and mortal condition – so wretched that nothing can console us when we really think about. We need some diversion that takes our minds off our mortality. Gambling, hunting, hustle and bustle, for example. We have a secret instinct driving us to seek diversion outside – an instinct that derives from resentment of these afflictions to which we are subject.

Cavell exhibits a fascination with Pascal's thought that the way to deal with the questions that torment us philosophically is just to sit quietly – to recognize our condition and to reconcile ourselves to it – but not get there prematurely. Rather, 'we will have to look at that sense of oppression itself', this sense of the oppressiveness of a philosophy which insists on bringing us back all the time to what may be said in ordinary language because 'such feelings [this sense of being oppressed] can come from a truth about ourselves which we are holding off'.[18] Thus, if we feel (as philosophers) that being limited to what can be said in ordinary language is an oppressive requirement, it may be because there is a truth about ourselves that we are avoiding.

In retrospect, Cavell allows that, from early on, he was already 'characterizing the tradition of Western philosophy ... as metaphysical diversion, distraction cosmicized'.[19] To the critical gaze of Cavell's ordinary-language philosopher, traditional metaphysical problems look like Pascalian *divertissement* – 'distraction cosmicized' – systematic and almost unstoppable avoidance of thinking about our mortality, about our unhappiness.

Now, of course, in the 1990s, ordinary-language philosophy is over and done with. Nobody would use the phrase, except when referring to a closed file. Cavell wants to say, however, that it has yet to make its legacy felt. Its deepest motivation, in Wittgenstein and in J. L. Austin, was – is – as a new criticism of the philosophical question of scepticism, so Cavell wants us to see. Those philosophers who are – were – most opposed to ordinary language are – were – the ones opposed to the very idea that the sceptical question remains 'a founding question for philosophy'. Ordinary language philosophy should be seen as a response to scepticism, to 'that anxiety about our human capacities as knowers that can be taken to open modern philosophy in Descartes'.[20]

## The truth of scepticism

The problems of philosophy that Cavell cares most about are as recurrent as human thought – problems pervaded by scepticism. 'For scepticism to be brought to an end, human nature would have to end'.[21] Scepticism is a place, 'perhaps the central secular place', 'in which the human wish to deny the condition of human existence is expressed'. The central 'secular' place, note: Cavell's version of self-transcendence incorporates, perhaps depends upon, some kind of contrast with religion, the sacred, and theology – 'and so long as the denial is essential to what we think of as the human, scepticism cannot, or must not, be denied'.[22]

If we sit quietly at home – if we stop being unhappy with our place – we cease to be human. That is Cavell's thought.

Again, 'an irreducible region of our unhappiness is natural to us but at the same time unnatural'.[23] This is an 'everyday condition', which Thoreau calls 'quiet desperation', Emerson 'silent melancholy', Coleridge and Wordsworth 'despondency' or 'dejection'. Heidegger speaks of it as 'our bedimmed averageness', Wittgenstein as our 'bewitchment', J. L. Austin both 'as a drunken profundity (which he knew more about than he cared to let on) and as a lack of seriousness'.[24]

The Romantic quest, which Cavell is happy to join, is 'to find what degrees of freedom we have in this condition' – 'to show that it is at once needless yet somehow, because of that, all but necessary, inescapable' – if you like: 'to subject its presentation of necessity to diagnosis, in order to find truer necessities'. In fact there is a 'history of devotion to the discovery of false necessity': Thoreau's *Walden* 'links with those works of our culture specifically devoted to an attack on false necessities' – Plato's vision of us as staring at a wall inside a cave, Luther's idea of us as captives, Rousseau's of us as chained, or the ways in which Marx and Freud strive to unmask our self-subjugation.[25]

'The quest for the inhuman is an essential part of the motivation to scepticism', which is why Cavell remains interested in scepticism – scepticism as 'forever an inherent aspiration of the thing we know as human'.[26] His conception of the place of scepticism in Western philosophy and in modern Western culture means that Cavell regards the sceptical impulse as one version, one inflexion, of an ineradicable element in human nature. That is to say, he sees the drive to deny the human as itself internal to being human – in effect, he sees human beings as riven, driven, by a desire to deny their nature in very much the way that the biblical doctrine of original sin imputes a flaw to human nature.[27]

What Cavell wants to uncover is what he calls the truth of scepticism. He is not trying to refute scepticism.[28] Nor is he simply diagnosing scepticism.[29] Nor is he half-heartedly out to abandon scepticism.[30] Rather, Cavell is engaging with scepticism, trying to uncover what sense of our condition – what experience of our condition – is voiced in versions of scepticism. The problem is 'to discover the specific plight of mind and circumstance within which a human being gives voice to his condition'.[31] Wittgenstein's later writing, which Cavell seeks to continue (albeit in a very different mode), involves, according to Cavell, registering how, 'in investigating ourselves, we are led to speak "outside language games", consider expressions apart from, and in opposition to, the natural forms of life which give those expressions the force they have'.[32]

## Metaphysical finitude as intellectual lack

What happens, according to Cavell, is that 'a metaphysical finitude' gets transformed into 'an intellectual lack'.[33] When we are assured that we can know the existence of material objects, or the thoughts and feelings of others, or that there is nothing 'hidden' to be known, all the familiar anti-sceptical stuff in first-year philosophy classes – then (Cavell fears) our real experience of our inability to see the world as a whole, apart from a partial perspective, is denied or repressed or diverted.[34] We are being assured that the problem of knowledge is either solved or simply unreal. In such responses to scepticism what we see is 'the attempt to convert the human condition, the condition of humanity, into an intellectual difficulty, a riddle'.[35] But something deeper and more worrying is at issue, Cavell thinks.

It is the human condition that Cavell wants to focus on, and how both the sceptical and the anti-sceptical bodies of philosophical work arise in reaction to it. The conditions of being human include such facts as that we experience our separateness from, and often lack of attunement with, one another, and sometimes we want to overcome these. Again, we are not (though in fantasy we may wish to be) self-sufficient masters of our experience and language in ways that would pre-empt the possibility of mistakes and surprises, and that would cancel the burden of responsibility we bear all the time for keeping our claims in alignment with the realities of the world and keeping ourselves in attunement with one another.[36] Our lives are open all the time to unpredictable injuries (liability to which we wish to avoid) from the world, from others, and from our own choices. Surrounded by such experiences, circumstances, fantasies and liabilities, philosophers who bluffly insist that we really do know all we could know (other people's pains are obvious in their faces, we are not isolated from one another because we could then never be brought together, fantasies of deep attunement with one another or of the perfect alignment of language with world, have no content – can just be dismissed) seem to be repressing essential elements of our humanity.

## The other's separateness

This misperception of our finitude as a lack is one version of scepticism. This miscasting of our experience of our condition as that of a problem to be solved by epistemology confuses the issue, Cavell thinks. Scepticism has the advantage (against its opponents) of at least registering a real and troublesome experience of our condition that cannot be escaped by knowing – by any cognitive exertion – indeed it cannot be escaped at all. Scepticism pictures knowing as the only way out of this condition – and then denies that knowing will ever free us anyway. For Cavell, of the two, 'the anti-sceptic's position [is] weaker: the sceptic has a fact which needs noticing and recording; the anti-sceptic has no fact of his own to compete with that, he has only some words to think about, and his words keep looking like they deny the facts'.[37] The sceptic certainly sees something – namely, that 'the human creature's basis in the world as a whole, its relation to the world as such, is not that of knowing, anyway not what we think of as knowing'.[38] This insight is what Cavell calls 'the truth of scepticism'. Our condition, its liabilities and the wishes and fantasies characteristic of it, are not to be overcome or controlled or altered by our acquiring knowledge. The sceptic is right – he 'has, or seems to himself to have, discovered that unless we can share or swap feelings, we can't know what that person is experiencing (if anything)'.[39] If I have to consider the question 'Can I have the same feeling as you have?' as if I did not already know the answer, then I am strongly tempted to say, 'No'. The question then becomes, 'Is there anything that gives rise to this question anyway?' What generates the thought that we must feel what the other feels in order really to know?

If, as Wittgenstein urged, the 'distortion between [mind and world, and between mind and mind] [is] straightened, in the appreciation and acceptance of particular human forms of life, human "convention" ... [then] the sense of gap [the sense that there is something we would have to know or feel in order to know the world or one another, of necessity] originates in an attempt, or wish, to escape (to remain a "stranger" to, "alienated" from) those shared forms of life, to give up the responsibility of their maintenance.'[40]

Behind the sceptic's questions, but also the anti-sceptic's replies to them, Cavell is claiming, is the wish not to have this responsibility: the wish (that is to say) for one's language to be wedded to the world *apart from having to make sense to others* – apart from having to face charges from them of *not making sense*. This desire to evade having to subject what one says to the rule of others would be one more version of the desire to become immune to the pressures and vicissitudes of life in community with others. It is the wish that one should be whole and sufficient to oneself – indifferent to the interpretations that others place on one's efforts to make sense. This is 'the threat, or the truth, of scepticism: that it names our wish (and the possibility of our wishing) to strip ourselves of the responsibility we have in meaning (or in failing to mean) one thing, or one way, rather than another'.[41]

What gives rise to this wish, and makes it ours? Is it something characteristic of human beings, rather than something either individuals or particular cultures occasionally have and might give up? After all, in practice we do bear responsibility for meaning one thing rather than another by what we say, within the conversation, within the conventions apart from which we can mean nothing. 'The phenomena which constitute the criteria of something's being so are part of those very general facts of nature or of human life against the background of which our concepts mean anything at all.'[42] But of course the criteria do not impose themselves – it is up to us, to anyone who speaks the language, to stick to them, go on with them, modifying them occasionally. We continue the series in this way rather than that – waiting –

facing 'the inevitable moment of teaching and learning, and hence of communication, in which my power comes to an end in the face of the other's separateness from me'.[43]

Will the child I am teaching go on? Have I made sense to him? 'The mind cannot be led at every point; teaching (reasons; my control) comes to an end; then the other takes over.'[44] We have all felt the anxiety of this moment – will they laugh at one's joke? Will the other 'take' our gift? Do your children find your ideals, your projects, your life and your values, worthwhile – worth imitating – or ridiculous and eccentric? If they do not go on with me, then I begin to doubt my way of doing things until now. In the end, I can be counted, by myself because by others, as meaning anything, only if enough of my suggestions are 'taken' by enough others. I have to find with enough others that we customarily make sense to one another. (Cavell compares the situation of any participant in the conversation as regards going on with and from criteria with the task of the modernist artist finding an audience in order to establish, including to himself, the intelligibility of his work.[45]) It is I, going on from our previous conversations, who establish criteria of intelligibility:

> but this is only on the condition that I count, that I matter, that it matters that I count in my agreement or attunement with those with whom I maintain my language, from whom this inheritance – language as the condition of counting – comes ... If my counting fails to matter, I am mad.[46]

## Theological motifs

Like Nussbaum, Heidegger, Murdoch, and Irigaray, Cavell has much more interest in religion than might at first appear – much more interest than any of his critics have noticed prior to the recent splendid book by Stephen Mulhall[47] – much more interest in religion than fashionable philosophers are supposed to have in our supposedly post-religious age.

In an essay on *The Winter's Tale*, Cavell writes of the final scene as – 'among other things' – 'a marriage ceremony',[48] and not simply 'a translated moment of religious resurrection', as people are more likely to think, with Paulina as a figure for St Paul, in whose domestic chapel there is the statue of Hermione, who has been dead sixteen years.

'Those that think it unlawful business I am about, let them

depart', Paulina says. 'It is required you do awake your faith', she says to Leontes, the widower whose accusations that she had betrayed him with another man killed Hermione in the first place but who has long since repented his scepticism. There is music, the statue unfreezes and Hermione and Leontes embrace: a second wedding ceremony right enough, and just how much resurrection there is in the scene is a matter for discussion. Hermione actually says that she had 'preserved [herself] to see the issue'.

How many readers, how many of the most ingenious commentators, ever regarded the coming to life of the statue of Hermione as much of a resurrection? This, anyway, is an interpretation that, though it does not satisfy Cavell, has to be incorporated, or so he believes. This translated moment of religious resurrection Cavell proposes to look for 'in a sense of this theatre' – Shakespeare's plays – as 'in competition with religion, as if declaring itself religion's successor'.[49]

The reason a reader like Santayana claimed to find everything in Shakespeare *except* an interest in religion, Cavell goes on to say, is simply because religion is *everywhere* in Shakespeare – so pervasive that it is invisible to readers like Santayana.[50]

Cavell has always had an often ambiguous and sometimes prickly relationship to Christian religious themes and topics. In the early essay on 'The availability of Wittgenstein's later philosophy', for example, he attacks as 'Manichean' the voluntarist-existentialist conception of language, and particularly of moral language as a game of rules that we decide and choose.[51] This is very much the conception of which Wittgenstein was out to uncover the bogus charms and of which he wanted to discredit the authority; but there are still philosophers who believe that something like this is his own 'theory'. In 1962 it was David Pole's book on Wittgenstein that Cavell was attacking (rather brutally, it has to be said). Exactly what Cavell understands by 'Manichean' is not wholly perspicuous; but the point must be that, on Cavell's interpretation, the later Wittgenstein is out to show that everyday language does not depend upon some a priori system of rules and that the absence of such a structure in no way impairs its functioning. Language is not in the least like a calculus with fixed rules. Such a conception would be 'Manichean' – displaying, then, some sort of dualistic metaphysics. This would be one more denigration of everyday language for its vagueness, coarseness, etc., in favour of some ideal system of perfection, clarity or translucence, understood by some élite – something like that, perhaps.[52]

In effect, much recent philosophy of language, extending to the preconceptions in our culture about the nature of language, would have hidden theological implications. Far more radically than the Heidegger of *Sein und Zeit*, with his claims about the continuing secret influence of Christianity on modern conceptions of the self, the later Wittgenstein, with the so-called rule-following considerations, might actually be getting at much deeper theological and religious motifs and paradigms at work in the kind of thing we are inclined to think when we think about thinking, language, meaning and so on. Perhaps that is what Cavell is suggesting.

## Samuel Beckett and T. S. Eliot

Cavell has an early essay on Beckett's play *Endgame*, where, after quoting the Pascal remark: 'All the evil in the world comes from our inability to sit quietly in a room' – roughly what he takes Beckett to be saying – Cavell goes on to say that he should really now confront his account of Beckett's sensibility with the kind of thing to be found in 'Christian writing' about birth, death, exhaustion of spirit and the inability to 'turn'.[53] He has wanted to bring Eliot's *Ash Wednesday* into his discussion – but he backs away – such a confrontation would be 'too webbed and delicate to be handled quickly'. However, in a penultimate long paragraph, Cavell does quickly outline his case.

Both Beckett and Eliot in *Ash Wednesday* begin with the experience of the truth of Ecclesiastes, that biblical text about the profitlessness of labour, the absoluteness of time, the uselessness of self-transcendence, we may perhaps say, the inescapability of finitude. Eliot's poem is a virtual transcription of some such position, Cavell says, but it includes the injunction to 'rejoice' and as the poem proceeds we move from the joy of surcease to the joy of surrender. 'The direction is up', but can that direction really be taken? Cavell asks. Is not Eliot here relying on his Christianity? Does not Eliot's Christianity raise 'raw' the fundamental aesthetic question of the relation of religious belief to art since, after all, Eliot's Christianity, in *Ash Wednesday* anyway, reveals his faith organizing his art and his art testing his religious beliefs? And if the direction that Eliot detects can really be described, Cavell says, then no doubt Beckett's vision can be encompassed within Christianity – 'we could explain why we lack words, and have too many'. 'We could understand the sense in which redemption is impossible, and possible' – 'impossible only so long as we live solely in history, in time, so long as we think that an event near 2000 years ago relieves us of responsibility rather than nails us to it – so long, that is, as we live in magic instead of faith'. 'But can we really believe all this', Cavell asks, 'or must these explanations be given in bad faith, blinding us to what we do believe?'

Beckett is the one who puts all this to the test, Cavell says, precisely because he is the contemporary writer complex enough to match Eliot. Their worlds, their visions of humanity, of transcendence and finitude (we may as well say), do not measure together – do not even 'scrape', as Cavell says – they 'eclipse' one another.

Cavell comes down on the side of Beckett. Maybe, he says in his final brief paragraph, we have to destroy our gods: 'Nietzsche said we will have to become gods ourselves to withstand the consequences of such deeds.' 'Camus said we will never be men until we give up trying to be God.' *'Que voulez-vous, Monsieur?* Which do you pick?', Cavell asks. 'We hang between', he answers.[54]

Cavell has a very sympathetic essay on Kierkegaard.[55] His interest is mainly in the way that Kierkegaard diagnosed the problem of the Christianity of his day as a form of amnesia about its own concepts – a failure to remember the significance of Christian forms of life. It is as if Kierkegaard anticipated by a hundred years the later Wittgenstein's insistence that concepts are kept alive by being rooted in practices and applied this insight to Christianity.

## The impossibility of religion

It becomes clear in the Kierkegaard essay, however, that, while on Kierkegaard's view religious concepts need to be reconnected with forms of life, Cavell assumes that religion is no longer a live possibility for us now. He suggests this quite frequently. Telling us that Descartes recovered from scepticism only by his detailed dependence on theology, Cavell notes in an aside that this happened 'in a way I judge no longer natural to the human spiritual repertory'.[56] 'Satisfaction [of our sense of subjectivity] is no longer imaginable within what we understand as religion,' he says on another occasion.[57] 'Respectable further theologizing of the world has, I gather, ceased,' he says elsewhere.[58] In such asides, and they usually are asides, Cavell speaks personally, affecting a certain distance from the state of affairs he is registering ('I gather').

All three of the asides quoted might be unpicked. I might agree that it is no longer natural to the human spiritual repertory to deal with scepticism 'only' by 'detailed' dependence on talk about God.

Indeed, come to think of it, I may object that appealing to nothing but theology never was a good way of dealing with scepticism about our knowledge of other minds, the external world and so forth. I might agree that satisfaction of our sense of subjectivity is no longer imaginable solely within religion – now that we have Henry James and Proust, a whole range of works of art, the kind of sexual experience appealed to by Irigaray, and what all. But that need not mean that religion no longer affords *any* sense of our subjectivity, that it makes *no* difference.

On the whole, as Stephen Mulhall says,[59] Cavell does seem to be inclined in these asides to assume that there has been a cultural shift which renders religious belief no longer intellectually respectable or spiritually feasible – no longer feasible for people like us, his readers. He is ignoring Christians in many other parts of the world, as well as followers of Islam, not to mention Buddhists in Tibet enduring appalling persecution while Western governments suck up to the brutal regime that persecutes them, and so on. Cavell is typical of the Western intellectual who insists, against all the evidence, that religion is declining – refusing to listen to what is no doubt happening a few streets away, in homes that he or she would never visit, let alone to what is rife in other cultures and societies.

There is an interesting set of references and allusions in Cavell's work to what he takes to be the Christian attitude towards the human body – towards the fact that human beings are flesh and blood. This aspect of human nature, our physicality, our embodiment, has been regarded by Christianity as 'requiring mortification'.[60] Scepticism about other minds, in particular, needs to be discussed together with a history of attitudes to the body, he suggests. Such a history would consist principally of a history of libels, he thinks – a history of attempts to undo certain libels against the body. Luther and de Sade made important contributions but Cavell's own hero here would be Blake:

> What is it men in women do require?
> The lineaments of Gratified Desire.
> What is it women do in men require?
> The lineaments of Gratified Desire.

This would be 'a brave acceptance of the sufficiency of human finitude', 'an achievement of the complete disappearance of its disappointment, in oneself and others', 'an acknowledgement of satisfaction and reciprocity'.[61]

There are certain philosophies in which 'a denial of the human *is* the human', Cavell says[62] – 'Call this the Christian view'. That is why Nietzsche strove to overcome the traditional task of overcoming the human with the task of overcoming this *denial* of the human – transcendence not by mortification but through joy, ecstasy, as the affirmation of the body (very much Irigaray's story, then).

## Cavell on the doctrine of original sin

Those who attempt to counter a dualistic view of mind and body by asserting the identity of body and mind would once again only be avoiding the problem. Here Cavell, quite independently of course, goes quite some way along the road taken by Luce Irigaray. What is happening, in writers from Blake through to Nietzsche, is 'the constructing of a mythology to rival that of Christianity, bone by bone' – which is what is required for 'the working through of secularization'.[63] 'Can a human being be free of human nature?' Cavell asks;[64] and having asked the question, he then quite characteristically moves into parentheses for the rest of quite a long paragraph:

> (The doctrine of Original Sin can be taken as a reminder that, with one or rather two exceptions humankind cannot be thus free' [evidently allowing for a Catholic/Orthodox doctrine of the status of the Virgin Mary] – Yet Saint Paul asks us to put off our (old) nature. What is repellent in Christianity is the way it seems to imagine both our necessary bondage to human nature and our possible freedom from it. In this, Nietzsche seems to me right, even less crazy than Christianity ... Christianity appears in Nietzsche not so much the reverse of the truth as the truth in foul disguise. In particular, the problem seems to be that human action is everywhere disguised as human suffering: this is what acceptance of the Will to Power is to overcome.)[65]

The theological assumptions at work in that paragraph would warrant detailed examination. St Paul's Christian denial is of our old nature, and so is in aid of the acquisition of a new nature. What Cavell finds repellent here is the Christian conception of that transformation – the way it is supposed to happen. The aspect of this conception that fouls the truth is its emphasis on suffering – suffering understood here as the negation of action, thus as a kind of passivity, perhaps as waiting. The doctrine of original sin captures all this in the sense that it registers the Christian sense that our bondage to our old nature is such that release from it cannot be achieved by human resources alone. This transformation has to be something that happens to us rather than something we can make happen – something that is and must be done for us. In short: the doctrine of original sin encapsulates an idea of human inadequacy because of human dependence on divine grace, which amounts to a denial of human self-sufficiency. The Christian tendency to deny the body is thus a denial of human finitude, or rather, a denial of human integrity and autonomy: 'This denial of finitude has also been taken as the mark of sin.' 'It was to free humanity of that libel of sinfulness that Blake and Nietzsche undertook, as it were, to deny the distinction between the finite and the infinite in thinking of the human'.[66]

Cavell has developed several variants of this criticism of Christianity. His point is always, one way or another, his opposition to the very idea of *grace*. In religion, certainly in Christianity, so it seems to Cavell, since he is familiar only with very traditional versions of Christianity (he has evidently not been introduced to demythologizing non-realist versions), truth can never finally be derived from or authorized by purely human sources and authorities. That is always to propose some radically non-human authority other than the human beings over whom this authority holds sway. To this extent, Cavell comes very close to the kind of liberal-individualism that Murdoch wants to displace with her emphasis on the need for us to rediscover the sovereignty of good. If it is right (as Mulhall maintains) that Cavell's work in ethics, aesthetics and political theory, has an ineliminably 'liberal inflexion', his presentation of the autonomy and integrity of the self as a provisional and always threatened achievement requires to be taken into account.[67] His liberal-individualist sense of the self cannot be described as atomist; on the contrary, individual identity is something that has to be worked at. It cannot be maintained in the absence of participation in a community, in particular within the forms of life that sustain its language.

## The absent other

But it is more complicated. Cavell's increasingly open objections to Christianity may be read as betraying his worry that Christianity is too close to his own project. In Christianity human beings are possessed by a nature which disposes them to sin and prevents them from escaping their bondage by relying entirely on their own resources. They cannot achieve their new nature except by a relationship with a particular source – with a particular human being, one through whom divine grace has been made available, one who exemplifies the humanity to which God seeks to attract everyone of us while respecting our liberty to refuse it, and so on. In brief, to be a self requires one to be in the gift of any other.

For Cavell, the manifold versions of scepticism reveal that human beings are possessed of a nature in which the sceptical impulse is ineradicable. What is needed, if it is to be contained, is a relationship with a particular human other – one who enables us to become more ourselves. For Cavell what is repellent in Christianity is that it is a twisted version of what he regards as the truth; or (if you like) the truth that Cavell wants requires an unravelling of Christianity.

The key notion is that of acknowledgement. If Christianity insists on the priority of a certain passivity over action, then Cavell too sees no way of overcoming scepticism about other minds and about the world other than a kind of passivity. His attempt, in his Carus Lectures, to hold John Rawls' liberal individualism together with Emerson's perfectionism shows what straits Cavell has got himself into[68] but already, in a remarkable passage on 'the convulsion of sensibility we call the rise of Protestantism', he suggested that, with the Reformation, what happens is that 'one manages one's relation to God alone' – 'in particular one bears the brunt alone of being known to God'. Again: I have 'an existence essentially unknowable to myself, namely, whether I am of the elect'.

'As long as God exists, I am not alone' – roughly what Descartes concluded, according to Cavell. But now – the thought that haunts Cavell – could not the human other suffer the fate of God? At least, doesn't the human other now bear the weight of God? Cavell says: 'I wish to understand how the other now bears the weight of God, shows me that I am not alone in the universe.' 'This requires understanding the philosophical problem of the other as the trace or scar of the departure of God.'[69]

Thus, it seems, our redemption from particular onslaughts of scepticism, of narcissism, of paranoia, is not feasible now without the idea and possibility and reality of our dependence upon the human other. And is that ever going to be enough? Is that a secure enough basis for self-transcendence, moral growth and so forth?

It is the problem of Other Minds, so fascinatingly explored by John Wisdom, in the wake of Wittgenstein no doubt. It is the problem, Cavell thinks, of the other as the problem of the trace, the scar, left by the departure of God.[70] To say the least, that is a way of reading the obsessive 'Other Minds' literature of the 1930s that few philosophers have ever yet attempted. What Cavell is suggesting, however, is that we take the whole set of problems conventionally discussed in Anglo-American philosophy under the heading of 'Other Minds' or 'external world scepticism' as reactions to the loss of belief in God.

## Animism

Cavell admits to being fascinated by Heidegger's lecture 'Das Ding'.[71] He reads it (rightly) as a meditation on Kant's way of dealing with finitude. Heidegger strives to transform Kant's conception of our being conditioned, of our conditionedness, a conception that involves the claim that we simply have no knowledge of what is unconditioned, of things in themselves – *das Ding an sich*. The bargain that Kant makes with 'external world scepticism' is to buy back knowledge of objects by giving up things in themselves.[72] In an imaginative leap, Cavell places Heidegger's essay in the context of Coleridge's *Ancient Mariner* and suggests that this is Romanticism's bargain with Kant – buying back the thing in itself by taking on what Cavell calls animism.

This is not quite an *anima mundi* doctrine, a version of panpsychism, at least in the sense that we attribute to, or perceive in, plants, natural phenomena and inanimate objects, some kind of soul. It is more like a revival of some Stoic sense of the logos in the cosmos. What Cavell is especially fascinated by is Heidegger's proposal, that, if we allow ourselves to be enchanted by his voice, then we find ourselves going in for a kind of thinking in which we are called by the thing *as the thing*.[73]

In effect, what Heidegger is out to do is to retrieve Western thinking from Kant's Copernican revolution. Rather than saying that in order for there to be a world of objects of knowledge for us a thing must satisfy the a priori conditions of human knowledge – whatever these turn out on philosophical investigation to be – Heidegger is suggesting, on the contrary, that in order for us to recognize ourselves as human beings, we must satisfy the conditions of there being things that make a world in the first place – whatever these then turn out to be – and not so much by philosophical investigation as by poetic meditation. Things need redemption from the way we human beings have come to think, and the

redemption (the return) of the things of the world is the redemption (the return) of human nature. That is Heidegger's
story, according to Cavell's surely very good recapitulation.[74]

Is this a philosophy of Romanticism? If it systematizes something
like the task of Romanticism in poetry; if Romanticism in poetry
has to do with redeeming things from the way we have come to
regard them; if this redemption of things cannot happen except in a
certain poetry; then Heidegger's lecture would be some kind of
contribution to the redemption of human nature from the grip of
misconceptions of itself as well as of things.

Here Cavell has a paragraph, again in parentheses, noting that,
about the time that Heidegger was writing, there were several
American poets and literary critics such as John Crowe Ransom,
Kenneth Burke, R. P. Blackmur and Paul Goodman attempting to
come to grips with positivism by connecting the fate of poetry with
the fate of the experience of the world. In particular, Cavell
mentions Ransom's book *The World's Body*.[75] But without attempting to reconstruct Heidegger's argument, to expound or explain it,
let alone to criticize it, Cavell simply notes that, to the Enlightenment mind, to his own mind, the kind of thing that Heidegger
says is very difficult to accept as *philosophy*. He finds himself inclined
to laugh – 'The thing things' and so forth – and yet there is
something in it, he suspects, at least if Heidegger's idea of the thing
as thing, as gathering and uniting the world, may be understood as
another form of *animism*.

Perhaps we have then reached the (questionable) idea that keeps
surfacing in Romantic texts: that is, that there is a life and death of
the world – dependent on what we human beings make of it –
which brings us perhaps to the bound of a hermeneutical circle.
Either we go with it or get off.[76]

But before we decide whether to go on or get off, Cavell introduces another text, about the price of animism as an aspect of the
Romantic settlement with Kant. Amazingly, at least to anyone
conventionally educated in recent philosophical classics, this text
is John Wisdom's 'Gods'.[77] This is the only writing Cavell knows
within the Anglo-American analytical tradition that offers, if only
in passing, something like a rational justification of the possibility
of animism – a new view, if you like, of rational justification.[78]

Once again, then, Cavell shows his fascination with an aside,
with what a writer says 'in passing'. His own resort to parenthetical
remarks, when he touches on theological matters, on the pretext
that he is saying something incidental, provisional, incomplete or

supplementary, seems defensive, placatory, even evasive. The brackets that supposedly contain the theological asides become signals for the entry of sensitive and contentious issues. The asides are more like traps in the middle of the road. Finding 'animism' in a text by John Wisdom is certainly exposing an extremely surprising seam of thought.

Wisdom investigates the possibility of animism, Cavell says, when he asks us to imagine a situation in which someone picks up some half-withered flowers and gently puts them in a jug of water and someone else, seeing this, says: 'You believe flowers feel' – suggesting, mockingly perhaps, reproachfully, or incredulously, that there is something in the way the man put them in the water which reveals an attitude to the flowers which may be appropriate to butterflies (say) but is quite inappropriate to flowers. 'He feels [the sceptic in Wisdom's story] that this attitude to flowers is somehow crazy just as it is sometimes felt that a lover's attitude is somewhat crazy even when this is not a matter of his having false hopes about how the person he is in love with will act.'[79]

> It is often said in such cases that reasoning is useless. But the very person who says this feels that the lover's attitude is crazy, is inappropriate like some dreads and hatreds, such as some horrors of enclosed places. And often one who says 'It is useless to reason' proceeds at once to reason with the lover, nor is this reasoning always quite without effect.

Wisdom describes in some detail how this may happen.

What Wisdom is up to, according to Cavell, by opening with the sceptic's remark – 'You believe flowers *feel*', is getting us to notice that the first man's gentle rescue of the half-dead flowers is being described in a way designed to invite – incite – the suspicion of pathetic fallacy. A sceptic cannot do anything else but imagine something like a projection of emotion here. He can see nothing else in the other man's gesture but a surrender to the delusion of crediting inanimate objects with human emotions. In the attempt to reason with the lover, or the man who treated the flowers gently, the sceptic may find, however, as Wisdom says, that all the points he has to make are already perfectly plain to the other – 'he has not denied them nor passed them off'. 'He has recognized them and they have altered his attitude, altered his love, but he still loves.' That is to say: 'We then feel that perhaps it is we who are blind and cannot see what he can see.'[80]

Thus Wisdom concludes. What is happening, according to

Cavell, is that we are being invited to hold off the belief that flowers feel – this hypothesis – which would have to be defended to make the attitude of reverence to the flowers comprehensible. We are being asked to imagine, rather, if we can, someone's finding himself or herself amazed by someone's treatment of flowers – handling them nervously, behaving with special decorum in their presence, refusing to cut them or whatever (Cavell extends the list of possibilities), or placing them gently in a jar of water –well, just let yourself be amazed, Wisdom would be saying. What one might allow oneself to be prompted to consider would be what flowers *are* – what it is that one takes oneself to know about what is, and what is not, appropriate in the way we treat flowers.

From there Cavell moves to Wordsworth's 'Intimations of Immortality from Recollections of Early Childhood'. Thus, there is this (fairly brief) consideration of Heidegger's conversion of our sense of being conditioned as being confined, cut off from the unconditioned for which we crave, into a sense of our being 'be-thinged', prodigiously impinged upon, enriched, opened up, sustained and so on, by the world as both separate from us and essential for our being. There follows this (even briefer) consideration of John Wisdom's example of the man suspected of believing that flowers have feelings – an example that brings into the open what must be anyone's suspicion, since the Enlightenment, about any attempt, however poetic, to retrieve or reveal things as things by generating prose that seems remarkably like an extended pathetic fallacy. From inside this kind of suspicion there are only two ways out: either the flower-lover has crazy beliefs or he projects inappropriate emotions on inanimate objects. So it seems, at least. But what John Wisdom is doing, Cavell means, is inviting us to see if we can think ourselves clear of that suspicion. Rather than simply operating with our general preconceptions about objects, we might allow ourselves to reconsider our attitudes and reactions. By reconsidering the treatment that objects elicit from us we might begin to see how they attract us. We might begin to see that we are drawn to them – we might reconsider what it is about them that draws us – and so we might begin to reconsider what they are. Things might have a value and an interest for us to which we are usually indifferent. It may be our loss. Instead of working with our usual interests and needs we might allow things – the world – to elicit a different set of responses. It would be a bit like being in love with the world. 'It is the seeing of objects as objects (i.e. seeing them objectively, as non-animated) that is the sophisticated development' – 'the natural (or, the biologically more primitive) condition of human perception is of (outward) things, whether objects or persons, as animated.'[81]

Here Cavell speaks of 'empathic projection'. His interest in Coleridge and Wordsworth in connection with Heidegger on things, and in John Wisdom on whether flowers have feelings, has to do with the question of whether the (perhaps biologically primitive) idea of perceiving objects as animated can ever be given a sophisticated development in anything more than a merely 'metaphorical' or 'poetic' sense.[82] Is there a way of being for us now, with our history, our metaphysics, our science, a way of being in the world, *poetically*? – as if we were all poets and artists, letting things show themselves, letting others give themselves, in terms neither of fact nor of value? Is there not, Cavell asks, 'between human existence and the existence of the world a standing possibility ... of a yearning at once unappeasable and unsatisfiable, as of an impossible exclusiveness and completeness ... the possibility of falling in love with the world, blind to its progress beyond our knowledge'?[83]

'A yearning at once unappeasable and unsatisfiable': the 'truth' of scepticism is that nothing is more human than our desire to disown our position in the world, but eliminating that desire would be to lose all that makes humanity what it is.

# CHAPTER SEVEN

# CHARLES TAYLOR'S MORAL ONTOLOGY OF THE SELF

There has always been an interest among Christian theologians in some philosophical conception of what it is to be a human being, some ontology of human existence. In the last fifty or sixty years we have been invited by many of them to join modern times – *die Neuzeit* – which often means endorsing something suspiciously like the liberal-existentialist individualism that has been unmasked and discredited by philosophers such as Heidegger, Iris Murdoch and Luce Irigaray. It would be a case of Christian theology catching up belatedly on the Cartesian/Kantian notion of the individual. More recently, however, a number of theologians have emerged who believe that, in what is now the postmodern era, we need to accommodate ourselves to the decentred self. Others, again, believe that the theological turn to the subject is a quite unnecessary mistake: we need to be neither modern with the liberal individual self nor postmodern with the decentred self. We should do better to be premodern, or antimodern. We shall return to these proposals in the last chapter.

Charles Taylor[1] challenges all three of these views. He accepts the case against the modern liberal-existentialist self but, although he has been familiar all along with contemporary French thought, in a way that few Anglo-American philosophers are, he refuses to celebrate the decentred subject, in the wake of Lacan, Foucault, Derrida, et al. On the other hand, for all his proximity to communitarianism, he clearly does not want to get back to that in any of its hierarchical or organicist versions.

## Individual rights and social obligations

In his work in political theory, Taylor has striven to uncover the effects of what he labels 'atomism': the doctrines of social contract theory dating from the seventeenth century and their successor doctrines, always trading on 'a vision of society as in some sense constituted by individuals for the fulfilment of ends which were primarily individual'.[2]

Theories, first developed by such thinkers as Thomas Hobbes (1588–1679) and John Locke (1632–1704), which insist on the primacy of individual rights, tend to sideline our obligation to belong to and sustain society. In the Middle Ages, in contrast, no one would have thought of starting a political theory, let alone of running a political campaign, on the basis of the rights of the individual. What has made this plausible, Taylor maintains, is the hold exerted on our culture by atomism – the doctrine of the self-sufficiency of the individual. This involves 'the postulation of an extensionless subject, epistemologically a tabula rasa and politically a presuppositionless bearer of rights'. Thus we return to the fantasy of the unbounded worldless self that we found exposed and resisted in the work of Barth, Heidegger, Murdoch, Irigaray and Cavell, whatever the variations in detail.

Taylor links the atomistic view of society that sees it as made up of disconnected individuals, each with rights which it is society's sole function to protect and release, with the epistemological project, which seeks to ground knowledge in the experience of the individual subject. He aligns himself, then, with such thinkers as Merleau-Ponty, Heidegger and Wittgenstein, for whom knowledge can only be the work of an embodied agent interacting with others. The difficulty with this view – the main reason that Locke challenged it – is that it easily lapses into a form of conventionalism, according to which what passes for knowledge, truth, etc., is no more than the shared beliefs of a particular restricted community. At worst, this would collapse into intimidated conformism in closed societies that thwart all dissent.

Against that, Taylor insists that some explanatory frameworks give us a better sense of reality than others. True, it is not easy to judge one superior to another without appealing to epistemological foundations that stand outside all frameworks, or merely to list the technological achievements of Western science (say). There can be no going back on the lesson of modern philosophy: we have no access to sources of knowledge independently of whatever conceptual scheme we have in place. But pragmatic success is not a good enough criterion either: for one thing, what counts as success may vary from one society to another.

On one side, Taylor wants to distance himself from the empiricist-liberal tradition which finds foundations for knowledge, truth, etc., in individual experience, and holds up individual rights and personal autonomy as what matters most in politics. On the other hand, he refuses to endorse 'half-baked, neo-Nietzschean theories', which he associates with Michel Foucault and Jacques Derrida, according to which all judgements, whether moral, epistemological or political, would be grounded on the interplay of power.[3]

In the ordinary sense of the word, Taylor is of course a liberal – deeply and irrevocably attached to the liberties that liberal societies at least aspire to embody. He wants simply to remind us that 'the identity of the autonomous, self-determining individual requires a social matrix' – one which, for example, through a whole network of hard-won practices, recognizes the right to autonomous decision, to the expression of dissent, and to the individual's having a voice in deliberation about public affairs. As Taylor puts it:

> I am arguing that the free individual of the West is only what he is by virtue of the whole society and civilization which brought him to be and which nourishes him; that our facilities can only form us up to this capacity and these aspirations because they are set in this civilization; and that a family alone outside of this content – the real old patriarchal family – was a quite different animal which never tended these horizons.[4]

That is to say, there is no way of affirming the value of personal freedom which does not include an equally basic affirmation of the obligation to *belong*.

## Realism in ethics

Taylor insists, with Iris Murdoch, that modern moral philosophy has concentrated far too much on what it is right to do – moral acts, obligation and so forth – rather than on what it is good to be.[5] He believes that we may leave behind emotivism, prescriptivism, projectivism and all the other fashionable forms of non-realism in moral philosophy. If that argument has not been won, and it certainly has not been, as a glance at current literature would show, it is equally obvious that realism in ethics is now a perfectly respectable position to hold. For Taylor, anyway, we need have no embarrassment about regarding moral philosophy as primarily to do with exploring the nature of the good life for a human being. That means, as he puts it, that we have to discover the place in our

138

conceptual system for the concept of the good as the object of our allegiance – of our love – the good as the privileged focus that draws our attention and opens our moral world.[6] In his own way, Taylor builds on Murdoch's seminal essay on 'the sovereignty of the form of the good'.

Taylor puts much effort into enlarging, or retrieving, modes of thought and description that have (as he thinks) misguidedly been made to seem problematic. A great deal of background has been theorized away, so that we are either embarrassed to appeal to it or we have even forgotten that it exists. Taylor is out to remind us of the richer background to ethics than is now commonly allowed. Our moral intuitions, he holds, are embedded in assumptions about our spiritual nature and predicament. He wants to take us back to an understanding of our place in the world which involves asceticism and spirituality as much as epistemological concerns. To that extent, perhaps one may say, he is inviting us into pre-modernity.

What we need to recall is the range of discriminations of right and wrong, better or worse, etc., which are not rendered valid by our desires, inclinations or choices, but which stand independently of these and indeed offer standards by which these can be judged. (Here Taylor's proximity to Murdoch's Platonism is obvious.)

For a start, there are the demands that we recognize as moral which have to do with respect for the life of other human beings. In this or that society it may not include *all* human beings. Elsewhere it may extend to some non-human animals. But there simply are certain moral intuitions, uncommonly deep, powerful, universal – rooted in instinct, you might be inclined to say – in contrast with other moral reactions which seem rather the product of upbringing and education. The reluctance to inflict death or injury on our own kind, the inclination to come to the help of the injured or endangered, seem to Taylor to cut across all cultural differences. There is something very deep about reluctance to kill our conspecifics: men – sane men – need a great deal of special training before they become comfortable with the idea of killing human beings.

Of course, the story may differ from one culture to another. The culture will often have a story, even a theory, explaining why we do not kill and eat one another with any pleasure. It may be held that human beings have immortal souls, or that they are rational agents with a dignity that transcends any other animal, which is why we owe such respect to one another. That we do not eat one another is grounded in a certain theology, you might say – as if we might eat one another but are inhibited by a theory. In contrast, we feel free to eat other animals, justifying this on the grounds (perhaps) that they have no immortal souls, they are not rational agents. (Actually it is not easy to explain why it is all right for us to eat other animals but not to eat one another.)

Our moral reactions at this level are very like instincts, Taylor wants to say, not unlike our love of sweet things, or disgust at stinking and rotting things, or our fear of falling. Such reactions can be modified, up to a point: we can be trained to resist sugar, you can develop a taste for well-hung game, and so on. But there surely are reactions at this level which can never be eradicated – leaving aside physical injury that deprives one of the sense of taste or of smell or whatever. Certain moral reactions – about not eating one another and suchlike – yield or endorse a story about the nature and status of human beings. Our reactions turn out to be affirmations of a certain ontology of the human.[7]

One influential line has long been to dismiss such claims about the natural-instinctive basis or form of morality. Such naturalist ontologies of the human are distrusted, for one thing, because of the use some of them have been put to – justifying the exclusion of certain practices and institutions. Claims that this or that sort of conduct is not 'natural' – not in accordance with human *nature* – have justified excluding certain *people* from society. Secondly, stories about how 'unspoiled human nature respects life by instinct' win little credence. Above all, all such naturalist ontologies lie under a 'great epistemological cloud' for all those who have empiricist or rationalist assumptions about knowledge 'inspired by the success of modern natural science'.[8]

In particular, Taylor resists the 'error theory' of moral values, espoused by J. L. Mackie, which depends on a form of the fact/value dichotomy.[9] According to Mackie, our 'gut' reactions in moral questions no doubt have survival value in a socio-biological perspective; but the belief that 'we are discriminating real properties, with criteria independent of our *de facto* reactions' is an illusion. We may hold on to these moral reactions, fine tune them, alter them, and so on, to make life more bearable; but there is no place for a view that 'certain things and not others, just in virtue of their nature, [are] fit objects of respect'.

Taylor appeals to 'the way we in fact argue and reason and deliberate in our moral lives'.[10] It is not just that we happen to have certain visceral reactions, or that the survival of the fittest has shown pragmatically that they are very useful. We actually believe that it would be utterly wrong – intrinsically wrong – to draw a line round the people in the human race whose lives we count as more worth respecting. Whatever was the case once, whatever it may be in societies very different from our own, when people say that some people's existence is less worthy of respect than others (Taylor says) we immediately ask what criteria they have for this discrimination. This is what we do with racists, for example. We try to persuade them that skin colour has nothing to do with that in virtue of which human beings command our respect. The racists will no doubt reply that certain defining human characteristics are genetically determined, some human beings, individuals or ethnic groups, are less intelligent, less capable of moral consciousness and so forth. That is to say, the racists make empirical claims about supposedly innate intellectual and moral differences. They cite statistics, research results, anecdotal evidence at least, and so on, to back their claims. All such claims, Taylor says, are 'unsustainable in the light of human history'. But the logic of the debate means that the objects of our moral responses (coloured people in this case) have to be described according to criteria which are independent of our *de facto* reactions. The racist's gut reactions to a coloured person will be rapidly extended or articulated into his or her own ontology of the human. The claims that he makes about the object of his contempt are not actually about the survival value or usefulness of his gut reactions. Rather, he makes assertions about the intrinsic properties of the objects of his 'moral' reactions.[11]

The main reason for denying this, Taylor thinks, comes from modern epistemology. There is a deeply misguided conception of practical reasoning according to which the various ontological accounts that attribute predicates to human beings – such as being God's creatures, emanations of divine fire, agents of rational choice, etc. – are regarded as analogous to theoretical predicates in natural science. In this sense they are remote from the everyday descriptions by which we deal with people around us and ourselves ('folk psychology', as thinkers in this line say) and, moreover, they make reference to our conception of the universe and our place in it.

Let us go back to Plato, Taylor says, for whom the ontology of the human underlying his conception of justice was identical with his 'scientific' theory of the universe – the theory of Ideas underlies physics as much as ethics.[12]

It seems natural to us moderns, however, to think that we have to establish ontological predicates about human beings in ways analogous to our physical explanations. We think we have to start from the facts identified independently of our reactions to them (prejudices about them) and then try to show that one underlying explanation would be better than others. But as soon as we make this move we have gone wrong – 'we have lost from view what we're arguing about'.[13] Ontological accounts 'articulate the claims implicit in our [moral] reactions': 'We can no longer argue about them at all once we assume a neutral stance and try to describe the facts as they are independent of these reactions', 'as we have done in natural science since the seventeenth century'.[14]

There is such a thing as moral objectivity, Taylor insists. Growth in moral insight often requires that we hold back or restrain some of our reactions; but restraining or enlarging our reactions to people is something we do precisely in order that these others may be more transparently identified in their otherness – 'unscreened by petty jealousy, egoism, or other unworthy feelings' (very much Iris Murdoch's story then). But it is never a matter of 'prescinding from our reactions altogether'.[15]

Moral argument takes place within a world shaped by our deepest moral responses – just as natural science operates on the assumption that we focus on a world where all our responses (fears, lusts, nausea, desire) have been neutralized. It is just a mistake to discuss morals as if we had a neutral perspective on ourselves as beings with moral reactions. 'If you want to discriminate more finely what it is about human beings that makes them worthy of respect, you have to call to mind what it is to feel the claim of human suffering, or what is repugnant about injustice, or the awe you feel at the fact of human life.' (Close to Nussbaum here.) No amount of argument can take you from this supposed neutral stance towards the world to insight into moral ontology – but that does not mean that moral ontology and its insights are pure fiction, as naturalists in ethics say. 'Rather we should treat our deepest moral instincts, our ineradicable sense that human life is to be respected, as our mode of access to the world in which ontological claims are discernible and can be rationally argued about and sifted.'[16]

This moral ontology of the human is the picture in the background of our spiritual nature and predicament that makes sense of our moral responses – this is Taylor's next step. This is what we appeal to – what we draw on – when we have to defend our responses as the natural ones, the appropriate ones, the right ones, in this or that situation. This is never easy or straightforward. For one thing you may not yourself be the best authority: the moral ontology behind anyone's reactions and views is largely implicit. It seldom emerges unless there is some challenge (somebody tells you that your views are dreadful, racist, sexist or whatever). Most people, most of the time, take it for granted that every human being has the same rights to life, security and so forth. 'The greatest violators [of people's rights] hide behind a smoke screen of lies and special pleading'.[17] Racist regimes believe in human rights but speak of separate but equal development for this or that scientifically or culturally justifiable reason. Dissidents in the former Soviet Union were just mentally ill. And so forth. It is difficult to find instances in which people would now deny the universality of human rights. Controversies such as the one about abortion involve one side in the argument denying not that certain human beings do not have the same rights as the rest of us but that certain beings are not human in the first place – and, as Taylor says, this is a case where the moral ontology, the background picture about our spiritual nature and place in the universe, comes very plainly to the fore, bringing theology with it, or not, as the case may be.

Usually the background remains unarticulated, unexplored. We react in the same way, morally, to so much of the suffering and challenge, to so many of the opportunities and misfortunes of human life, that our ontology of the human need never be consulted, exposed or expounded. But often there is resistance to exploring it, Taylor argues. There is often a gap, a lack of fit, between what people officially and consciously believe and what they need to include in order to make sense of some of their moral reactions. The philosophers who set moral reactions aside as folk psychology, after all, go on arguing like the rest of us about what objects deserve respect, what reactions are appropriate, and so on. The idealist will teach his children the word 'chair', after all, for of course he wants them to do this and that, e.g. fetch a chair, as Wittgenstein remarked in an analogous connection.[18] The idea that the first attitude of all can be – ought to be – directed towards a possible disillusion, the idea that we have to begin by being taught a false certainty, is exactly the idea that there 'must be' some neutral stance that Taylor wants to dislodge from moral philosophy.

His main claim here is that 'there is a great deal of motivated suppression of moral ontology' – partly because the pluralist nature of our societies make it much easier to live that way but also because of the epistemology and the spiritual outlook associated with it.[19]

Before getting into that, Taylor insists on two great characteristics of our moral ontology of the human now in Western societies.

First of all, he notes the emphasis we put on avoiding human suffering – not that we have ceased to inflict pain, to torture prisoners, starve them in camps, and so on, but such horrors are now far more widely regarded as aberrations. In societies like ours we could no longer have executions in public. Part of the reason for this change in sensibility is negative, in the sense that we no longer believe in ritually undoing a terrible crime in an equally terrible punishment. The whole notion of a cosmic moral order which was outraged and had to be compensated has faded. As that kind of belief has declined, especially with the utilitarian Enlightenment, we protest against unnecessary suffering – executions have to be as painless as possible, and so on. There is no larger cosmic drama in which the punishment of a human being plays a part.[20]

Positively, however, this emphasis on minimizing human suffering has a source in the New Testament,[21] so Taylor claims. Indeed, it is one of the themes of 'Christian spirituality'. This is one of the most fundamental features of Christian spirituality in the modern era – 'the affirmation of ordinary life' – Taylor's term of art meaning roughly the life of production and the family.

## Affirmation of the ordinary

For Aristotle and in the Middle Ages work and family life were 'infrastructural' – necessary background and support to the Good Life of contemplation and the political action of the free citizen. One of the innovations of the Reformation, so Taylor holds, is this 'Christian-inspired sense that ordinary life was . . . the very centre of the good life'.[22] The crucial issue becomes whether ordinary everyday life is led in a God-fearing way or not: and the life of God-fearing people is lived out now, not in celibacy and contemplation, but in marriage and avocation. Taylor regards this affirmation of ordinary life (cf. Nussbaum on Molly and Leopold Bloom!) as 'one of the most powerful ideas in modern civilization' – underlying so much concern with welfare issues in the Western democracies, but, in a different way, with its 'apotheosis of man the producer' powering the ideology of Marxism.[23]

In these reflections on the concern to minimize suffering, Taylor joins Nussbaum in thinking that this may well be largely the effect of the Christian God who becomes a human being who suffers and dies. But, while Nussbaum certainly had her vision of Molly and Bloom in bed together at the end of James Joyce's *Ulysses* as a transfiguration of everyday life, Taylor goes much further, though not in the direction of Irigaray's celebration of the couple's sexual difference in ecstatic instasy. He insists that the rehabilitation[24] – perhaps he really means the discovery – of married life, starts with the first Reformers. In his prayer book of 1549 Cranmer adds a third reason to the two traditional ones for marriage: as well as the avoidance of fornication and the procreation of legitimate children, marriage is recognized as being the 'mutual society, help and comfort, that the one ought to have of the other, both in prosperity and adversity'. With Puritanism especially, Taylor argues, and especially in North America, there was a new emphasis on the intrinsic spiritual value of the marriage relationship and of the love and companionship, the friendship, it involves – 'the indisputable Authority, the plain Command of the Great God, requires Husbands and Wives, to have and manifest very great affection, love and kindness to one another'.[25] There he is quoting Benjamin Wadsworth but he has quotations from Jeremy Taylor, John Cotton and several others. If the later seventeenth century was producing the Cartesian subject, the precursor of the liberal-existentialist self with problems about solipsism, believing in other minds and so on, as well as with the will to project whatever values he likes on the intrinsically valueless world into which he has been thrown – it has to be allowed that, in same late seventeenth century, above all out of the Puritan strand in Protestantism, there developed a new ideal of companionate marriage which, as Taylor puts it, is 'ancestral to our whole contemporary understanding of marriage and sexual love'.[26]

It is a pleasure to find a philosopher who sees something else besides Cartesianism in the seventeenth century. It is also a pleasure to see how much we owe to Protestantism and especially to Puritanism (however idealized). But above all it is worth remembering that this modern ideal of friendship-marriage is a historical creation, which emerged at a certain point. It has not prevailed everywhere, it may even be passing away as obsolete in many places, often the same places as it is only beginning to take hold and transform people's lives. One wonders just how much this ideal of friendship-marriage depends on having a fair range of other ideals and practices in place, many of which may have to be 'Christian'. But Taylor's main point here is that this new understanding of marriage is a new understanding of people, a new sense of the worth of men and women and children, in fact all part of a new sense of the sanctification of ordinary life. 'To know/ That which before us lies in daily life/ Is the prime wisdom', Taylor quotes from *Paradise Lost*.[27]

Taylor does not argue directly that religion should play a central or constituent role in our moral lives. He just wants to show that, with a lot of qualification, it could do so and indeed that it actually does so. 'I believe in God', Taylor says,[28] 'because I sense something which I want to describe as God's love and affirmation of the world, and human beings. I see this refracted in the lives of exceptional people, whom I'll call for short saints, as well as hearing faint echoes in my own prayer life.' At once he speaks of 'the confused searching, alternation of doubt and confidence, hope and despair, which actually constitute what one might call my spiritual life'. We see the caution but also the astonishing audacity in a philosopher's telling us that he has some kind of prayer life!

Of course we could pick over what he says. Taylor has a very conversational casual style of writing – disarming even: 'I believe ... because I sense something ... something I want to describe ... to describe as God's love ... affirmation of the world ... affirmation of human beings ... something I see ... see refracted in the lives of exceptional people.' It is not difficult to see how philosophers of a positivist or non-realist turn of mind would want to put pressure on most of the words in Taylor's remarks. 'What I believe in', he goes on to say, 'is what figures in my best account of the world, history, and my experience as a moral and spiritual being.' So it is 'my best account' – it is personal testimony – he is open to the possibility of developing a better account.

His account of religious belief is, he says, 'quintessentially modern'.[29] He explains this as follows. He has no time for the Five Ways of proving the existence of God propounded by Thomas Aquinas – at least if such arguments are meant to convince us quite independently of our moral and spiritual experience. If one is supposed to take these arguments as an unbeliever would, as showing the inescapable logical cogency of certain conclusions, regardless of their spiritual meaning to people going through the arguments, they mean nothing to Taylor. Whether that is how such arguments should ever have been taken is, he says, by no means unproblematic. If you take that line it is always going to annoy philosophers who think that religion is meaningless because there are no valid arguments for the existence of God – they need the arguments to be intended to work regardless of people's moral and spiritual condition.

Taylor is interested in what actually makes one's spiritual outlook plausible to oneself. 'We can be deluded about this.' Indeed, if there are people who base their religious belief on the validity of proofs for the existence of God understood in the disengaged way just described, Taylor would regard them as deluded: 'They would never find them remotely convincing, if they weren't already moved to do so by their feel for what makes sense of their moral and spiritual experience.'[30] He permits himself the comment that nobody ever was convinced by such 'disengaged' arguments.

## Taylor's argument for God

In his paper 'From Marxism to the dialogue society', Taylor approaches Marxism as 'an answer to a question which arises in the historical dialectic of European humanism':[31] 'Why is it that rational control over nature which has grown with the European philosophical and technological achievement has nevertheless produced such antihuman results?' Marx, like Hegel, wanted to 'save the essence of the Enlightenment' from its critics: 'Ever since the Romantics, the basic spiritual stance of the Enlightenment has been under constant attack' – that stance being understood as 'a way of treating nature ... as material which waits to be transformed or manipulated in order to produce certain results' – results, goals, 'dictated by man and ... imposed on the material from without'.

Although no doubt caricatured in the critique, this basic stance, Taylor thinks, is obviously central in much modern Western thought: in the means-ends relation central to utilitarian ethics; in the dualism of Cartesianism-empiricism, where the body is seen as being in interaction with the mind, source of goals and values; and in the achievement of the sciences, since part at least of the criterion for success is that the phenomena investigated become more amenable to control.

'Man is the source ... of "values"' – hence what Taylor calls 'frenetic attempts' to eliminate the picture of man as both object and subject, whether attempts by behaviourism or by idealism; hence the 'embarrassed attempt to hold facts apart from values' – mystification about 'value-freedom' in the social sciences; and so on.

From the first Romantics on – on to such diverse figures, as Taylor calls them, as D. H. Lawrence and Heidegger – this basic stance has been denounced and derided again and again for cutting human beings off from their living relations to nature, cutting them off from relations of meaningful solidarity with one other, cutting them off from their own nature, crushing their individuality, blunting their creativity, killing their spontaneity, and so on.[32]

Marxism has seemed attractive Taylor thinks, because it refuses any outright rejection of the Enlightenment's basic stance: gaining rational control over nature is an immense gain. Indeed it is part of the essential realization of human nature. But Marxism takes up also the Romantic conception, or family of conceptions, of human activity as being the expression through change of self or surroundings of an inner nature. The Enlightenment stance takes all activity on the means-ends model, Taylor insists; but the notion of expression, the bringing into existence of significant reality, obviously belongs to another dimension, it is not just a return to the models of human action as the realization of virtues or vices – 'action conceived of as realizing a virtue' is not the same as 'action seen as expressing an essence'. Activity realizes a virtue by struggling against disorder towards some inner equilibrium, but activity expresses an essence by breaking through a barrier and achieving control over some external reality.

On the first story you realize a potentiality. With expression theories, on the other hand, Taylor argues, you break through a barrier. And this second family of theories is very widespread in our culture – in Marxism, as for Hegel, the essence cannot be said to be until expressed in external reality. For Marx, man may be said to construct his own nature by transforming nature and thus himself. His being cut off from himself is a matter of his being cut off from transformed nature, and that means that this transformed nature, this second nature, no longer expresses him. It is something alien. So we get the notion of alienation: 'a disharmony between the conditions of man's transformatory action, social production, and the exigencies of class society, private appropriation'.[33]

The problem with Marxism, however, is that it is not true.[34] It rests on an illusion about the human condition: 'The promise that it holds out of complete reconciliation of man to other men, his creation and himself, all in one act, is unfulfillable.' All criticisms of Marxism, Taylor holds, come back to this one.

The promise is unfulfillable, first of all, because human beings will never be transparent to themselves – partly for the reasons that Freud has explored: 'lucidity and creative sanity is [sic] won in a difficult and fundamentally unendable struggle/negotiation with the archaic'. More generally than the Freudian point, however, 'man's being plunges right down into the depths of nature considered as a scale of life ... so that he or his works can never have the transparency of pure project, thrown in front of him into the future, as it were, but always lie partly hidden behind him'.

But secondly, related to this of course, the promise of total reconciliation is unfulfillable because 'man needs, in order to come to creative terms with the archaic, to reach beyond himself and renew contact with the non-human, and I must add the more than human'.[35] We have to transcend ourselves, by renewing contact with the more-than-human.

In this perspective, Marxism is no better than the Enlightenment *tout court*: 'man reaching out for some living source comes only into contact with the genus' – man collectively – 'the creative meaning is that of the genus'. 'Men are to live in a purely human, man-made world' – and now – what will such a world express? – 'Man'. 'But there is something ultimately tail-chasing, self-referring in an infinite regress, about this.' 'Man can celebrate himself as the being who understands and can transform, but the celebration has no point unless the understanding glorified is of something, and the transformation is inspired by something else.' That is to say, Taylor concludes, Marxism belongs within the circle of the whole European voluntarist-metaphysical tradition which underlies Enlightenment thought: 'in raising man above nature (including his own nature) it leaves him without interlocutor and therefore with nothing to say' – and that can be, Taylor says, as devastating an error when we take man generically as when we take him individually.

Without reproducing the whole argument, we may say that, for Taylor, what is wrong with Marxism as with the capitalist societies of the West has to do with their not being dialogue societies – societies, that is to say, wherein we have to come to terms with our own instinctual base, which means discovering authentic forms of expression for our basic drives. We cannot disown the archaic in our nature; and that involves relating ourselves to a greater reality outside – 'that from which one has received and to which one gives in return'.[36]

'Men are led to define themselves in terms of some more ultimate reality.' For some (humanists) this greater reality might be the human race as an ideal community. But what is important here is Taylor's discussion of what he calls the recipient/donor relation to ultimate realities.[37] He is concerned about how this relation has atrophied in capitalist/technological societies – how the springs by which the presence of the sacred in human life was periodically renewed have dried up. One of the principal ways in which people found contact with the sacred was the community itself, so that the community, or the tribe, was both that from which one received and that to which one gave in return so that the tribe and the sacred

149

were identical. Even as they became differentiated, he says, one mediated the other as earthly authority might be thought to have a divine foundation. People have also found the sacred in the extra-human world around – in Nature. But we have a completely desacralized vision of the cosmos, and the community itself is not regarded as sacred. On the contrary it exists largely to serve productive goals, it is an instrument designed for the furtherance of individual happiness, at least on the standard liberal view. To all this there have of course been responses – one of the great themes of the Romantic movement was to rediscover a relationship of meaning with Nature; some forms of nationalism have involved the (re)sacralization of the community (*Volk*, racialism).

With nature and society desacralized you might think that mediation of the sacred would concentrate in the churches. Taylor believes, however, that there has instead been 'a spread of a diffuse, unstructured, publicly unexpressed and inexpressible spirituality or sense of the divine'.[38]

But his main theme is that 'Generic man is not the ultimate reality'. 'Man can never be fully in control of his generic nature because it extends out of his reach into the prerational and the pre-human' – 'On my view the Marxist promise of transparency is a kind of collectivised and historicised Cartesian dream.' 'Like the original Cartesian dream, it is breached both above and below, both in being immersed in a less-than-human nature and in being placed before a more-than human ultimate reality'.[39]

## Isaiah Berlin on Taylor

Isaiah Berlin speaks very highly of Taylor as a philosopher.[40] The chief difference between them (they have discussed philosophy together off and on for nearly forty years) is, Berlin says, that Taylor is 'basically a teleologist – both as a Christian and as a Hegelian'. That is to say, Taylor believes, as so many in the history of thought have done and still do, that 'human beings, and perhaps the entire universe, have a basic purpose – whether created by God as religious Christians and Jews believe' – or created by Nature, as Aristotle held and as perhaps Hegel taught (Berlin thinks Hegel is somewhat ambivalent about this). The upshot is that, for Taylor, as Berlin puts it, 'everything he has written is concerned with what people have believed, striven after, developed into, lived in the light of, and, finally, the ultimate goals towards which human beings as such are by their very natures determined to move'.

Berlin mentions the interest in, admiration for, Herder that he shares with Taylor, mentioning Herder's central idea that to belong to a society is an intrinsic human need, like the need for food or security or shelter or freedom. Indeed: self-realization cannot be obtained in isolation from social life but only in the framework of the organic structure of the culture or society into which we are born and to which we therefore cannot help belonging. This commits neither Berlin nor Taylor nor for that matter Herder to any kind of cultural relativism in which one is enclosed in one's culture never able to escape, dissent, transcend and so on. But beyond this Berlin parts company with Taylor. He believes that societies and cultures develop in a certain fashion – he has spent much of his life reconstructing such developments – but he believes that 'purposes are imposed by human beings upon nature and the world, rather than pursued by them as part of their own central natures or essences'. 'I think that Taylor believes in essences, whereas I do not.' That is to say, spelling it out:

> I believe that it is human beings, their imagination, intellect and character that form the world in which they live ... but that this is in a sense a free, unorganised development – which cannot be causally predicted ... It is not part of a determinist structure, it does not march inexorably towards some single predestined goal, as Christians, Hegelians, Marxists and other determinists and teleologists have, in varied ... ways, believed and still believe to the present day.[41]

Berlin gestures towards his own well-known view – that there are incompatible moral goals and values in our society, in any society – 'so that the notion of one world, one humanity moving in one single march of the faithful, *laeti triumphantes*, is unreal'. Rather, it is what human beings do and suffer, not some 'cosmic plan' that determines what the total outcome of human behaviour must be.

Every word invites attention. Isaiah Berlin is operating with a pretty clear conception of what Christian theology involves. No doubt there are distinctions to be made between Aristotelians and Hegelians, Hegelians and Marxists, and so forth – and between all of those and Christians. Unmistakably, however, for Berlin, Christian theology means a belief in human essences, such that the world we form by our imagination, intellect and character, is not a free, unorganized development but something that can be causally predicted. It is part of a determinist structure, it is one single march towards some single predestined goal. Here we have, in one of the most influential thinkers of our time, a very clear and surely very contestable theology. It is perhaps going too far to say that Isaiah Berlin's liberal-pluralist moral philosophy is in any decisive way shaped by his conception of Christian theology – it is other totalitarianisms, I think, that he is reacting against – but there is no doubt about his conception, or misconception, of Christian theology.

The striking thing, however, is that Taylor, in his two pages of response to Berlin, says nothing about Berlin's view of Christian theology as a causally predictable deterministic march to some predestined goal. Taylor in fact seeks to play down the differences between himself and Berlin – 'I'm not sure the gap is as wide as it seems in his description'. Fair enough: Charles Taylor is an optimist – though it must be particularly irritating to someone like Isaiah Berlin whose most distinctive thought is that there are equally valid and totally incompatible outlooks. But the next remark that Taylor makes is even more worrying: he is not sure the gap is as wide as Berlin paints it – or rather, as he says, 'the differences run very deep metaphysically and theologically; but they narrow somewhat in the practical judgements about our situation in society and history'.[42]

Taylor is utterly opposed to 'the modern vogue of ethical thinking, which tends to try to derive all our obligations from some single principle'. He usually has utilitarianisms in mind when he says this kind of thing elsewhere. Indeed, that is what he likes in Berlin who has insisted so strongly on the irreconcilable conflicts we frequently face between different goods and goals we cannot help subscribing to – 'I very much agree with him on this: human beings are always in a situation of conflict between moral demands.' 'We are torn two ways ... We don't have any formula ... We can only make difficult judgments in which ... demands are balanced against each other, at some sacrifice to one or both'. On all this Taylor agrees with Berlin. He even goes so far as to say that 'in this regard ... Berlin's thinking has been a surer guide than mainstream moral philosophy'[43] – mainstream moral philosophy no doubt being Kant with his universalizability principle, the utilitarians with their calculus, the non-cognitivists and non-realists with their criterion 'if it feels right then it is right'. Where Taylor disagrees, he says, and Berlin had already pointed this out, is that Taylor is reluctant to take Berlin's perception of the incompatibility of equally valid goals and goods as the last word: 'I still believe that we can and should struggle for a "transvaluation" ... which could open the way to a mode of life, individual and social, in which these demands could be reconciled' – demands in concrete social and political dilemmas between freedom and control, protecting the environment and creating jobs, and so forth – 'I don't think this is totally chimerical'. 'We have made some such advances in history'.

The example Taylor gives, the only one (but he has only a paragraph left in his reply to Berlin), is that for centuries human beings could not imagine how public order and popular sovereignty might be reconciled: 'Now the most law-abiding societies are democratic.' 'That this may have been achieved at the cost of other values has to be allowed' – and there, I think, from what he has written elsewhere, Taylor would be conceding that democracy brings popular culture and that frequently means trivialization of the human spirit. 'But the original dilemma was not insurmountable' and of course there was – is – a conflict at the theoretical level in this case but really it might be a case of our agreeing that for practical purposes keeping public order and depending on popular sovereignty need not conflict – on the contrary – although we might still have deep metaphysical and theological differences running between us. Taylor then allows that the whole history of the twentieth century shows how dangerous the aspiration to reconcile conflicting values can be – precisely Berlin's point. Leninist 'democracy', Taylor says, is a clear case of 'the too quick belief in a specious solution', which 'can wreak terrible destruction', and he concludes that 'the distinct nature of the [originally conflicting] demands, in their full richness and power, have [sic] to be kept before our eyes, lest we trick ourselves that we have met them with cheap substitutes'.[44] This is where Berlin's 'immensely eloquent and penetrating work is and will remain indispensable reading for a long time to come'.

But the gap between Taylor and Berlin is surely pretty wide. Berlin's central point is that the only way of saving humanity from oppression of some kind or other is precisely to give up once and for all the aspiration to resolve our moral and political differences completely. Of course we can and ought and indeed already all the time do work away at reducing the conflicts of goals and goods in our private lives, in our friendships and other relationships, in business, in international relations and so forth. Berlin's desire to eradicate all hope of achieving complete and final harmonization of goals and values does not commit him to some kind of quietism – he has plenty of room for reducing differences, provided we acknowledge that there will always be some. If you want there to be complete unity you will have to expel a lot of dissenters from your society, you will have to liquidate a lot of people – the story of the twentieth century, which is what dominates Isaiah Berlin's moral philosophy all the way through.

It remains astonishing, and disappointing, that, even within the confined space of a couple of pages, Taylor did not question Berlin's conception of Christian theology as involving a deterministic teleological metaphysics. This is not one of the conceptions of Christian theology that Nussbaum identifies and questions. It is not unlike caricatures of Barth's Calvinism – but caricatures: there is plenty of room in the *Church Dogmatics* for human autonomy.[45] It is a conception of Christian theology which is not unlike Heidegger's picture of it as onto-theo-logical metaphysics – replaced in Heidegger's case by a pretty deterministic or anyway fatalistic internal-teleological dance of non-human forces. But it surely is a conception of Christian theology that Taylor should have challenged. He is not a theologian, he might say, but one of the main points I am trying to make is that there needs to be far more investigation of the religion in much of the most impressive and influential philosophy, whether these philosophers are professionally, confessionally, Christian or establishing their own views over against what they take, or mistake, religion to involve.

One of the good things about Nussbaum, I think, is that, starting from a position of no sympathy whatsoever for the Christian religion, she has moved some way towards clarifying her understanding. Murdoch by comparison has what looks like a pretty unshakeable non-realist story about the Christian religion. Irigaray, with her belief that Feuerbach was right about religion as a human projection but that, far from this being some kind of criticism of religion, we have rather to notice that it has been an androcentric projection and what is needed now is a women's religion, also belongs in the non-realist camp. But when we get to Charles Taylor, the only one of my clutch of major philosophers who is actually a religious Christian (in Berlin's phrase), it is somewhat disconcerting to find him failing to challenge what surely seems to any Christian theologian a pretty unsatisfactory conception of the Christian religion. In effect, it is a conception of the Christian religion which rules out in advance any serious participation in history by human beings. It is a well-known story: either God does it all and human beings are automatically marching towards their final destiny like an army of puppets; or else we are free and moving in a pretty disorganized fashion, one step forwards two steps sideways, but helping God to bring the process to some eventual happy end – an end that will surprise God as much as it will surprise us. Isaiah Berlin's remarks take it absolutely for granted that the Christian story has no place for real human autonomy, imagination, creativity and so forth. It is such a familiar misconception that one is a bit surprised that Berlin himself, after all the most distinguished historian of ideas alive, has not noticed it – but, stranger still, Taylor seems to feel no need to query or resist Berlin's version of Christian teleology.

## Taylor on Heidegger

Taylor has written a good deal about Heidegger. If you know something about Heideggerian themes already you can detect variations on them in much of Taylor's apparently standard Anglo-American analytical philosophy.[46]

In particular, Taylor writes very sympathetically about what might be called Heidegger's philosophy of ecology – the proximity of some of his later work to what is now called deep ecology.[47] Heidegger's philosophy is anti-subjectivist, antihumanist, anti-non-realist, in the sense that he holds that there is no future for us human beings unless we understand that nature makes demands on us – that something beyond the human makes demands on us.[48] Mostly Taylor works this out in terms of Heidegger's conception of language, a good way into Heidegger's work; but the upshot is to challenge the idealism, the non-realism, that is there (Heidegger thinks) in the founding figures of modern philosophy – Descartes, Locke – culminating in Nietzschean claims to the effect that reality is simply what we human beings make of it, or project on it. The world worlds, as Heidegger would say, only in virtue of our being here – no doubt pre-Kantian metaphysicians failed properly to acknowledge our role; but any activity of ours, any description or representation of things and situations that we achieve, takes for granted what non-realists forget – namely, that it is a mistake to think that meanings are all in our heads. Through language a world is disclosed, a world in which objects of specifically human emotions impinge on us, threaten us, attract us, and so on. Some of these goods attract us in ways that prompt the variety of enterprises we now call science. Others provoke, evoke, other kinds of response, other kinds of discourse, including in their own way stories and mythologies as well as music, painting and so forth. In the West, according to Heidegger's story, we tend to see language as our instrument and the space of meaning, the world as an order of intelligibility, as something that happens in us that we generate – something that simply reflects our goals and purposes. But what we are – and here Taylor is happy to accept talk of our nature, our essence – is to be found, or made, in the ways in which we are attentive to how language opens up a space of meaning, which is not something that we arrange or impose. It is not there without us, but it is there as the context for all our making and acting. We can act only in so far as we are already in the midst of things.

Our role is, in Heidegger's later terminology, a secondary one. Human beings are not the first cause of the world of meaning we inhabit. In old-fashioned theological language, we operate as secondary causes. Once again Heidegger is transforming traditional Christian theology. For him, in other words, non-realism makes us God – creating the order of meaning out of nothing, by an act of will – whereas our role is one, rather, of taking care (*pflegen*), of sparing (*schonen*). The human agent is a shepherd of Being, in his famous phrase.[49]

If we deny that – if we act as if we had the initiative, as if we were the creator of the space of meaning we inhabit – then, for Heidegger, we go against our essence, and this cannot but be destructive. Our essence, our nature, is not derived from our being the animals with rationality, with ideas in our heads. Our nature is derived from our being animals possessing or rather possessed by language – but language as one of the ways in which we are related to (what we saw in Chapter 3) the fourfold.[50] In the end, Taylor takes up Heidegger's claims about the space of meaning (*die Lichtung*, as he calls it: the clearing, as in a forest[51]). This is conceived as something that *happens*, that keeps happening, as we human beings let certain things *be*. Such things appear, not simply as objects (although there is nothing wrong about their doing so in the appropriate circumstances) not, even less, as raw material entirely subject to human will. Rather, the thing about a thing is that in being handled, in being visible, in being paintable, it co-discloses the world. As the jug, the decanter, the chalice, fulfils its role in our life, in our community, it is heavy with the human activities in which it plays a part – the pouring of wine at the common table for instance. 'The jug is a point at which this rich web of practices can be sensed, made visible in the very shape of the jug and its handle which offers itself for this use.'[52]

Somewhat controversially, Taylor takes it that the sacred dimension that is revealed is, for example, at least the way that some things make a claim on us. They are what he calls strong goods, matters of intrinsic worth. Heidegger envisages this dimension, this connection, Taylor says, as arising from the ritual of pouring wine from a jug in certain circumstances. The modes of conviviality that the decanter co-discloses are shot through with religious and moral meaning, even if no one has said grace at the beginning of the meal. The jug is something shaped and fashioned for human use – it is always already a locus. It stands on and stands in, emerges from, a vast domain, a field of potential further meaning – our future life together – open-ended, unforeseeable, perhaps ending in an unexpected death in a few hours. But it also has a history – a past – ultimately it depends on the clay, thus on the earth. The whole round of interdependent relationships that the jug gathers into itself, and extends to all who participate in using it, is open (Heidegger thinks) to cosmic forces far greater than anything that we human beings can form. These forces either allow our activities to flourish or sweep them away: the alternation of day and night, storms, floods, earthquakes, or their benign absence – these are what define the space.[53]

Heidegger is on to something very important, Taylor concludes. His understanding of what it is to be human as ultimately the gift of something non-human offers the basis for an ecological politics. This would be a politics founded on something deeper than instrumentalist calculation of the conditions of our survival. We have to think of the claims that things put on us to let them be, to let them disclose themselves in a certain way. It is a manner of letting things be, which in crucial cases (Taylor says) is quite incompatible with the approach of will to power over everything.

Take for example any region of wilderness. If the rain forests are simply standing reserves for timber production that is one approach and that is already annihilation. Of course there is exploration as well as exploitation. We can identify the species and geological forms that the wilderness contains, retaining and indeed deepening our sense of the inexhaustibility of their wilderness surroundings: 'Our goals here are fixed by something which we should properly see ourselves as serving.' 'So a proper understanding of our purposes has to take us beyond ourselves.'[54] Properly understood, the shepherd of Being can never be an adept of triumphalist instrumental reason – that is why learning to dwell poetically among things may amount literally to 'rescuing the earth': 'At this moment when we need all the insight we can muster into our relations to the cosmos in order to deflect our disastrous course, Heidegger may have opened a vitally important new line of thinking'.[55]

We need not go to Heidegger to get this kind of deep ecological politics – we know of many other sources. And although Taylor certainly mentions Heidegger's failure to grasp the significance of what happened in his native land between 1933 and 1945, much more would need to be said about the ambiguities inherent in this kind of non-anthropocentric ontology of the human which appeals to a relationship to something non-human as the defining feature of our essence. Perhaps it is somewhat more paradoxical than Taylor acknowledges when he connects human flourishing with responsibility for the environment (as of course he is absolutely right to do) by invoking the work that Martin Heidegger was producing from about 1936 onwards. But the main point for Charles Taylor is that we human beings need to be in touch with – have to be receptive and open to – the non-human creatures in this world of ours, this world of theirs, if we are to hold on to our own identity as humankind.

Deep ecology, then, together with realist ontology of the human, the affirmation of ordinary life, and religious belief as a sense of our needing – our having – some interlocutor not ourselves, some other – that is Charles Taylor's version of the self-transcendence manifest in our lives already.

# CHAPTER EIGHT

# NATURAL DESIRE
# FOR GOD

It is no part of the argument of this book that recent philosophy, whether Anglo-American analytical or Continental post-phenomenological in tendency, is irretrievably theological. Theological motifs would be difficult to trace in most currently fashionable philosophers.

Perhaps it would not be impossible. 'All true philosophy outside Christianity', the Catholic theologian Hans Urs von Balthasar claims, 'is at bottom theology.' Philosophy 'lives and is kept alive by a point, a gravitational pull, external to itself, that mysterious Absolute that lies beyond the purview of merely human reason and that alone makes thought worthwhile'.[1] A good deal would turn on what counted as 'true' philosophy. We should have to be thinking of metaphysics, ethics, political theory and so on, presumably, rather than of logic, at least if it may be regarded as a system of techniques. Secondly, we might wonder how much philosophy, at least since Augustine's day, has been 'outside Christianity'. We might concede that, historically, modern philosophy derived from late-medieval theology, and that its origins may exercise much more influence than is often acknowledged.[2] Thirdly, if we regarded philosophy as essentially metaphysics, we might agree with Iris Murdoch that, from Plato onwards, it has always been essentially a religious enterprise.

It might be tempting, at this point, to cross the border from the philosophy of religion to seek a grand narrative that would incorporate the traces and reconfigurations of Christian theology, however misconceived and sidelined, that we have uncovered in some recent philosophical projects. A brief recapitulation of what we have seen, however, would surely show the impossibility of amalgamating the diverse views that we have examined in an all-embracing harmonious account.

159

## Seven versions of transcending humanity

Martha Craven Nussbaum's work (Chapter 1) includes a variety of ways of dealing with the desire to transcend humanity that has long seemed natural at least in Western metaphysics and culture. She rejects Diotima's recipe, in Plato's *Symposium*, for concentrating desire on the abstract non-human good, and favours a fairly low-key transfiguration of the everyday world; she prefers the guilt-free playfulness of the birds and the bees to the sex-hating and body-loathing effects of a certain (mis)conception of the doctrine of original sin; she favours a secularization of the same doctrine, quite differently understood, in an endlessly deepening knowledge of one's tragically flawed existence; she entertains the possibility of a god who might accept the conditions of human life, suffering and mortality; and throughout she fears any project of transcending humanity which translates us into the life of any sort of non-human being. Within Nussbaum's writing, perhaps we may say, the pull of the absolute is ubiquitous, and she has incommensurable ways of dealing with it.

That need not be an objection. On the contrary, a self-consistent monolithic way of dealing with our immortal longings might be exactly what is *not* the most satisfactory solution. Martin Heidegger's project (Chapter 3) might be exactly the kind of thing that Nussbaum most fears (she only mentions his name once or twice). His way of dealing with the solitary soul's desire to ascend to unmediated communion with the absolute is to immerse the self – disperse the self, we might even say – in the mirror-game, *das Spiegel-Spiel*, by which the non-human realities of sky, earth, death and the sacred, joined in a kind of round dance, open the space for the human being to be both finite and transcendent, both situated and decentred, at one and the same time. To Nussbaum, this radical decentring of the self would surely seem as humanly alienating and destructive as Diotima's project. In either case the human being as conceived in the Cartesian/Kantian picture of the self-directing agent disappears, either into the impersonal absolute or into something that lies in the gift of a quartet of non-human realities.

On the other hand, Iris Murdoch's project (Chapter 4), with her emphasis on the human being as prey to egoistic fantasy, sees the Platonic project of liberation by perpetual submission to the always greater ideals of the good, the true and the beautiful, as the only hope for human beings to become fully and properly human. Far from feeling threatened by Diotima's project (as Nussbaum understands it), we need precisely that metaphysical ascent to discover and maintain any sort of humanly congenial and worthy moral life. By gradually stripping away our selfish and prejudiced subjectivity we may at last gain the freedom of obedience to something objective.

In contrast, according to Luce Irigaray (Chapter 5), Diotima's project, largely misunderstood by Socrates, offers a glimpse of eros as the divine intermediary, as the coincidence of bodiliness and spirituality in the finite transcendence, the ecstatic immanence, of the encounter between sexually different beings. In effect, the event of a meeting between man and woman – woman at last enabled to be herself and not a man's mirror image –would itself be *divine*.

If Heidegger invites us to find our true selves by participating in the dance of the quaternity, and if Murdoch directs us to disciplined subjection to the sovereignty of the form of the good, the true and the beautiful, then Irigaray invokes sexual difference as the suprahuman 'given', with respect to which human beings may at last come into their own in practical acknowledgement of their otherness.

Heidegger, Murdoch and Irigaray, with the quaternity, the form of the good and *la différence sexuelle* respectively, offer variations on Diotima's ascent of love which, contrasted with Nussbaum's explorations, all seem extremely, even frighteningly, monolithic.

Stanley Cavell's resting with 'a yearning at once unappeasable and unsatisfiable' (Chapter 6) and Charles Taylor's retrieval of 'sources of the self' (Chapter 7) bring us back into a conversation in which the voices are, like Nussbaum's, a good deal more tentative and self-doubting. Cavell seems vulnerable to the attractions of the liberal-existentialist self; he cannot take religion seriously as a possibility for intelligent people; and yet his insistence on the 'truth' of scepticism as the endless interrogation of ultimate values is, in its way, an unstoppable oscillation between immanence and transcendence. Taylor, by contrast, makes no bones about his Catholic beliefs, though, on present evidence, his theology seems rather thin compared with his neo-Romantic ecological consciousness.

Karl Barth comes in between Nussbaum and Heidegger (Chapter 2). If Nussbaum displays a range of ways of dealing with aspirations to transcend humanity, settling for none and leaving a good deal of unresolved tension, Heidegger offers a very coherent and single-minded project for securing the insertion of humanity in the finitude of the self-transcending fourfold. Barth too has a monolithic solution to Diotima's dream, but far from being a descent into the confines of the world remythologized as the mirror-game of the quaternity, as in Heidegger, he invites us to remember that the only absolute there is has become one of us and opened the way, in an unexacted and unanticipatable dispensation of grace, for us to become more fully human than ever in comnmunion with the only truly human being there has ever been. The historical event of the incarnation, death and resurrection of Jesus Christ, the one whose human nature is united hypostatically – really and ontologically, not just psychologically and morally – with the divine nature, seizes the ancient quest for the absolute and turns it on its head.

Plainly, it is impossible to reconcile these different versions of transcending humanity. But should we expect to be able to do so – even to grade them according to some scale of plausibility or proximity to the truth? Any attempt would have to be measured against the traditional Christian recognition of the powerlessness of finite mortal life to fulfil our natural desire for transcendence in a way that respects our humanity *without grace*.

## Christianity or nothing?

According to Hans Urs von Balthasar,[3] in one of his moods, Christianity has been so successful in our culture that the religious experience of the world that people used to have, and that people outside post-Christian cultures still have, has been devalued and marginalized. Three or four centuries have been needed, he thinks, but the diffuse sense of the sacred, once taken for granted, has all but faded away, leaving us with nothing but the choice between the story of Christ crucified and raised from the dead and, on the other hand, the *tabula rasa* of an empty universe upon which we simply have to impose what values we can conceive.

This has no doubt sharpened our sense of the uniqueness of the gift – of the Christian dispensation of grace; but it leaves that gift – that grace – completely isolated. The God of natural religion, once found in one form or another everywhere, has become definitively and uniquely located in Jesus Christ in such a way that the alternative now is nothing but 'the great void'. 'Finite human freedom, with its superhuman aspirations, has been treated as absolute.'[4] The alternative to acceptance of the Christian economy of grace, it would appear, is simply idolatry of human will – liberal-existentialist voluntarism, we may say.

It is always a good question to ask what a philosopher fears. Von

Balthasar's highly implausible claim that the success of Christianity has wiped out all other forms of religion and metaphysics is tied up with his suspicions of Karl Rahner's theology. He fears that the deity of natural religion is 'the kind of God whom now, in the post-Christian age, modern transcendental theology would like to reinstate'. The metaphysical perspective, inherited from Stoicism and Neoplatonism, has been 'rolled up and set to one side'.

This state of affairs has a good as well as a bad side. For example, it explains why the cosmological arguments for God's existence remain valid but have become unconvincing for people for whom nature is no longer manifestly ordered and sacred.[5] It means, on the other hand, that, since we no longer regard our natural environment with reverence, we treat it as raw material for technological exploitation. This desacralization of nature, however, affords new opportunities for Christian faith. Finding ourselves alone in this demythologized universe, we discover that we human beings are the only sources of ultimate value. When we regard another human being as of such unique and intrinsic worth, we begin to suspect that this becomes visible only in the illuminating perspective of the Christian tradition. The collapse of religion clears the stage for the appearance of Christianity in all its specificity. Indeed, previously, the biblical world itself was 'almost like an episode, clarifying and symbolizing the deep embrace of infinite and finite freedom', seldom or never allowed to stand out in its historical particularity.

The religious world picture is irretrievably lost. What angers von Balthasar about 'today's transcendental theologians' is that they 'would like to interpret Christ as the "highest, unsurpassable instance" of a self-disclosure to man on God's part that is coterminous with creation as such'.[6] But these theologians – Karl Rahner, above all – come too late on the scene: 'the stage's background has already been cleared'. With perceptible glee, von Balthasar concludes that Rahner's theology 'still thinks in terms of a fundamental religious instinct in man' – an instinct 'that may already be defunct'.[7]

This is a pretty wild story. Rahner's transcendental argument about the a priori conditions of our subjectivity does not result in anything that might fairly be called a religious 'instinct'. Von Balthasar, we may note in passing, is equally dismissive of the other major projects in recent Catholic theology. In particular, he denounces liberation theology, which 'builds the gospel (in which cross and resurrection have become superfluous) into the temple of humanity it is trying to erect', as well as what is evidently the work of Edward Schillebeeckx: 'a soteriology backed up by exegesis' that 'shifts the accents in the picture of Jesus to his "solidarity" with the oppressed and the marginalized, to such an extent that today the Cross ... is nothing more than the logical expression of this solidarity'. These two projects, at least as he characterizes them, depend on his view of modern man's desacralized world. They are wrong headed because they water down Christian revelation; but at least they are not grounded, like Rahner's theology, on an appeal to 'a fundamental religious instinct in man'.

What has surely emerged from our study of a half-dozen recent philosophers is how important theological motifs and considerations are in the development and articulation of their projects. Besides that, they are all engaged, in no doubt very different ways, in recreating, rediscovering, something like the religio-metaphysical conception of human life into which Christianity erupted. Also, they all believe, and argue, that as moral agents, as subjects, we are indebted to something other than ourselves. In one way or another, they believe that human life as a moral and spiritual enterprise is essentially *responsive*. However tentative, provisional, off centre and misguided they may be, their projects cannot be dismissed as posturings against the void. But that is not the main point. Von Balthasar's refusal to acknowledge the continuing existence and validity of religious and metaphysical views is dictated by his determination to discredit Karl Rahner's theology.

## The nature/grace controversy

Hatred among theologians is legendary – *odium theologicum*! The bitterest dispute in Roman Catholic theology this century has been over the proper way to characterize the relationship between nature and grace. In its most acute form, it is the question of what we are to say, in a theological perspective, about the longings that human beings naturally seem to have for some sort of transcendence of finitude.

In neo-Scholastic jargon it is the question of the point of insertion of supernatural life into human nature.[8] In the Reformed tradition, in Karl Barth's attack on the notion of the *Anknüpfungspunkt*, the point of contact between the Christian gospel and human nature,[9] we have an equally vigorous debate. (How far the partisans of the two debates were aware of one another's work is hard to say from the published evidence.)

For Barth, there could be nothing already existing in our nature to which the gospel might appeal. On the contrary, conversion to Christ 'consists in a miracle performed upon man, in a miracle which makes it not a phrase but literal truth to say that he has become a new man, a new creature'. He quotes St Paul: 'there is a new creation whenever a man comes to be in Christ' (2 Corinthians 5.17). While accepting the traditional doctrine that human beings are created 'in the image and likeness of God', he holds that this image has been so radically defaced by the fall as to leave nothing behind. We remain human, 'even as a sinner man is man and not a tortoise', Barth quaintly says. But we are no more receptive than a tortoise to the call of God until, through the gift of faith in Christ, the image of God is created in us *de novo*.

## Political implications of the debate

Few Catholic theologians in France, Germany or elsewhere, were as explicit as Barth in uncovering the wider political implications of the debate. Natural theology, left at the Reformation as an open question, turned, in the late nineteenth and early twentieth centuries, he believed, from 'a latent into an increasingly manifest standard and content of Church proclamation and theology'.[10] When the Evangelical Church in Germany was confronted in the political events of the year 1933, for example, by the demand to recognize in 'the form of the God-sent Adolf Hitler a source of specific new revelation of God, demanding obedience and trust', it found itself tempted by a new form of natural theology, so Barth thought. Within a few years this resulted in 'the transformation of the Christian Church into the temple of the German nature- and history-myth'. So many Christians in Germany were vulnerable to the blandishments of National Socialism in the first place, however, because the way had been prepared, Barth insists, by centuries of Christian theology during which it was claimed that 'side by side with its attestation in Jesus Christ and therefore in Holy Scripture the Church should also recognize and proclaim God's revelation in reason, in conscience, in the emotions, in history, in nature, and in culture and its achievements and developments'. 'Happy little hyphens were used', Barth notes, conjoining reason and revelation, nature and grace etc., but the crisis confronting the Church in the racist doctrines of Nazism revealed how dangerous such juxtapositions finally were. Barth gestures towards a whole history – Stoic humanism in the early eighteenth century, idealism and Romanticism in the nineteenth century. The infiltration of Christianity in Germany with ethnic considerations, though perhaps too blatant for Christians elsewhere, could nonetheless easily be paralleled by movements 'in England and America, in Holland and Switzerland, in Denmark and the Scandinavian countries', in the strongholds of the Reformation.[11]

Some of the leading Catholic theologians of Barth's generation feared that a dualism of nature and grace had struck deep roots in ordinary piety and morality. They were just as aware as he was of the ways in which theological presuppositions can weaken people's resistance to wickedness in the domain of social ethics and political decisions.

The debate among French theologians offers the clearest example. The nature/grace controversy needs to be placed against the background of the bitter struggle that dominated politics in France in the later nineteenth and early twentieth centuries between supporters of the Third Republic with their increasingly anti-clerical 'laicism', as it was called, and adherents of traditional Catholicism with their monarchist nostalgia and ultramontanist inclinations. The conflict was centred on the education system, with one side fearing that church schools were not forming children in loyalty to the ideals of the Republic (and thus of 1789), while the other side regarded state schools as seedbeds of militant atheism. In the widest theological terms, the problem was to do with how to respect the autonomy and intrinsic value of the ordinary world of human nature without reducing the Church to the sphere of purely private religion.

But the theology, however remotely, had real effects in people's lives. The German invasion of Belgium in 1914 united France, at least for the duration of the war. While the politicians were mostly republican, the generals were often devout Catholics. But the majority of Catholics and their clergy kept their distance from the Third Republic right into the upheavals of the 1930s. Many of the clergy remained in sympathy with the counter-Revolutionary programme of the leader of the movement Action Française, Charles Maurras, in spite of the fact that Catholics were banned from membership in 1926. Anti-Semitism was central to the programme. Maurras believed that the Jews were responsible for infecting people with the liberal-individualist conception of the self; indeed he blamed the Jews for Protestantism. He called, in the name of a return to order, for monarchism, Catholicism, and extreme economic and cultural nationalism. In 1940, after France collapsed, the Third Republic was voted out of existence by the National Assembly at Vichy, and replaced by a state which, initially at least, with its triple ideal of 'Work, Family and Country', and with its generous attitude to church institutions, had a great deal of appeal for many Catholics. In effect, under the Vichy government of 1940 to 1944, Maurrasian ideas came into their own. (Maurras was tried in 1945, sent to prison, and died in 1952, reconciled with the Church.)

Much more might be said about the background.[12] The important thing to note, however, is that, without exception, theologians like the Dominicans Marie-Dominique Chenu and Yves Congar and the Jesuit Henri de Lubac,[13] who were to become so influential in French theology in the late 1940s, and, through the Second Vatican Council (1962–65), in Catholic thought more generally, were never among supporters of the Vichy state. De Lubac, who took a leading part in denouncing the anti-Christian character of Nazi neo-paganism and anti-Semitism, even spent six months in hiding in 1943, when the Gestapo was looking for him. From the outset his theology immunized him against the attractions of the Vichy state, but it also helped to explain why so many of his fellow Catholics succumbed.

The main purpose of de Lubac's first great book, *Catholicisme*, was to correct what seemed to him an extremely individualistic and privatized religious sensibility by reminding Catholics of the inherently social nature of Christianity. He saw a double failure on the part of his co-religionists. On the one hand, they were too often satisfied with a purely conventional religion, which was little more than the socially useful 'religion for the people' that Maurras admired. On the other hand, in Renan's phrase, many people both inside and outside the Church seemed to regard Christianity as 'a religion made for the interior consolation of a few chosen souls'. To counter these opposite deviations, de Lubac sought to show, by a wealth of quotations from patristic and medieval literature, that, for example, Catholicism, unlike many modern theories, refuses to sacrifice the individual to the community or vice versa. He would have no truck with either totalitarian collectivism or liberal individualism. The key to understanding the infinite value of a person is to recognize that he or she is created in the image of God. That is why a person has a freedom over against all totalitarian claims. But it also means that being the image of God is not something extra added on from outside to a life lived in accordance with natural or secular principles. That secular humanist view of human life, de Lubac suggested, was largely the creation of a certain dualistic theology.

In a brilliant chapter on the effects of doing theology against others – 'we have learned our catechism too much against Luther' – de Lubac homes in on what would be the topic of *Surnaturel*, his most controverted book, in the following words:

> [F]or about three centuries, faced by the naturalist trends of modern thought on the one hand and the confusions of a bastard Augustinianism on the other, many could see salvation only in a complete severance between the natural and the supernatural. Such a policy ran doubly counter to the end which they had in view ... the supernatural, deprived of its organic links with nature, tended to be understood by some as a mere 'super-nature', a 'double' of nature. Furthermore, after such a complete separation what misgivings could the supernatural cause to naturalism? For the latter no longer found it at any point in its path, and could shut itself up in a corresponding isolation, with the added advantage that it claimed to be complete.[14]

This theology, as it imagines itself overcoming naturalism, humanism, materialism, etc., actually only clears the ground for positivism, deism, etc. Instead of preserving the supernatural-transcendental dimension in the midst of immanent-everyday realities, this 'separatist' theology, as de Lubac calls it, exiles the former and leaves the latter in possession.

Thus, what de Lubac showed, in *Catholicisme*, was that the anti-clerical laicism of the Third Republic was simply the mirror image of a supernaturalist religion that was either the empty shell of cultic practice and external observance or individual retreat into a spirituality of private interiority – either way, isolating faith from effective engagement with the real world. Indeed, more challengingly than that, de Lubac was to suggest in his *Surnaturel* that the grace/nature dualism in Catholic theology, invented to protect nature against Lutheranism and grace against Enlightenment humanism, was itself the creator of deism and atheism.

The central thesis of *Surnaturel*, positively put, is that in the whole Catholic tradition until the sixteenth century the idea of humanity as the image of God had prevailed. Neither in patristic nor in medieval theology, and certainly not in Thomas Aquinas, was the hypothesis entertained of a purely natural destiny for human beings, something less than the supernatural and eschatological vision of God. There is only this world, the world in which our nature has been created for a supernatural destiny. Historically, there never was a graceless nature, or a world outside the Christian dispensation – precisely what Karl Barth said.

As a historian of theology, de Lubac showed that, in the sixteenth century, a new conception of the relationship of grace to human nature appeared. The traditional conception of human nature as always destined for grace-given union with God fell apart between attempts on the one hand to secure the sheer gratuitousness of the economy of grace over against the naturalist anthropologies of Renaissance humanism and, on the other hand, resistance to what was perceived by Catholics in the Tridentine period as the Protestant doctrine of the total corruption of human nature by original sin. The split between Catholic faith and agnosticism in France, and finally between Church and State, was not so much the work of the rationalist philosophers of the Enlightenment as, more profoundly, that of theologians themselves. The conception of the autonomous individual for which the philosophers of the Age of Reason were most bitterly criticized by devout Catholics was, de Lubac suggested, first invented by theologians.

According to de Lubac, modern Roman Catholic theology had introduced a distinction between nature and grace that ruined the premodern understanding of the inner orientation of the human spirit to the beatific vision. Philosophers could now proceed without taking any account of the longing for God that had hitherto been taken to be natural to the human creature. On the other hand, much more serious for Catholicism internally, the loss of the patristic-medieval sense of the internal relationship between the order of creation and the dispensation of grace led to a conception of grace as something so totally extraneous and alien to human nature that anything and everything natural and human was downgraded and demeaned. In particular, when questions about politics or sexuality (say) were detached from the traditional unitary theology of grace as fulfilling nature, it would not be surprising (de Lubac would have thought) if politics was treated with cynicism and sexuality with suspicion and disgust. When the dispensation of divine grace was no longer assumed to have resonance and even roots in some kind of natural desire for God, human nature – and that means reason, feeling, and the body – become temptingly easy to dismiss. When grace is conceived as wholly extrinsic to human nature, there is a temptation towards a dualist and ultimately Manichaean kind of asceticism and piety. It would not be surprising either if theologians, as the experts on divine revelation, kept everyone else out of the conversation – nor if the clergy, as ministers of grace in the sacramental system, maintained an extremely hierarchical and authoritarian church.[15]

## Vatican II

If the Roman Catholic Church may be said to have come out 'into the world', at the Second Vatican Council, acknowledging the presence of grace in the 'signs of the times', there can be no doubt that theologians like Henri de Lubac, summoned to take part at an early stage, exercised a decisive influence in the composition of the conciliar texts. There was an unexpected and irreversible opening to ecumenical dialogue and to recognizing the ecclesial reality of other churches. There was repentance for anti-Semitism. There was an opening towards non-Christian faiths and religions. In particular, in the pastoral constitution *Gaudium et Spes*, 'the holy synod proclaims the noble calling of humanity and the existence within it of a divine seed, and offers the human race the sincere cooperation of the church in working for that universal community of sisters and brothers which is the response to humanity's call-ing'.[16] That certainly sounds like a reaffirmation of the premodern understanding of the internal and quasi-organic relationship of nature and grace in the actual historical order, which must have delighted Henri de Lubac (even if he did not draft it!).

Karl Barth, as he explains in his memoir *Ad Limina Apostolor-um*,[17] was too unwell to accept the invitation to take part in the Vatican Council but he spent the summer studying the texts before visiting Rome in 1966 for lengthy discussions with theologians representing diverse views of its achievements. Five out of the seven general questions that Barth raised with his hosts deal with what he regarded as the menace of a subjugation of the Church by the world. In reaction against the experience of the Church as self-isolated and hostile towards the modern world, so he feared, Catholics seemed tempted towards endorsing whatever movements in culture and society seemed most promising for natural flourish-ing. 'Is it so certain that dialogue with the world is to be placed ahead of proclamation to the world?' Is the 'thorough optimism' of the Constitution *Gaudium et Spes* over the possibilities of the development of the world really in tune with New Testament expectations?

Although Henri de Lubac believed that the conciliar texts register the premodern vision of graced nature, it has to be said that he too, certainly by 1967, was deeply troubled by what he could not but regard as rampant secularism in the Catholic Church, particularly in France. The Church that had been introvertedly supernaturalist was now in danger of becoming worldly. In *The Mystery of the Supernatural*, he justified his return to the theme, concerned now, however, to insist on the distinction between nature and grace, each in its own integrity, whereas his earlier emphasis was on the continuity between them. That only shows how difficult it is to get the right balance between the world and the gospel, creation and salvation, nature and grace. It also shows that, far from being a merely academic and somewhat abstruse problem, the theological understanding of the relationship between nature and grace has a deep effect on the spirituality and liturgical experience available to the ordinary believer.

## Von Balthasar against Rahner

The nature/grace controversy, and the question of whether the desire for God is inserted in human nature as such or in human nature as already divinely graced, if that is a real distinction, have ramifications far beyond what we have sketched. Enough has perhaps been said to show that we are not dealing with a purely academic issue. There are no serious theological issues which do not have repercussions elsewhere.

Theologians who might seem to be on the same side could also be deeply divided. Von Balthasar insists that Rahner's transcendental theology is nothing more than a version of Neoplatonism:

> God's merciful turn toward a lost world, in Jesus Christ and, earlier, in the election of Israel – this fundamentally dramatic act of God in his freedom (*dieser in seiner Freiheit ur-dramatische Akt Gottes*) – becomes the undramatic, permanent, essential constitution of a God (*wird zur undramatisch zuständlichen Wesensverfassung eines Gottes*) who, as in Plato and Plotinus, and later in Spinoza and the Enlightenment, is (and always has been) the eternally radiant 'Sun of Goodness' (*die ewig ausstrahlende 'Sonne des Guten'*). Accordingly, the picture of man is primarily determined, not by his frail finitude in which, nonetheless, he must accomplish things of ultimate value (*nicht durch die ihn bannende Aporie der Endlichkeit, in der doch End-Gültiges geleistet werden müsste*), but by a resignation with which he commends himself to the unfathomable mystery of his being (and of all

being) (*sondern durch eine resignierte Selbstübergabe an das unerforschliche Geheimnis seines und alles Seins*); this is an attitude to death that overflows into all his finite acts; it is a Stoicism with Christian trimmings.[18]

Von Balthasar is thinking of Rahner, though without naming him at this point. It seems even wilder than the claim that Rahner is out to revive a supposedly obsolete religious 'instinct'. The best that philosophy can do, von Balthasar has been arguing, is to reach the horizon of an abstract absolute 'in the presence of which' the historical takes place – whether this absolute is regarded as the all-overwhelming *theion* or *nirvana*. Philosophers can no doubt sketch a religio-metaphysical background to the 'pathos' of the human beings on the stage; and in doing so it deprives these historical figures of their 'pathos'. The 'pathos of historical worldedness' is raised to another level, in this metaphysical perspective; but, paradoxically, the 'dramatics of finitude' (*die Dramatik der Endlichkeit*), is neutralized by the very move that acknowledges its grandeur. What von Balthasar seeks here is 'the Christian solution' of this 'baneful dilemma' – the impasse of human finitude. The metaphysical project that places the finite being in the context of the absolute, and thus displays the possibility of transcending finitude, is the very move that deprives the finite being of the pathos and drama of finitude.

Von Balthasar's aim, in his last great work, has to be to show how insolubly 'tense' (*verspannt*), our historical situation in the world remains. We are always on the lookout for a solution – a redemption – but it cannot be constructed or even suspected from our side. 'In retrospect, of course, it is not difficult to create a pseudo-harmony by putting forward Christian philosophies of history that contain the a prioris that emerge from Christian theology.' But such projects render innocuous 'the ultimately hopeless situation of finite existence in the face of a transcendence that does not automatically disclose itself' – 'in the face of the as yet hidden world plan whereby God becomes man (which implies that God "becomes pathos") and shows himself, through this Incarnation, to be the triune God'.

However we deal with the aporia of finitude, the one thing we must not do, von Balthasar says, is to invoke notions like 'the supernatural existential'. That is a way of refusing to allow the dilemma to take its dramatic form. Of course, as it actually is, the world has been created with a view to being redeemed. But we must not speak as if this redemption is something of which human beings have always already had some awareness, even if only transcendentally. That is Karl Rahner's language. The drama of human existence, the historical character of our life, the pathos, the aporia, are overlooked by the metaphysical theology which is repeatedly suggested to be Rahner's. Indeed, the picture of human existence in his theology would set us off towards a resigned self-abandonment to the unfathomable mystery of being, very like the submission to the absolute that Nussbaum fears, and not altogether unlike what Murdoch defends.

Will this attack on Rahner really do? Von Balthasar's opposition goes back a long way, to his review of Rahner's first book *Geist im Welt*.[19] His rage, regarded by some as a scandal, came to a head in his little book *Cordula*,[20] in which he attacked the notion of 'anonymous Christians' based on the thesis of the 'supernatural existential', supported in turn by 'transcendental theology'.

## Rahner's jargon

Three things need to be sorted out: anonymous Christianity, the supernatural existential, and transcendental method in theology.

A transcendental argument is one that starts with the undeniable existence of some state of affairs and argues from the fact to the a priori condition(s) for the very possibility and intelligibility of such a state of affairs. Rahner argues from our experience of subjectivity, and particularly of knowing and willing, to what must be the a priori condition(s) for the very possibility of what we do all the time. He has nothing dramatic in mind. In every act of knowing and willing, he argues, we show ourselves to be oriented towards an infinite horizon, independent of us, from which the light comes that enables us to be subjects in relationship to objects in the first place. All the time, in everyday ways, we reach out beyond ourselves and our finite world, towards that which confers the possibility of our world's being intelligible and lovable. In our most immanent activities we are always already transcending ourselves, since we cannot but be pulled towards the horizon that enables us to see things as intelligible, desirable, etc. The horizon that opens us to truth, goodness, being, and so on, so Rahner goes on to say, is to be identified with what Christians know as God. But there is a relationship to God – implicit, unreflective, unthematic, deniable by any individual but actually indestructible and unavoidable, in every act of knowing what is true or of loving what is good. Human beings are by nature, that is to say, always already transcending their finitude in their relationship to the absolute.

For this metaphysics of knowledge, Rahner says, there is no great difficulty in seeing that the transcendence towards being, truth, goodness, etc., that transcendental reflection on our subjectivity uncovers, cannot be clearly distinguished now, since Christian revelation, from the openness of the human being informed by the gift of grace that directs him or her towards the absolute self-revealed as the triune God. Whether they know it or not, indeed even if they reject the very idea, everyone now lives within the open horizon of transcendence towards the God of Christian revelation. Any morally good action, for example, is a super-naturally redeeming and sanctifying one:

> Our whole spiritual life is lived in the realm of the salvific will of God, of his prevenient grace, of his call as it becomes efficacious: all of which is an element within the region of our consciousness, though one which remains anonymous as long as it is not interpreted from without by the message of faith.

Hence, for Rahner, we have not the theoretical possibility but the inescapable reality of 'anonymous Christians':

> Thus when man is summoned by the message of faith given by the visible Church, it is not the first time that he comes into spiritual contact with the reality preached by the Church: such conceptual knowledge of it is not primary ... The preaching is the express awakening of what is already present in the depths of man's being, not by nature, but by grace. But it is a grace which always surrounds man, even the sinner and the unbeliever, as the inescapable setting of his existence.[21]

So much for the transcendental method and anonymous Christians.

As regards the supernatural existential, an expression first mentioned by Rahner in 1950, thus at the height of the nature/grace controversy, we may say that it is his way of steering between the extrinsicism of the neo-Scholastics and the suspected 'Modernism' of such theologians as Henri de Lubac. To speak of an existential was to borrow a piece of early Heideggerian terminology for an essential feature of human existence: not any particular phenomenon, certainly not anything psychological, but one of the a priori conditions in order that human existence should exhibit some phenomenon or other. Thus, while open to discovery by transcendental reflection on human existence, particularly on knowing and willing, it could not be reduced to, or aligned with, any 'feeling', 'illumination', 'religious instinct', or other psychological 'experience' (which a Catholic Modernist might be thought to favour). Yet such a feature of human existence certainly has to be regarded as intrinsic to human nature, thus excluding any extrinsicist conception of grace as something imposed on human nature without any point of contact (*Anknüpfungspunkt*). On the other hand, this modality of human existence has to be 'supernatural', in the sense that it is concretely realized in a dispensation within which the human being is destined and called, unanticipatably, to supernatural/eschatological beatitude – a modality prior, that is, to its particularization, either as acts of love or something else.

## Cartesian inclinations?

As recently as 1967, Karl Rahner insisted that there must be no going back, in theology, on 'modern philosophy's transcendental anthropological change of direction since Descartes, Kant, German Idealism (including its opponents), up to modern Phenomenology, Existentialism and Fundamental Ontology'.[22] That might sound as if he wanted Catholic theology to submit to radical rewriting in function of Cartesian/Kantian doctrines of the self, just about the time when the half century of neo-Thomist resistance to modern philosophy had collapsed, and when the postmodern decentring of the self-conscious moral agent was already on the way. But Rahner was not so naive. This whole tradition, with some exceptions, is 'most profoundly anti-Christian', in the sense that it 'pursues a transcendental philosophy of the autonomous subject, who stands aloof from the transcendental experience in which he experiences himself as continually dependent, with his origin in and orientation towards God'. Rahner had no doubt about the impossibility of incorporating the ideal of any worldless self into Christian theology. But there is no way that theology can avoid the turn to the subject, paradoxically, because this philosophy is also 'most profoundly Christian'. On any properly Christian theology, Rahner insists, 'man is not ultimately one factor in a cosmos of things, subservient to a system of co-ordinate ontic concepts drawn from it' (which might include Heidegger's rich picture of human identity as an element in a cosmic game just as much as some stripped-down behaviourist materialism). Rather, we need to think of 'the subject on whose freedom as subject hangs the fate of the whole cosmos'. Without some such conception, neither history nor the history of

God's dispensation of grace could have 'cosmological significance' – 'Christological cosmology would be infantile concept-poetry'. The ambivalence of the self in modern philosophy – its 'inner divided-ness' – is nothing new, Rahner thinks. On the contrary, it is a symptom of philosophy in all ages. There is a more 'dramatic' side to Rahner's metaphysics of the human agent than some have been tempted to think.

It has been maintained that Rahner's 'most characteristic theological profundities are embedded in an extremely mentalist-individualist epistemology of unmistakably Cartesian provenance'. In essence, Rahner is charged with refusing to 'own our finitude'.[23] But will this interpretation of Rahner do? What if his remark about the ambivalence of the philosophy of the autonomous self were to be taken seriously? In fact, suppose that Rahner's theology were replaced in the context of the controversies about the relationship of grace and nature, in which of course he was involved – what then?

## From anthropology to mystery

The usual story is that Rahner's theology is a system, founded on transcendental analysis of the individual person's subjectivity. In his first book *Geist in Welt*, he would have started by developing a theory of knowledge from consideration of the cognitive experi-ence of the self-conscious subject. This enabled him to uncover the a priori condition of subjectivity, which is the pull of the absolute by which the human spirit is always already drawn and directed. Our experience as finite beings would thus be inescapably self-transcendence towards the absolute. In turn, that provided Rahner with the key to his theological system. Every essay that he ever composed would be a variation on the theme of human nature as orientation towards the absolute. In particular, he would be able to overcome all docetic temptations to think of the centre of the Christian faith as 'the myth of God incarnate' by situating the case of Jesus Christ in terms of the supreme instance of the dynamic openness of humanity to the pull of the absolute. There would be nothing mythical or arbitrary about the incarnation – just the opposite: Christology should be regarded as the fulfilment of metaphysical anthropology, and anthropology as a defective Christology. (In a way, then, Rahner's ontology of the self is as radically Christological as Barth's, though of course the starting point is completely different.)

One of the best commentators voices 'sheer admiration at the unity and metaphysical coherence of Rahner's thought'. According to this view, the early philosophical work, and specifically the metaphysics of knowledge, underlies and sustains the theological essays, however diverse they may seem. The philosophy is even described as the 'basis' of his theology: 'On the basis of his metaphysics, grounded on man's inner experience, Rahner structures the data of Scripture and and tradition into the synthesis of his theological anthropology.' As another fine critic notes, Rahner is not suggesting that we can 'deduce' the birth or character or destiny of Jesus of Nazareth from any philosophical understanding of human nature – it is only that 'we can demonstrate from the transcendental analysis of spirit that he does in fact fulfil the conditions there apprehended for a concrete manifestation of the absolute'. If the human spirit is radically constituted by desire for the absolute and unconditional, something that is displayed in ordinary everyday acts of love and knowledge, men and women turn out, not very surprisingly, to be 'authentically spiritual, self-transcending subjects, responding to the inner pressure of unconditional claims'. We have in advance at least the outline of a profile to help us to place Jesus Christ: a human being, who lives out unreservedly and wholeheartedly the response to the call of the absolute, will be the complete realization of human nature, and will thus express humanly the unconditional presence of the absolute in the world.[24]

This way of reading Rahner's work needs some re-examination. It may be noted, first, that Rahner stresses that this supernaturally-orientated transcendence of the human spirit should not be discussed – 'as it too often is' – in connection only with knowledge.[25] On the contrary, if God is love and not Aristotle's self-referential act of thinking, 'no understanding of man and of the absolute fulfilment of his being (by grace) can succeed, unless man is considered as freedom and love, which again may not be considered just as a by-product of the act of knowledge'. Those who would read Rahner's work as irretrievably controlled by a preconception about the knowledge-seeking self need to reflect on such remarks.

More fundamentally, however, it needs to be asked whether Rahner's theological system is founded on his philosophy – indeed whether there is a system at all. His own contemporaries, evidently including von Balthasar, seem to have taken for granted the unity of his thought, and in particular that his theological work all depends on the way that he lays bare the transcendental conditions of our acts of knowing and willing. It has been assumed that his theology was founded on his transcendental anthropology and that, if that turns out to be unacceptable, the whole of his theology collapses.

But what if Rahner's anthropology allows for an element, if not of von Balthasar's notion of the dramatic and the tragic, at least for a certain ambivalence? What if his theology is not a superstructure that he erected on the foundations of his early metaphysics of knowledge? What if his essays are much more unsystematic than they have been allowed to appear?

An alternative reading along such lines is already establishing itself, as Karen Kilby has noted.[26] She suggests, with J. A. DiNoia, that Rahner's work is actually quite fragmented and benefits from being read unsystematically.[27] With Nicholas Healy, she wants to read Rahner as an 'ad hoc apologist'.[28] Instead of treating all the essays, from about 1950 onwards, as building blocks in some totalizing work in progress which he left unfinished, they should be read as 'internal apologetics' (a phrase she owes to Healy). Most of Rahner's work is directed to those who are already within the Church, but even when he addresses himself to those who are not yet Christians his concern is usually to look for affinities between Christian claims and other matters which are either self-evidently true or anyway open to discovery by transcendental reflection on what is the case. Again and again, he tries to show that, far from being something arbitrary and alien to people with an Enlightenment background, Christianity is something to which we are always already attuned.

Convinced of the impotence of the neo-Scholastic theology which he inherited to bring people to God, since it was regarded by the people whose faith he sought to deepen as precisely the kind of metaphysical speculation that Kant was thought to have ended, Rahner placed the fundamental experience of the presence of the absolute at the centre of his essays. He sought to show how Christian claims, however bizarre and disorientating they may seem, actually fit with ordinary everyday human experience. This is, of course, something to be seen only in retrospect. The absolute mystery to which all knowledge and loving are related, as transcendental analysis of human subjectivity discloses, has in fact been revealed by the dispensation of grace in the history recorded in the Bible. Given that this self-revelation of God has occurred, Rahner wants to discover what must be true about the structure of human knowledge and loving for such a revelation to be recognized and received. For many people, including many brought up within the Catholic Church, nearly always Rahner's intended readership, God's self-revelation often seems something which asserts itself from outside everyday life and thus appears optional and even quite irrelevant. Rahner, then, wants to present a version of Christianity which shows how deeply connected it is to other aspects of our life. In effect, he is out to free people from the extrinsicist conception of grace. In this respect he is an apologist: he wants to remove one of the principal obstacles to religious belief, for Christians as well as non-believers: the fear that Christianity as a system of belief is fundamentally alien to our real everyday lives. He wants to show that, on the contrary, it is the articulation of something very deep in us.

Of course Rahner's frequent references to, and repeated emphasis on, transcendental reflection on human subjectivity cannot be denied. But it needs to be situated. In the first place, he wanted to make the possibility of Christian faith at least plausible, or at any rate less bizarre and esoteric, to people brought up in post-Enlightenment culture – Catholics especially. Much of his work aims at overcoming the more or less concealed intellectual schizophrenia from which many Christians suffer, at least in the West. More radically, he wanted to make his own contribution to the discussion within neo-Scholastic theology about the relationship between nature and grace, or about the natural and the supernatural orders. Though never alluding as explicitly as either Barth or de Lubac to the deleterious political effects of a theology that sets the two orders against one another, he worked hard at every point 'to display the continuities between the human order and the divine purposes and activities in its regard, without subverting the confession of their utter gratuity and transcendence as pure grace'. For Rahner, that is: 'The divine purposes and activities are not alien to human well-being, even though surpassing human possibilities and merits utterly'.[29]

If any single topic offers the best access to Rahner's immensely prolific and varied work, it is surely the nature/grace controversy. Now, as Kilby says, it is hard to see why a theologian, who was so determined to undermine the two-tier grace/nature structure in general, should have been happy with a two-tier structure in his own work. Of course, since theologians (like everybody else) are sometimes oblivious to logs in their own eyes, of which they have detected splinters in the eyes of others, we might argue that Rahner simply failed to see that his theology depended on a certain philosophy for its foundations. On the other hand, as Kilby shows in detail, there is not such a smooth transition from the early theological anthropology to the mature essays as the hitherto prevailing reading of his work assumes. It is just a mistake to regard his theology as 'founded' on the philosophy, she argues. One of the advantages that she sees in taking this line is that it would release those, brought up in a different philosophical tradition, who find transcendental Thomism unattractive, from feeling obliged to go into it so that they can read Rahner's theology. Allowing that his theology *can* indeed be read as foundationally dependent on a particular philosophical anthropology, she insists that it *need* not be so read. The option – of reading everything that Rahner published on the assumption that he believed completely in the possibility of a theological system based on the kind of transcendental analysis of human subjectivity worked out in the early books – will remain. In that case, however, everything that he says in the writings of the 1960s and 1970s about inescapable pluralism in philosophy and theology is impossible to take seriously. On the other hand, if one takes his remarks about the inescapability of pluralism with the seriousness with which he seems to make them, and assumes that he himself understood his transcendental theology as one approach among others, we open up a way of reading his work which we might (with Kilby) call modest, postmodern – in a word: 'non-foundationalist'.[30]

Michael Purcell, rereading some of the best known essays in the light of the work of Emmanuel Levinas, insists that, while the ontology which sustains Rahner's epistemology is one in which being and knowing are essentially related, with a background in transcendental Thomism, the finite spirit is less to be understood in terms of Cartesian self-presence than as transcendence towards what is other than the self, towards the alterity of exteriority.[31] Theologically, this comes out in Rahner as the dispensation of grace, where God communicates himself to the essentially open and receptive subject, while remaining himself uncompromised by his offer. The other to whom the self relates is, that is to say, with respect to the self, elusive and unencompassable. Above all, the relation to the other, whether the absolute or being, is not primarily comprehension but mystery. It is ' mystery not mastery', in Purcell's phrase, which guides the development of subjectivity.

In *The Ordinary Transformed*,[32] Russell Reno places Rahner's theology very firmly in the context of the nature/grace controversy. He too sees Rahner's theological vision as formed by the problem of extrinsicism, striving to preserve the neo-Scholastic separation of nature from grace while seeking to bring out the affinities and continuities between human nature and the Christian economy of grace. In Reno's terminology, Rahner refuses both radical transcendence and pure immanence. There is no need to choose between repudiating the ordinary in order to affirm the extraordinary and denying the extraordinary in order to focus on the ordinary. For Rahner, according to Reno, philosophy is always already proto-theological, yet still an independent enterprise. In this respect, it mirrors the relation of God to the human creature – being both internal and external. Just as nature is included within the economy of grace, yet has its own identity, so Rahner's philosophy would have its own specificity while being at the same time interwoven with his theology. The connection between the philosophy and the theology in Rahner's writing would not be that the theology is founded on the philosophy, any more than the historical dispensation of grace should be regarded as resting on the foundations of the natural order.

However else this new generation of readers will help us to see in Rahner's work, they are surely right to focus on his concept of mystery, and to set his theory of knowledge in the context of that concept. In his fine essay on 'The hiddenness of God', written in honour of Yves Congar in 1974, in which he speaks of himself as a 'systematic theologian', and even proposes to outline a 'synthesis',[33] Rahner begins, as so often, with criticism of the neo-Scholastic theology that he inherited, in this instance objecting to the desire for 'theoretical understanding' in the standard way of treating the question of the 'incomprehensibility' of God. The conception of knowledge and truth at work in the discussion is based on a model of knowledge in which objects are 'penetrated and mastered'. To say that God is 'incomprehensible' is to say that our knowledge of God remains deficient, even in heavenly beatitude – 'God is, unfortunately, always incomprehensible'! – as if we almost but not quite have the cognitive reach to 'entirely or exhaustively grasp God'. In this ideal of knowledge, so Rahner thinks, the Platonic desire for absolute knowledge combines with the modern conception of knowledge as a process of mastery. Thus, the incomprehensibility of God becomes 'the ground for the permanent finitude of the creature' – finitude 'negatively conceived'. The assertion of this finitude certainly gives God due glory – something we must note in case we might be tempted either 'to make human subjectivity the event of absolute consciousness' or 'to suppress the pain of being finite'. There is no need, in other words, either to yield to the temptation to make ourselves the authors of all the meaning in the world or to deny that our finitude can be a constraint. What concerns Rahner most, however, is whether the predominance of the desire for theoretical understanding does not encourage acknowledgement of God's incomprehensibility to turn into a kind of practical atheism – an indifference on our part towards something which we cannot understand. If our capacity for knowledge is fulfilled in comprehensive mastery, do we not simply have to be 'resigned to being trapped within [our] finite capacity of knowledge in the face of the incomprehensible God'?

We need to return to an older understanding of knowing, Rahner argues. Of course, if knowledge – 'taken in the sense usual in western tradition' – is essentially mastery, then it will 'founder on the alien and inhospitable rock of God's incomprehensibility'. But if knowing is pictured, not as 'seeing through' an object, but as 'a possible openness to the mystery', we should be able to see ourselves not in terms of 'the dominant, absolute subject', but as 'the one whose being is bestowed upon him by the mystery'. Indeed, 'the essential human capacity for truth' is unfolded and established by the 'overwhelming mystery' which is now revealed as the 'hidden God'. Instead of conceiving ourselves in terms of the self-conscious autonomous subject who is striving to ascend to the absolute, we should think of ourselves rather as the gift of the mystery.

This, Rahner tells us here, is what the early studies in the metaphysics of knowledge were about! Perhaps he is rewriting them; but at least we must take seriously his reading of them as generating, not any mentalist-individualist philosophy of the subject, but rather as registering a conception of the self as 'the openness to the mystery' which – moreover – is 'given radical depth by grace'.

Rahner, like Cavell, thinks that we are haunted by an inhuman ideal of human knowledge. The difference is that, for Cavell, what is required is 'an acknowledgment of human limitation which does not leave us chafed by our own skin' – chafed, then, 'by a sense of powerlessness to penetrate beyond the human conditions of knowledge'.[34] For the neo-Scholastics, Rahner argues, God is hidden precisely because of the inadequacy of human knowledge. God is incomprehensible, we may say, only because human beings lack the intellectual power to comprehend him. The dominance of an ideal of knowledge as total comprehension, which Rahner seeks to demythologize as determinedly as Cavell, thus distorts theological understanding of the hiddenness of God. But Rahner wants to locate the incomprehensibility of the divine mystery properly, not just to free us from illusory ideals of knowledge. The divine mystery is not to be viewed as something to be mastered. 'We must understand that this *reductio* [*in mysterium*] constitutes not a regrettable imperfection in theology, but rather that which is most proper to it of its very nature'.[35]

In these 'Reflections on methodology in theology', originally prepared for a theological symposium in 1969,[36] Rahner starts by insisting on the situation of the Catholic theologian. 'The individual theologian in his work today is the theologian who is alien, alone, and isolated' – because he is 'conditioned by an uncontrollable pluralism of theologies'. He expresses his 'decided and radical mistrust of any attempt to reduce theology in any adequate sense to the methodology employed in it' – and goes on, specifically, to speak of transcendental theology as not claiming to be anything more than one aspect of theology. He returns to his favourite theme: if divine revelation is to be heard as something more than a word uttered about God and caused by God – if it is to be heard as the word of God himself – then the condition which makes this possible in those who listen has to be that 'God himself through his own act of self-communication upholds this act of hearing as an intrinsic principle'. This is what is called 'the supernatural grace of faith'. 'But this faith is not indoctrinated into us *ab externo*', Rahner insists, once again repudiating an extrinsicist doctrine of grace as an arbitrary intrusion of something radically alien. It is indeed 'only through revelation *ab externo* that it is brought to its full self-realization and certainty at the level of conscious thought', but 'supernatural grace and the theological virtues', 'once they are recognized', have a 'point of contact with the transcendental experience of the human spirit'.

Thus Rahner sketches once again his analysis of human subjectivity as always already transcending itself in every finite act of knowledge and loving. But he goes on to insist, against Wittgenstein,[37] that we should not simply be silent about things about which we cannot speak clearly. True enough, theology must not understand itself as 'that science which develops itself more and more in a systematic drawing of distinctions down to the last possible detail'. On the contrary, it has to be understood as 'that human activity in which man, even at the level of conscious thought, relates the multiplicity of the realities, experiences, and ideas in his life to that mystery, ineffable and obscure, which we call God'. There may be some justification, Rahner concedes, for conceiving theology on the model of 'a logically developing system in which ever finer distinctions are drawn'. Perhaps that was, to some extent, Thomas Aquinas's ideal; perhaps it is 'almost two thousand years' old. Now, Rahner thinks, it is 'drawing to its close'. Now, he insists, we have to allow that 'every theological statement is only truly and authentically such at that point at which man willingly suffers it to extend beyond his comprehension into the silent mystery of God'.

The human being, understood as spirit in the world, thus both transcendent and immanent, is finally characterized by Rahner as 'the being of the holy mystery'.[38] Precisely where we are dealing with what is within hand's reach, ordinary familiar things which are 'amenable to a conceptual framework', we are always 'confronted with the holy mystery'. That is to say, it is not something upon which we may happen to stumble if we are lucky (or unlucky!). Nor is the holy mystery to be understood as something in which one might choose to take an interest, as if it were something over and above the regular items in one's field of vision. On the contrary, we live by the holy mystery all the time, even where and when we are unaware of this. 'The lucidity of [our] consciousness derives from the incomprehensibility of this mystery.' Again: 'the freedom of [our] mastery of things comes from [our] being mastered by the Holy which is itself unmastered.'

Rahner goes on to develop explicitly Christian implications of his concept of mystery, but just before doing so he recapitulates what he has been saying in these words:

> The mystery is self-evident. That it is unattainable has already been said. Existentially, and for a theory of knowledge, it is at once a menace to man and his blessed peace. It can make him chafe and protest, because it compels him to leave the tiny house of his ostensibly clear self-possession, to advance into the trackless spaces, even in the night. It forces upon him the dilemma of either throwing himself into the uncharted, unending adventure where he commits himself to the infinite, or – despairing at the thought and so embittered – of taking shelter in the suffocating den of his own finite perspicacity.[39]

Powerfully stated; yet memories of the several different versions of transcending humanity that we have examined suggest that it is overstated. We do not have to choose between the leap in the dark of radical transcendence and hiding in the pure immanence of the familiar world. That is perhaps a theologian's dilemma that a philosopher of religion would hope to set aside.

# NOTES AND REFERENCES

## Preface

1. *Must We Mean What We Say? A Book of Essays* (Charles Scribner's Sons 1969), p. 61.
2. *Nicomachean Ethics*, Book 10, Chapter 8: 1177b 32ff.


## 1. Transcending humanity: Nussbaum's versions

1. Martha Craven Nussbaum (born 1948), currently Professor of Law and Ethics at the University of Chicago, published Aristotle's *De Motu Animalium* (Princeton University Press 1978), the Greek text with translation, commentary and interpretive essays, but it was with *The Fragility of Goodness: Luck and ethics in Greek tragedy and philosophy* (Cambridge University Press 1986) that she established herself as a major voice in Anglo-American philosophy. Since then she has published *Love's Knowledge: Essays on Philosophy and Literature* (Oxford University Press 1990), a collection of studies including her Read-Tuckwell Lectures at the University of Bristol (1989) and *The Therapy of Desire: Theory and Practice in Hellenistic Ethics* (Princeton University Press 1994). The Gifford Lectures which she delivered at the University of Edinburgh in 1993 have been announced as *Upheavals of Thought: A Theory of the Emotions* (Cambridge University Press, forthcoming). Little has been written about the theological implications of her work but see L. Gregory Jones, 'The Love which Love's Knowledge knows not: Nussbaum's evasion of Christianity', *The Thomist* 56/2 (April 1992): 323–37.
2. 'The speech of Alcibiades: a reading of Plato's *Symposium*', *Philosophy and Literature* 3 (1979): 131–72, revised as Chapter 6 of *The Fragility of Goodness*. Subsequent discussion is too prolific to cite here but see John Finlay, 'The night of Alcibiades', *The Hudson Review* (Spring 1994): 57–79.
3. *Symposium* 210B – 211E.
4. 'Beatrice's "Dante": Loving the Individual?', *Apeiron* 26 (1993): 161–78, p. 168. As she notes, Nussbaum is developing the suggestions in the 'wonderful ground-breaking article' by Gregory Vlastos, 'The Individual

185

as Object of Love in Plato', in his *Platonic Studies* (Princeton University Press 1973), which brought the topic of love back on the agenda, opening up matters of interest to moral philosophers as well as classicists: Vlastos characterizes Plato's conception of love as 'spiritualized egocentrism' and argues that Aristotle's notion of friendship as well as the Christian doctrine of charity do more justice to the particularity of the beloved. Nussbaum's Gifford Lectures are the latest contribution to the question.

5. 'Beatrice's "Dante" ', pp. 171–2.

6. 'Beatrice's "Dante" ', pp. 176–7.

7. 'Beatrice's "Dante" ', p. 178. The problem with Dante, according to Nussbaum, is that 'his Aristotelianism is heavily qualified by the Catholic doctrine that the body is created separately from the soul, which is the source of our worth, and made by a separate act of God', cf. p. 176.

8. 'Transcending Humanity', *Love's Knowledge*: 365–91. Taylor's review is to be found in *Canadian Journal of Philosophy* 18 (1988): 805–14.

9. 'Narrative Emotions: Beckett's Genealogy of Love', *Ethics* 98 (1988): 225–54, reprinted in *Love's Knowledge*: 286–312; 'Non-Relative Virtues: An Aristotelian Approach', *Midwest Studies in Philosophy* (1988); review of Alasdair MacIntyre, *Whose Justice? Which Rationality?*, *New York Review of Books*, 7 December 1989.

10. Elaine Pagels, *Adam, Eve, and the Serpent* (Weidenfeld & Nicolson 1988).

11. *Love's Knowledge* [LK], p. 370; in 'Changing Aristotle's Mind', in *Essays on Aristotle's De Anima* ed. Martha C. Nussbaum and Amelie Oksenberg Rorty (Clarendon Press 1992), Nussbaum and Hilary Putnam go quite some way to defend Aquinas's view of the soul, against Miles Burnyeat's notion of 'the Christian view' as irretrievably 'dualist', pp. 51–5.

12. *LK*, p. 370.

13. *LK*, p. 306; see 'Beyond Obsession and Disgust: Lucretius on the Therapy of Love', *Apeiron* 22 (1989): 1–59; revised as Chapter 5 of *The Therapy of Desire*.

14. *LK*, p. 307.

15. *LK*, pp. 293–7.

16. Samuel Beckett, *Molloy* (1955), *Malone Dies* (1956), *The Unnamable* (1958); Nussbaum draws attention to the 'marvellous discussion' of the theological aspects of Beckett's work in Stanley Cavell, 'Ending the Waiting Game', *Must We Mean What We Say?* (Charles Scribner's Sons 1969), *LK*, p. 298 footnote. Cavell argues that, far from 'marketing subjectivity, popularizing angst, amusing and thereby excusing us with pictures of our psychopathology', etc., Beckett is out to dismantle eschatology, finally to renounce all final solutions, 'ending this world of order in order to reverse the curse of the world laid on it in its Judeo-Christian end', p. 149.

17. *LK*, p. 313. Nussbaum regards the enterprise of writing metaphysics as itself an attempt to erect a *monumentum aere perennius*; she even suspects her own act of writing about the beauty of human vulnerability, over against Diotima's project of enabling lovers to become invulnerable to anything but the sovereignty of the good, as itself 'a way of rendering

oneself less vulnerable and more in control of the uncontrolled elements in life', *Fragility of Goodness*, p. xv.

18. *LK*, p. 298.
19. *LK*, p. 299.
20. Without explicitly saying so, Nussbaum seems to think of rural Catholic Ireland in the 1930s as the society in Beckett's novel – perhaps, though Beckett was born in Dublin in a comfortably off middle-class Protestant family and left Ireland for good in 1932.
21. *LK*, pp. 302–4.
22. *LK*, p. 304.
23. *LK*, p. 305. Compared with his hero Proust and Henry James, a key figure for Nussbaum, for neither of whom is religion important, 'nor is religion's disgust with the body a major source of emotional life', Beckett seems to her to have 'a deeply religious sensibility' (*LK*, pp. 308–10). What this means, according to Nussbaum, is that 'mere human beings are powerless to make, on account of the fact that there is something very much more powerful in this universe that does all the making'. Believing in religion means accepting that we are puppets. Secondly, on the religious view, 'finitude, and our emotional responses to it, are themselves necessarily suffused with a sense of guilt and of disgust' – the complete absence of any 'joy in the limited and the finite', in Beckett's work, 'is an expression of a religious view of life'. Finally, there is 'one further religious prejudice', in Beckett's work: 'the prejudice against that which is made in society and in favour of the pure soul, the soul before and apart from all social constructing'. The intolerance of society and rejection of shared forms of life and language in Beckett's work, Nussbaum insists, reveals 'the grip of a longing for the pure soul, hard as a diamond, individual and indivisible, coming forth from its maker's hand with its identity already stamped upon it'. We reject shared language because we 'long for a pure language of the soul itself by itself and for pure relationships among souls that will be in no way mediated by the contingent structures of human social life'. 'Deep religiosity', and 'the Christian picture', generate a 'despair', because one is 'gripped by the conviction that nothing man-made and contingent could ever stand'. Even if Nussbaum is right about Beckett's understanding of the Christian religion one might have expected her to show more sign of suspecting it to be a fairly radical misunderstanding.
24. 'Flawed Crystals: James's *The Golden Bowl* and Literature as Moral Philosophy', *New Literary History* 15 (1983): 25–50, reprinted as Chapter 4 of *Love's Knowledge*.
25. *LK*, p. 133.
26. *LK*, p. 148.
27. *LK*, p. 135, cited from the preface to *The Princess Casamassima*.
28. *LK*, pp. 373–4: A solitary good life that does not need other human beings because it does not have the forms of dependency and neediness that lead human beings to reach out to one another would not be a human life.
29. *Nicomachean Ethics* 1097b 7–11, discussed in *Fragility*, Chapter 12.
30. A life without friends would not be worth living: 1169b 3ff.

31. *LK*, pp. 378–9.
32. *LK*, p. 375.
33. *LK*, p. 376.
34. *LK*, p. 378.
35. *LK*, p. 379.
36. *Fragility*, pp. 373–7; *Nicomachean Ethics* 10, 6–8: 1177b 31–4.
37. *Fragility*, p. 375.
38. *Fragility*, p. 377.
39. *Fragility*, p. 377.
40. See, for example, Jonathan Lear, *Aristotle: the desire to understand* (Cambridge University Press 1988), where it is insisted that, far from being 'an unworked-out appendage, perhaps (one hopes) tacked on by a witless editor', the theology at the end of the *Ethics* is an essential part of Aristotle's metaphysical anthropology: 'By realizing what is best in him man transcends his own nature: he no longer lives the life that it is best for man to live; he simply lives the life that is best', p. 318.
41. *Nicomachean Ethics* 1159a 10–12: 'If it was rightly said that a true friend wishes his friend's good for that friend's own sake, the friend would have to remain himself, whatever that may be; so that he will really wish him only the greatest goods compatible with his remaining a human being'; and 1166a 20: 'No one would choose to possess every good in the world on condition of becoming somebody else'. Cf. *Fragility*, p. 376: Nussbaum is very insistent that the good for us must remain within our species identity.
42. *LK*, p. 379.
43. *LK*, p. 380.
44. *LK*, p. 391, a postscript to the William James Lecture, insisting on how novels, with the right readers, can 'immerse them in the characteristic movements of human time and the adventures of human finitude – in the form of life in which it is natural to love particular people and to have concern for the concrete events that happen to them'. But 'the forms of vision and concern that inhabit the human form of life ... would be unavailable to beasts, uninteresting to gods' (which gods?).

## 2. *Karl Barth's Christological metaphysics*

1. Karl Barth (1886–1968) first became famous with his commentary on Paul's Epistle to the Romans (1919, English 1933), in which he attacked liberal Protestantism for believing that human beings could reach religious understanding by reason; he took the lead in drawing up the Barmen Declaration (1934) against the pseudoreligious claims of Nazism; his *Kirchliche Dogmatik* [KD] (1932–67), translated as *Church Dogmatics* [CD] (T & T Clark 1936–69), uncompleted at his death, is widely recognized as the greatest work of Protestant theology this century.
2. *KD* III/4, p. 651; *CD* III/4, p. 567.
3. *CD* III/2, p. 563.
4. *KD* III/2, p. 683.
5. *CD* III/2, p. 563.
6. *KD* III/2, p. 49; *CD* III/2, p. 43.

7. CD III/2, p. 48.
8. CD I/1, p. 99.
9. Barth refers us to *Confessions* Book X.
10. CD III/2, p. 58; KD III/2, p. 67.
11. CD III/2, p. 58.
12. CD III/2, § 46: 'Through the Spirit of God, man is the subject, form and life of a substantial organism, the soul of his body – wholly and simultaneously both, in ineffaceable difference, inseparable unity, and indestructible order'.
13. CD III/2, § 44: 'The being of man is the history which shows how one of God's creatures, elected and called by God, is caught up in personal responsibility before Him and proves itself capable of fulfilling it.'
14. CD III/2, § 47: 'Man lives in the allotted span of his present, past and future life. He who was before him and will be after him, and who therefore fixes the boundaries of his being, is the eternal God, his Creator and Covenant-partner. He is the hope in which man may live in his time.'
15. KD, III/2, p. 69; CD III/2, p. 59.
16. CD, III/2, p. 54.
17. Barth directs us to Amandus Polanus (1561–1610), born in Silesia, brought up as a Lutheran but became a Calvinist, professor of Old Testament at Basel; his *Syntagma theologiae christianae* (1609) is one of the major Calvinist texts.
18. CD III/2, p. 72.
19. CD III/2, p. 103.
20. CD III/2, p. 121.
21. KD III/2, p. 127; CD III/2, p. 108.
22. CD III/2, p. 113.
23. CD III/2, pp. 112f.
24. CD III/2, p. 113.
25. CD III/2, pp. 122ff. Although Emil Brunner (1889–1966) supported Barth in opposing theological liberalism he believed that a limited knowledge of God might be gained from reflection on creation, which famously roused Barth's ire in his pamphlet *Nein! Antwort an Emil Brunner* (1934), included in Emil Brunner and Karl Barth, *Natural Theology*, tr. Peter Fraenkel (Geoffrey Bles 1946). Barth's objection here to Brunner is very like Iris Murdoch's, in her classic discussion with Ronald Hepburn in the supplementary volume of the *Proceedings of the Aristotelian Society* (1956), when they both argued, against the utilitarianism, Kantianism, prescriptivism, existentialism etc., of the time, that morality is a matter of vision as well as of choice. Barth's mockery of the autonomous self in the early-Heideggerian existentialism of the Lutheran theologian Rudolf Bultmann (1889–1976) breaks out hilariously much later (CD IV/1, pp. 434–5, dating from 1953), in a discussion of the serpent in the Adam and Eve story, where he ascribes to the serpent the thought that 'it is time for man to be enlightened and to come of age' – 'It is time for him ... to do a little demythologizing, to pass from the decision of obedience to God to that of his own choice, from service in the garden to rule' – to make the

movement 'from dependence to independence, from heteronomy to autonomy'.

26. CD III/2, p. 132.
27. CD I/2, p. 197. See my essay 'Cartesianism according to Karl Barth', *New Blackfriars* (July/August 1996): 358–68.
28. CD I/2, p. 45.
29. *KD* I/2; *Confessions* XI, 14f; 'temporality as care (*Sorge*)', in *Sein und Zeit* § 65 (1929).
30. *De civitate dei* XI, 6; cf. XII, 25.
31. *Confessions* XI, 20.
32. CD I/2, p. 46.
33. CD I/2, pp. 47ff.
34. CD I/2, p. 50.
35. CD I/2, p. 55.
36. CD I/2, p. 117.
37. CD III/2, pp. 440ff.
38. CD III/2, p. 441.
39. *KD* III/2, p. 529; CD III/2, p. 441.
40. 1 John 1.1–2; cf. *CD* III/2, p. 448: 'The Resurrected is the man Jesus, who now came and went among them as such, whom they saw and touched and heard, who ate and drank with them, and who, I believe, was still before them as true man, *vere homo* ... It is impossible to erase the bodily character of the resurrection of Jesus and His existence as the Resurrected. Nor may we gloss over this element in the New Testament record of the forty days, as a false dualism between spirit and body has repeatedly tried to do. For unless Christ's resurrection was a resurrection of the body, we have no guarantee that it was the decisively acting Subject Jesus Himself, the man Jesus, who rose from the dead.'
41. CD III/2, p. 445: 'Jesus and His disciples were not identical in the Easter event. He Himself was with them in time, in this time, beyond the time of His earthly life between His birth and death, in this time of revelation. This is what really took place. In our view, we do violence to the texts of the New Testament if we take a different line, as Bultmann does.'
42. *KD* III/2: p. 537; CD III/2, p. 448.
43. CD III/2, p. 451.
44. CD III/2, p. 456.
45. CD III/2, p. 463.
46. *KD* III/2, p. 556; CD III/2, p. 463.
47. *KD* III/2, p. 557; CD III/2, p. 464.
48. CD III/2, pp. 442ff.
49. CD III/2, p. 449.
50. CD III/2, pp. 452–4.
51. CD III/2, pp. 455f.
52. CD III/2, pp. 511–53.
53. CD III/2, p. 555.
54. CD III/2, p. 556.
55. CD III/2, pp. 557f.
56. *KD* III/2, p. 678; CD III/2, p. 559.

57. CD III/2, p. 562: 'Life as an endless process, and therefore space for it, is the last thing any one conscious of the humanity of his life can desire. Rather, he will appreciate the fact that the exact opposite, life confined to a set span, is what he has been granted, and that in comparison with that other possibility it is not only equally good but far better.'

58. CD III/2, p. 565.

59. CD III/2, p. 565: 'Man would not be this man, here and now, the concrete subject of this history, if his life did not have this outline and contour, if it did not have these limits and boundaries. A being in unending time would be centrifugal. It would not be that of a concrete subject to whom God can be an equally concrete Counterpart and Neighbour, with whom He can enjoy communication and intercourse.'

60. CD III/2, pp. 562ff.

61. CD III/2, p. 566.

62. CD III/2, p. 571.

63. Friedrich Schleiermacher, *The Christian Faith* (T & T Clark 1928), translated from the second edition (1830) pp. 243f: 'If we think away the gradual decay of organic powers, the possibility that the organism may be destroyed by external forces of nature, and disappearance through death, what we are thinking of is no longer beings of our kind, while yet real human history would only begin when all these things were present ... neither the Old Testament story nor the relevant indications in the writings of the New Testament compel us to hold that man was created immortal.'

64. CD III/2, pp. 596–7: 'Of death as it actually meets us we certainly cannot say that it is an inherent part of human nature as God created it and as it is therefore good ... our standing under this sign is not something intrinsic to our human nature. For God did not create us to exist under this impending threat of being hewn down and cast into the fire. It does not correspond to our determination to have no other prospect but a being in outer darkness and eternal torment.'

65. CD III/2, p. 597: 'If there is anything natural about it; if it belongs in any sense to man's divinely appointed creaturely status that his time should have an end; if death is not intrinsically and essentially a curse and a misery, then its intrinsic and essential quality is for us at any rate unfathomably and inaccessibly concealed beneath the unnatural and even anti-natural guise in which it now comes to us ... It is never the natural being of man, but always man doubly deluded who speaks of death's reaper as though it were a kindly angel of light. Since death is the sign of divine judgment, man as he naturally is can face it only with sorrow. If we are to tackle honestly the question of the meaning of the finitude of our time, this is the first thing to see and accept.'

66. CD III/2, pp. 609f.

67. CD III/2, pp. 614f.

68. cf. CD III/2, pp. 632f.

69. CD III/2, p. 632: 'Man as such ... has no beyond. Nor does he need one, for God is his beyond. Man's beyond is that God as his Creator, Covenant-partner, Judge and Saviour, was and is and will be his true

Counterpart in life, and finally and exclusively and totally in death'; *KD* III/2, p. 770: '*Der Mensch als solcher hat also kein Jenseits; denn Gott ist sein Jenseits*'.

70. CD III/2, p. 633.

71. CD III/2, p. 633: Man as this being who 'clings here and now to God who as the One who is the Creator has set him these limits and given him this allotted span, and who now in the concrete form of the appearance and work of Jesus Christ is his only full and perfect hope . . .knows that already in the totality of his own this-sided existence, alone and beyond which there is no other, he is claimed by and belongs and is committed and thankful here and now to the God who as his gracious Judge and therefore his Saviour from death is his true beyond'.

72. CD III/4, p. 567.

73. KD III/4, p. 651; CD III/2, p. 568.

74. CD III/4, p. 566.

75. CD III/4, p. 566. In case we might be tempted to fall into the sort of Roman Catholic natural theology that is so roundly denounced on earlier occasions, especially at CD I/2, § 22 (1932), Barth cautions us that the 'mutual co-ordination' between us and God is known a posteriori and by reflection on what has happened in the Christian dispensation, and in no other way.

76. CD III/4, p. 567.

77. KD IV/2, p. 533; CD IV/2, p. 472.

78. KD IV/2, pp. 428f; CD IV/2, pp. 382f.

79. KD IV/2, p. 452; CD IV/2, p. 401.

80. CD IV/2, § 60.

81. CD IV/2, p. 404.

82. In effect this is a generalization of the monastic bugbear of *accidie*, though Barth does not refer to it. The first vice which stands against the joy of charity, according to Thomas Aquinas, *Summa Theologiae* 2a 2ae, 35, is *acedia*, traditionally translated as sloth, but as Thomas Heath notes, 'spiritual apathy' seems better to catch the phenomenon: 'a bored indifference towards religious and spiritual matters': tracing analysis of this vice from Evagrius of Pontus and John Cassian, Heath never mentions Barth's prolix disquisition on the theme but makes the attractive suggestion that Emily Dickinson might well be described as 'the poet of *acedia*' (Blackfriars edition, Eyre and Spottiswoode, volume 35, 1972, Appendix 1).

83. KD IV/2, p. 458; CD IV/2, p. 407.

84. KD, IV/2, p. 522; CD IV/2, p. 462.

85. KD IV/2, p. 522; CD IV/2, p. 463.

86. KD IV/2, p. 529; CD IV/2, p. 468.

87. CD IV/2, p. 469.

88. It can plausibly be maintained, as for instance by Catherine Mowry LaCugna, *God for Us: The Trinity and Christian Life* (HarperCollins 1991), p. 252, that Barth's God remains one Subject who exists in three modes as revealer, revelation and revealedness, and is thus vulnerable to the charge of modalism; but even more damagingly to the modern critic, this God

would be the Absolute Subject, the mirror image then of the autonomous self of Enlightenment philosophy. God's sovereignty might anyway be a predictable Calvinist emphasis. However that may be for the first volume (CD I/1 and I/2), it is surely arguable that Barth's insistence on understanding 'the form of the divine being in its triunity, the beginning and ending which do not mean that limitation of Him who begins and ends, a juxtaposition which does not mean any exclusion, a movement which does not signify the passing away of anything, a succession which in itself is also beginning and end' as 'the absolutely real time' (CD II/1, p. 615) indicates that the Christian doctrine of God as Trinity has nothing to do with the notion of God as a static and solitary being that so many philosophers take for granted.

89. CD III/2, p. 189.
90. *The Modern Theologians: An Introduction to Christian theology in the twentieth century*, ed. David F. Ford (Basil Blackwell 1989) volume I, p. 46. But see also Robert W. Jenson, *Alpha and Omega: A Study in the Theology of Karl Barth* (Thomas Nelson & Sons 1963), p. 140: 'To put it somewhat crudely, Barth has solved the problem of the disappearance of the timeless by retaining the general structure of classical theology but putting the historical event of Jesus' existence in the place formerly occupied by changeless "Being" ... Thus where "is" stood there now stands "becomes". Where "Being" stood there now stands Jesus Christ. Where "Beauty", "Goodness", "Truth" in the abstract stood there now stands the life-history of Jesus. To be is to become, to become a brother of Jesus, to share in His story.' Cf. Eberhard Jüngel, *Karl Barth: A Theological Legacy* (The Westminster Press 1986), p. 68 for a somewhat different account of how Barth 'used the Platonic framework to insist polemically that the temporal (finite) cannot by itself conceive of the eternal (infinite)'.

## 3. Heidegger's cosmogonical myth

1. Martin Heidegger (1889–1976), no doubt the most famous German philosopher of this century, was brought up a Catholic, for health reasons gave up the idea of becoming a priest, and by 1915 had distanced himself from Catholicism through study of Paul, Luther, Kierkegaard and Eckhart; *Sein und Zeit* appeared in 1927; teaching at Marburg in the 1920s he became a close friend of Bultmann, who believed he had a good knowledge of current Protestant theology including Barth's work; he succeeded Edmund Husserl (1859–1938) at Freiburg in 1928 but had by then developed his own phenomenological method; he supported the Nazi Party and never expressed public regret for doing so; his later meditations on language often rework Christian themes; and to the end he remained fascinated by Christianity. See John D. Caputo, 'Heidegger and theology', *The Cambridge Companion to Heidegger* ed. Charles Guignon (Cambridge University Press 1993): 270–88.
2. *Sein und Zeit* (Max Niemeyer 1927), translated as *Being and Time* by John Macquarrie and Edward Robinson (SCM Press 1962); Gilbert Ryle's

perceptive review, *Mind* 38 (1929), is reprinted in Gilbert Ryle, *Collected Papers*, volume 1 (Hutcheson 1971). The review by T. F. Torrance deserves attention, *The Journal of Theological Studies*, (October 1964): 471–486.

3. In the next few paragraphs I draw on my essay 'Getting the Subject back into the World: Heidegger's Version', in *Human Beings* ed. David Cockburn (Cambridge University Press 1991): 173–90.

4. *Being and Time* [BT], p. 48.

5. BT, e.g., p. 56 'das Geistding', p. 116 the 'bare subject without a world', p. 118 the 'isolated subject', p. 119 'das Ichding', p. 206 the 'worldless subject' – very much Barth's picture of the unbounded self as in Fichte.

6. BT, p. 190 footnote, where Augustine, Luther and Kierkegaard are named.

7. BT, p. 199 footnote.

8. BT, p. 249 footnote.

9. *The Essence of Reasons*, tr. Terence Malick (Northwestern University Press 1969), p. 51.

10. '... Poetically Man Dwells ...', in *Poetry, Language, Thought* tr. Albert Hofstadter (Harper & Row 1971), pp. 213–29, the text of a lecture that Heidegger gave in 1951. The standard story about the later Heidegger has been overthrown by the remarkable book by John van Buren, *The Young Heidegger: Rumor of the Hidden King* (Indiana University Press 1994), which demonstrates convincingly that the famous 'turn' after *Sein und Zeit* was actually a re-turn to earlier though then unpublished ways of thinking.

11. BT, p. 68.

12. 'The Origin of the Work of Art', in *Poetry, Language, Thought* [PLT] (Harper & Row 1971), pp. 17–87, the 1950 version of a much revised and expanded lecture first given in 1935.

13. *PLT*, p. 22.

14. *PLT*, p. 26.

15. *PLT*, p. 26.

16. *PLT*, pp. 33f.

17. *PLT*, p. 61.

18. *PLT*, p. 35; It is not a matter of describing, explaining, reporting or observing, as if the picture were an object in front of us; but rather of our being brought under the spell of the picture in such a way that we find ourselves – suddenly – jolted into a different place from our customary one in the world.

19. *PLT*, p. 42; cf. *Holzwege* (Vittorio Klostermann 1963[4]), p. 31.

20. *PLT*, p. 44. As J. E. Malpas puts it, more beautifully than Heidegger could ever be rendered in English, in *Donald Davidson and the Mirror of Meaning: Holism, truth, interpretation* (Cambridge University Press 1992), p. 276: 'This is not some especially esoteric or exotic experience (though perhaps it may take on a mystical air), but an experience that is part of the everyday. It is the experience of being in a world – a world of richness and variety, of darkness and light, a world which is open to us in the earth beneath our feet and the sky above our heads, in those others whom we

encounter before and around us. It is an experience of the world as a world
– as a place wherein we find ourselves, which bounds and constrains and
which also involves and engages us.'

21. 'The Thing', in *PLT*, pp. 165–86, the text of a lecture given in 1950.

22. *PLT*, p. 166: 'Man stares at what the explosion of the atom bomb could
bring with it. He does not see that the atom bomb and its explosion are the
mere final emission of what has long since taken place, has already
happened ... What is this helpless anxiety still waiting for, if the terrible
has already happened.' The terrible (*das Entsetzliche*), is something
unsettling (*das Entsetzende*), and, according to Heidegger here, is the
way in which, in our culture, we have lost all sense of distances in time and
space: 'Man now reaches overnight, by plane, places which formerly took
weeks and months of travel. He now receives instant information, by
radio, of events which he formerly learned about only years later, if at all ...
Distant sites of the most ancient cultures are shown on film as if they stood
this very moment amidst today's street traffic ... The peak of this abolition
of every possibility of remoteness is reached by television, which will soon
pervade and dominate the whole machinery of communication,' etc.
Television has already taken the world away from us – unsettled and
estranged us: a nuclear holocaust (we are after all in 1950 with this lecture)
would only be the final sputter (*Auswurf*) of the irreversible process.

23. *PLT*, p. 172.

24. *PLT*, pp. 172–3.

25. *PLT*, p. 174.

26. *PLT*, p. 178.

27. *PLT*, pp. 179–80; so the story is that in the metaphysical tradition we think
of human beings in terms of animals with rationality whereas with
Heidegger's non-metaphysical way of thinking we figure human beings
as mortals – but that means mortals in relationship with earth, sky and the
beckoning messengers of the godhead. We have to discover a way of being
in the world as participating in the game (*Spiel*) of the fourfold (*das
Geviert*). Whether Plato's *Gorgias* is a text in the metaphysical tradition or
not, one of the rare anticipations of the concept – conceit – of the fourfold
is to be found there at 507E, where Callicles is reminded by Socrates that
the world as a whole has been called *kosmos* (by the Pythagoreans) because
'heaven and earth and gods and humans are held together by communion,
friendship, orderliness and temperance and justice'. Perhaps the failure to
call human beings mortals suggests that this is already a metaphysical text,
resiling anthropocentrically from the reality of death.

28. *PLT*, p. 180.

29. *PLT*, p. 180.

30. *PLT*, p. 181; *Vorträge und Aufsätze* (Neske 1954), p. 179.

31. *PLT*, p. 182. Heidegger's world is evidently a world with pitchers of wine
and comfortable benches, footbridges over country streams and ploughs at
the side of fields; but not just of such man-made things, it extends also to
trees, ponds, streams, hills; animals such as heron, deer, cattle and horses,
as well as looking-glasses, buckles, books, pictures (images?), crowns (on

statues of the Virgin?) and crosses (on the altar?): a rural Catholic landscape such as he knew in his childhood.

32. *PLT*, p. 181.

33. *PLT*, p. 181; we have to move, or allow ourselves to be moved, from the domain of representing and explaining what is the case to a different kind of thinking which Heidegger connects with 'vigilance' (*Wachsamkeit*), and 'recollection' (*andenken*). Watching and vigils are traditionally religious customs; in oldfashioned Catholic parlance *Andacht* was evening devotions and *andenken* is the word for remembering the dead in one's prayers. Here, as so often, Heidegger borrows religious language for his remythologization of the world: the other kind of thinking seems to be a kind of prayer – addressed, however, to the world itself.

34. *An Introduction to Metaphysics*, tr. Ralph Manheim (Doubleday 1961), p. 171 – 'the essent' is a somewhat desperate rendering of '*das Seiende*', Heidegger's jargon for 'anything and everything that exists'.

35. *The Epistle to the Romans*, tr. Edwyn C. Hoskyns (Oxford University Press 1933), p. 36: 'The activity of the community is related to the Gospel only in so far as it is no more than a crater formed by the explosion of a shell and seeks to be no more than a void in which the Gospel reveals itself.'

36. *Identity and Difference*, tr. Joan Stambaugh (Harper & Row 1969), p. 72.

37. In *Nein!*, curiously, Barth attacks Brunner for misrepresenting the Catholic conception of natural theology as 'a self-sufficient rational system, detachable from the *theologia revelata* and capable of serving it for a solid foundation' (*Natural Theology*, pp. 95–6). On the contrary, Barth insists, 'a true knowledge of God derived from reason and nature is de facto never attained without prevenient and preparatory grace'. But Heidegger is not the only one to react against what he regarded as an irretrievably rationalistic natural theology. Ludwig Wittgenstein (1889–1951) seems to have a similar reaction: consider, for example, his contempt (arguably less than entirely justified) for 'Father O'Hara' – 'one of those people who make [religious belief] a question of science', *Lectures and Conversations on Aesthetics, Psychology and Religious Belief* ed. Cyril Barrett (Basil Blackwell 1966), pp. 57–9.

38. *PLT*, p. 178; but what god needs to be withdrawn from all comparison with occurrent entities? Evidently not the God of Thomas Aquinas: '*deus non est in aliquo genere*' – '*Deus non est in genere substantiae*' (*Summa Theologiae* 1a, 3, 5). Aquinas's God is thus not an item in any genus, not even in the category of substance. On the religious significance of Heidegger see John D. Caputo, *Demythologizing Heidegger* (Indiana University Press 1993).

# 4. Back to Plato with Iris Murdoch

1. Iris Murdoch (born 1919) has published two dozen novels since *Under the Net* (1954); she taught philosophy from 1948 to 1963 in Oxford; her Gifford Lectures at the University of Edinburgh in 1982, much revised and expanded, appeared as *Metaphysics as a Guide to Morals* (Chatto & Windus 1992), but her importance as a philosopher was established by

*Sartre: Romantic Rationalist* (Bowes & Bowes 1953) and especially by three lectures collected as *The Sovereignty of Good* (Routledge & Kegan Paul 1970), and *The Fire and the Sun: Why Plato Banished the Artists* (Oxford University Press 1977). See R. Gillies (ed.), 'Iris Murdoch's Giffords': A *Study of the 1982 Gifford Lectures* (Theology in Scotland Occasional Paper 1, St Andrews: St Mary's College 1995).

2. *Metaphysics as a Guide to Morals*, p. 491.

3. 'The Idea of Perfection', originally in *The Yale Review* 1964, in *The Sovereignty of Good*, pp. 1–45, cf. p. 1. Both early (*Sovereignty*, pp. 4–11) and late (*Metaphysics*, pp. 269–86) Murdoch evinces deep suspicion of the later Wittgenstein's work, mainly on the grounds that it tends to take away 'the inner life'; but she certainly seems to share his belief that what would otherwise be obvious to everyone has often been 'theorized away' by determined and influential philosophers. Cf. *Metaphysics*, p. 497: 'People know about the difference between good and evil, it takes quite a lot of theorising to persuade them to say or imagine that they do not'.

4. For acknowledged indebtedness to Murdoch in the revival of moral realism see Mark Platts, *Ways of Meaning* (Routledge & Kegan Paul 1979); Sabina Lovibond, *Realism and Imagination in Ethics* (Basil Blackwell 1983); Charles Taylor, *Sources of the Self: The Making of the Modern Identity* (Cambridge University Press 1989); Hilary Putnam, *Realism with a Human Face* (Harvard University Press 1990); Cora Diamond, *The Realistic Spirit: Wittgenstein, Philosophy, and the Mind* (MIT Press 1991), pp. 373–77; several uncollected essays by John McDowell; and, for a general introduction, David McNaughton, *Moral Vision* (Basil Blackwell 1988).

5. *Sovereignty*, p. 35.

6. *Sovereignty*, p. 38.

7. *Sovereignty*, p. 37.

8. 'Existentialism and Mystics', in *Essays and Poems Presented to Lord David Cecil*, ed. W. W. Robson (Constable 1970), pp. 169–83.

9. *The Fire and the Sun*, p. 36.

10. *Sovereignty*, p. 72.

11. *Metaphysics*, pp. 452ff.

12. *Metaphysics*, p. 449, citing Friedrich von Hügel, *The Mystical Element in Religion as studied in St Catherine of Genoa and her Friends* (1908) volume 2, p. 260.

13. *Metaphysics*, p. 451, evidently dismissing centuries of theological effort to make something other than doceticism out of the doctrine of the incarnation.

14. *The Fire and the Sun*, p. 52; *Metaphysics*, p. 442, a somewhat inadequate doctrine of the Trinity. Cf. *Metaphysics*, p. 145.

15. *Metaphysics*, p. 472.

16. *Metaphysics*, p. 453; Don Cupitt, *Taking Leave of God* (SCM Press 1980).

17. *Metaphysics*, p. 455.

18. *Metaphysics*, p. 455, evidently dismissing the 'Deus non est in genere substantiae' thesis unexamined.

19. *Metaphysics*, p. 455, evidently ignoring recent discussion about whether

God is to be described as 'a person' at all, as well as centuries of argument about the meaning of the term 'person' in the theology of God as Trinity.

20. *Metaphysics*, p. 454.
21. 'Above the gods: A dialogue about religion', in *Acastos: Two Platonic Dialogues* (Chatto & Windus 1986), pp. 67–121; severely reviewed, not without reason, by Martha Nussbaum, *The Times Literary Supplement*, 15 August 1986, p. 881.
22. *Metaphysics*, p. 455.
23. *Taking Leave of God*, p. 40.
24. *Sovereignty*, pp. 17–28.
25. *Sovereignty*, p. 26.
26. *Sovereignty*, p. 31.
27. *Sovereignty*, p. 40.
28. *Sovereignty*, p. 41.
31. *Sovereignty*, p. 41.
32. *Metaphysics*, pp. 391–430.
33. *Metaphysics*, p. 396.
34. *Metaphysics*, p. 397, citing Barth's *Epistle to the Romans*: 'Plato in his wisdom recognized long ago that behind the visible there lies the invisible universe which is the Origin of all concrete things.'
35. *Metaphysics*, p. 399.
36. *Metaphysics*, p. 399.
37. *Metaphysics*, p. 400.
38. *Metaphysics*, p. 400.
39. *Metaphysics*, p. 428.
40. *Metaphysics*, p. 429.
41. *Sovereignty*, p. 41.
42. *Metaphysics*, p. 430.
43. *Metaphysics*, p. 428, thus, far from wanting to relieve us of the ideal of perfection Murdoch believes that we already try to obliterate it and can only be fully human if we allow it to have its sway.
44. *The Fire and the Sun*, p. 33.
45. *The Fire and the Sun*, pp. 34–5.
46. *The Fire and the Sun*, p. 36. Whether Murdoch's insistence on our native condition of selfishness, greed, fantasy etc. owes a good deal to the Christian doctrine of original sin is a question that will have to remain on the table; it certainly bears comparison with Nussbaum's 'secular analogue' thesis. Cf. *Sovereignty*, pp. 28 and 52. 'In the moral life the enemy is the fat relentless ego. Moral philosophy is properly, and in the past has sometimes been, the discussion of this ego and of the techniques (if any) for its defeat. In this respect moral philosophy has shared some aims with religion.'

# 5. Irigaray and the sensible transcendental

1. Luce Irigaray (born 1930), philosopher and psychoanalyst, published her work on linguistic collapse in senile dementia (1973) and then her doctoral thesis (1974), tr. Gillian C. Gill as *Speculum of the Other Woman*

(Cornell University Press 1985). Many of her subsequent books have appeared in translation: *This Sex Which Is Not One*, tr. Catherine Porter with Carolyn Burke (Cornell University Press 1985); *Marine Lover of Friedrich Nietzsche*, tr. Gillian C. Gill (Columbia University Press 1991); *An Ethics of Sexual Difference*, tr. Carolyn Burke and Gillian C. Gill (The Athlone Press 1993); *Sexes and Genealogies*, tr. Gillian C. Gill (Columbia University Press 1993) – among others, not yet including, unfortunately for our purposes, *L'Oubli de l'Air chez Martin Heidegger* (Minuit 1983), where she suggests, in the midst of much criticism, that Heidegger's attempt to disconnect thinking from '(patriarchal) theology' could be an opening for a new way of being in which, among other things, the human subject would be *sexué* (whatever all that means). The best general introduction in English is Margaret Whitford, *Luce Irigaray: Philosophy in the Feminine* (Routledge 1991); but for theological discussion see Elizabeth Grosz, *Sexual Subversions: Three French Feminists* (Allen & Unwin 1989), Chapter 5; Serene Jones, 'Divining Women: Irigaray and Feminist Theologies', *Yale French Studies* 87 (1995): 42–67; and Graham Ward, 'Divinity and Sexuality: Luce Irigaray and Christology', *Modern Theology* 12 (1996): 221–37 and 'A Theology of Sexual Difference: Beyond von Balthasar', in *Von Balthasar at the End of Modernity* (T & T Clark, forthcoming).

2. Nussbaum has no patience with the wilder forms of American feminism, such as the claim (by a woman with a university post in philosophy) that *modus ponens* [if p then q; p; therefore q], one of the basic laws of logic, is a male patriarchal creation oppressive of women (see Nussbaum's long review, *The New York Review of Books*, 20 October 1994); but she has been concerned with feminism from the start, suggesting even that Plato 'has a good claim to be called the first feminist philosopher' (*The Fragility of Goodness*, pp. 3–4). Murdoch has always insisted on the difference between philosophy and fiction as modes of discourse, and (rightly or wrongly) on the distinctiveness of her practice in each mode: like Nussbaum she would regard her philosophical work simply as a contribution to *philosophy*, and certainly not to some kind of *écriture féminine* (Irigaray), maternal thinking (Sara Ruddick), or whatever. Her novels, however, which usually have a male narrator, often deal with gender-identity and transgression of gender boundaries, as Debora Johnson explores, with the help of Irigaray's ideas as it happens, in her book *Iris Murdoch* (The Harvester Press 1987). Barth has not attracted much feminist-theoretical interpretation so far; but consider Serene Jones, 'This God Which is Not One: Irigaray and Barth on the Divine', in *Transfigurations: Theology and the French Feminists*, ed. C. W. Maggie Kim, Susan M. St Ville, Susan M. Simonaitis (Fortress Press 1993), pp. 109–41. Heidegger, perhaps surprisingly, has been discussed very interestingly by Jean Graybeal, *Language and 'The Feminine' in Nietzsche and Heidegger* (Indiana University Press 1990), using Julia Kristeva's theories as a framework, reading Heidegger early and late, highlighting feminine, maternal and erotic imagery, and suggesting that his overcoming or

sidelining of traditional (Platonic) metaphysics may also contribute to the task of moving beyond androcentric thinking.

3. This passage is not in the text of Hegel's *Philosophy of Right* (1821) but in notes taken at the lectures that he gave using the book, intercalated by the editor of the 1833 edition (tr. T. M. Knox, Clarendon Press 1942, p. 263).

4. Nussbaum, *The Fragility of Goodness*, pp. 1–20.

5. Murdoch, *Sovereignty*, p. 74.

6. Peter Conradi, *Iris Murdoch: The Saint and the Artist* (Macmillan 1986), p. 6.

7. 'God must be questioned and not simply neutered in the current pseudoliberal way. Religion as a social phenomenon cannot be ignored', *Sexes and Genealogies* (Columbia University Press 1993), p. v.

8. *An Ethics of Sexual Difference* [ESD], p. 5.

9. See 'Sorcerer Love: A Reading of Plato, Symposium, "Diotima's Speech"', in *ESD*, pp. 20–33. Socrates recalls his conversation with Diotima at *Symposium* 201D–212B. For a brilliant and very damaging critique of Irigaray's reading see Andrea Nye, 'The Hidden Host: Irigaray and Diotima at Plato's Symposium', in *Revaluing French Feminism: Critical Essays on Difference, Agency, and Culture*, ed. Nancy Fraser and Sandra Lee Bartky (Indiana University Press 1992), pp. 77–93.

10. *ESD*, p. 25.

11. *Symposium*, 207E.

12. *ESD*, p. 30.

13. *ESD*, p. 82.

14. *ESD*, p. 87, citing Descartes, *The Passions of the Soul*.

15. *ESD*, p. 13.

16. *ESD*, p. 13.

17. *Metaphysics as a Guide to Morals*, pp. 146, 253, 343–5.

18. 'To demand equality as women is, it seems to me, a mistaken expression of a real objective. The demand to be equal presupposes a point of comparison. To whom or to what do women want to be equalized? To men? To a salary? To a public office? To what standard? Why not to themselves?', in *je, tu, nous: Toward a Culture of Difference* (Routledge 1993) tr. Alison Martin, p. 12.

19. *Sexes and Genealogies* [SG], p. 75.

20. *SG*, p. 64.

21. On Girard's thesis that every human group is constantly renewed on the basis of some cathartic immolation see Fergus Kerr, 'Revealing the Scapegoat Mechanism: Christianity after Girard', in *Philosophy, Religion and the Spiritual Life* ed. Michael McGhee (Cambridge University Press 1992): 161–75. For Irigaray the thesis seems to depend on the model of male sexual behaviour as described by Freud: tension, discharge, return to homeostasis, etc.

22. *SG*, p. 76.

23. *SG*, p. 78.

24. Logocentrism+phallocentrism: the supposedly dominant metaphysical a priori in all Western thinking, with logos, logic, reason, knowledge, etc.,

insisting on a logic of identity that colludes with the exclusion and binary polarization of difference, together with an exaltation of the human male as patriarch, progenitor, etc., reducing women to versions of masculinity, either through negation, assimilation or unification into a greater whole.

25. SG, p. 21.
26. SG, p. 21.
27. On the New Testament, note Irigaray's critical review of what she would regard as the liberal-feminist work of the Catholic biblical scholar Elisabeth Schüssler Fiorenza, originally in *Critique* 480 (mai 1987), available as 'Equal to whom?', in *differences* 1 (1989): 59–76.
28. *ESD*, pp. 114f.
29. *ESD*, p. 140.
30. *ESD*, pp. 144, 146.
31. *ESD*, p. 148.
32. *Marine Lover*, pp. 181f.
33. *Marine Lover*, p. 181.
34. 'Having a God and becoming one's gender go hand in hand. God is the other that we absolutely cannot be without. In order to *become*, we need some shadowy perception of achievement; not a fixed objective, not a One postulated to be immutable but rather a cohesion and a horizon that assures us the passage between past and future ... To have a goal is essentially a religious move ... Only the religious, within and without us, is fundamental enough to allow us to discover, affirm, achieve certain ends', *Sexes and Genealogies*, p. 67.

# 6. Stanley Cavell and the truth of scepticism

1. Stanley Cavell (born 1926), who has taught at Harvard for many years, published 'The Availability of Wittgenstein's Later Philosophy', *The Philosophical Review* (1962), and reprinted it in his first major collection *Must We Mean What We Say? A Book of Essays* (Charles Scribner's Sons 1969). Among much else he has published *The Claim of Reason: Wittgenstein, Skepticism, Morality and Tragedy* (Clarendon Press 1979); *In Quest of the Ordinary: Lines of Skepticism and Romanticism* (University of Chicago Press 1988); *Conditions Handsome and Unhandsome: The Constitution of Emersonian Perfectionism* (The University of Chicago Press 1990), and *Philosophical Passages: Wittgenstein, Emerson, Austin, Derrida* (Basil Blackwell 1995). There are two good books about Cavell's work: Richard Fleming, *The State of Philosophy: An Invitation to a Reading in Three Parts of Stanley Cavell's The Claim of Reason* (Associated University Presses 1993) and Stephen Mulhall, *Stanley Cavell: Philosophy's Recounting of the Ordinary* (Clarendon Press 1994), which includes a valuable discussion of Cavell's relationship with Christianity.
2. See for example Bertrand Russell, *The Problems of Philosophy* (1912, frequently reprinted).
3. Immanuel Kant's *Critique of Pure Reason*, translated by Norman Kemp Smith (1929, frequently reprinted), A 735/ B 763.
4. Kant, *Critique*, A 795/ B 823.

5. Kant, *Critique*, A 796/ B 824.

6. Ludwig Wittgenstein, *Philosophical Investigations* (Basil Blackwell 1953): § 116, translation modified.

7. Manuscript 109 (August 1930 to February 1931) in Von Wright's numbering.

8. See Garth Hallett, *A Companion to Wittgenstein's 'Philosophical Investigations'* (Cornell University Press 1977), pp. 203ff; 'I have tried to convince you of just the opposite of Descartes' emphasis on "I"', *Wittgenstein's Lectures: Cambridge, 1932–35*, ed. Alice Ambrose (Basil Blackwell 1979), p. 63.

9. *The Claim of Reason*, p. 207. We have to account for 'the human temptation to deny the conditions of humanity, or in other words, the will to be monstrous', *In Quest of the Ordinary*, p. 141.

10. *In Quest of the Ordinary*, p. 129.

11. *In Quest of the Ordinary*, p. 161. 'Other Minds', first published in 1946, is in J. L. Austin, *Philosophical Papers* (Oxford University Press 1961).

12. *In Quest of the Ordinary*, p. 161.

13. *In Quest of the Ordinary*, p. 162.

14. Wittgenstein, *Philosophical Investigations*: § 124.

15. Cf. *Must We Mean*, p. 2, cf. p. 161.

16. Pascal, *Pensées* tr. A. J. Krailsheimer (Penguin Books 1966) p. 67; *Oeuvres Completes* (Editions du Seuil 1963), p. 516.

17. Pascal, *Pensées*, p. 67.

18. *Must We Mean*, p. 2.

19. R. Fleming and M. Payne (eds), *The Senses of Stanley Cavell* (Bucknell University Press 1989), p. 38.

20. *Stanley Cavell*, p. 46.

21. *Stanley Cavell*, p. 48.

22. *In Quest of the Ordinary*, p. 5.

23. *In Quest of the Ordinary*, p. 9.

24. *In Quest of the Ordinary*, p. 9.

25. *In Quest of the Ordinary*, p. 9.

26. *In Quest of the Ordinary*, p. 138: 'I have claimed that scepticism is our philosophical access to the human wish to deny the conditions of humanity, relating this, as well as to Kant's vision, both to Christianity's and to Nietzsche's hopes for the human to be overcome.'

27. As Mulhall notes, *Stanley Cavell*, p. 299: Cavell 'offers a picture of human beings as language animals essentially riven by a desire to deny their essence in just the way that the reviled doctrine of Original Sin imputes a necessarily non-integral human nature.'

28. See Don Mannison and Lloyd Reinhardt, 'Critical Notice: *The Claim of Reason*', *Philosophical Investigations* 5 (1982): 227–44.

29. Barry Stroud, 'Reasonable Claims: Cavell and the Tradition', *The Journal of Philosophy* 77 (1980): 731–44.

30. Richard Rorty, 'Cavell on Skepticism', *The Review of Metaphysics* 34 (1980–81): 759–74.

31. *Must We Mean*, p. 240.

32. *The Claim of Reason*, p. 207.

33. *Must We Mean*, p. 263.
34. *Must We Mean*, p. 238.
35. *The Claim of Reason*, p. 493.
36. *The Claim of Reason*, pp. 351f.
37. *Must We Mean*, p. 255.
38. *The Claim of Reason*, p. 241.
39. *Must We Mean*, p. 247.
40. *The Claim of Reason*, p. 209.
41. *In Quest of the Ordinary*, p. 135.
42. *The Claim of Reason*, p. 106.
43. *The Claim of Reason*, p. 122.
44. *The Claim of Reason*, pp. 122, 358.
45. *The Claim of Reason*, p. 121.
46. *In Quest of the Ordinary*, p. 127.
47. See Mulhall, *Stanley Cavell*, pp. 283–312 for an extremely illuminating discussion of Cavell on religion and on Christianity in particular.
48. *In Quest of the Ordinary*, p. 99.
49. *In Quest of the Ordinary*, p. 99.
50. *In Quest of the Ordinary*, p. 99.
51. *Must We Mean*, pp. 47f.
52. Clearly, Wittgenstein believed that we (he at least) felt the temptation to regard the language of every day as 'somehow too coarse and material for what we want to say' (*Investigations*: § 120); an 'immaculate meaning' and a 'perfect language'(§ 98); something 'pure and clear-cut' (§ 105); not the things of everyday thinking but 'extreme subtleties' (§ 106); 'crystalline purity' (§ 107–8); etc.
53. *Must We Mean*, p. 161.
54. *Must We Mean*, p. 162.
55. *Must We Mean*, chapter 6.
56. *Disowning Knowledge In Six Plays of Shakespeare* (Cambridge University Press 1987), p. 198.
57. *Disowning Knowledge*, p. 27.
58. *Disowning Knowledge*, p. 36 footnote.
59. *Stanley Cavell*, p. 288.
60. *The Claim of Reason*, p. 471.
61. *The Claim of Reason*, p. 472.
62. *The Claim of Reason*, p. 493.
63. *The Claim of Reason*, p. 494.
64. *The Claim of Reason*, p. 416.
65. *The Claim of Reason*, p. 352.
66. *The Claim of Reason*, p. 455.
67. Mulhall, *Stanley Cavell*, pp. 267–82.
68. *The Claim of Reason*, p. 470.
69. *The Claim of Reason*, p. 470: 'This descent, or ascent, of the problem of the other is the key way I can grasp the alternative process of secularization called romanticism. And it may explain why the process of humanization can become a monstrous undertaking, placing infinite demands upon

finite resources. It is an image of what living our skepticism comes to' – 'alternative', presumably, to scientistic materialism of some kind.

70. Cavell keeps coming back to God, far more often than we can cite here. We have a 'craving for *totality*', which is an expression of the way that 'we want to know the world as we imagine God knows it. And that will be as easy to rid us of as it is to rid us of the prideful craving to be God. – I mean to *rid* us of it, not to replace it with a despair at our finitude' (*The Claim of Reason*, pp. 236f). This is very reminiscent of some of the things we heard Karl Barth say!

71. *In Quest of the Ordinary*, p. 65.

72. *In Quest of the Ordinary*, p. 65.

73. *In Quest of the Ordinary*, p. 66.

74. *In Quest of the Ordinary*, pp. 65–8.

75. *In Quest of the Ordinary*, p. 67.

76. *In Quest of the Ordinary*, p. 68.

77. John Wisdom (1904–93), while teaching at St Andrews, published a series of articles on 'Logical Constructions' (*Mind* 1931–3), which took 'philosophical analysis' in the wake of G. E. Moore to the point of no return; in 1934 he was shocked by Wittgenstein's classes at Cambridge into completely changing course, and his series on 'Other Minds' (*Mind* 1940–43) is the classical treatment of scepticism and solipsism; unlike many of his colleagues at the time he was deeply interested in art, literature, psychoanalysis and religion (not to mention the turf!). Cavell recommends the 'experience of John Wisdom's *Other Minds*' (*The Claim of Reason*, p. 353); but he already refers to his work respectfully in footnotes to the 1957 paper 'Must We Mean What We Say?', the first chapter of the volume of that title. Wisdom's 'Gods' appeared in *Proceedings of the Aristotelian Society*, 1944, and is reprinted in his *Philosophy and Psycho-Analysis* (Basil Blackwell 1969).

78. *In Quest of the Ordinary*, p. 68. 'Animism' is perhaps not the happiest term: Wisdom himself does not use it; D. Z. Phillips uses it of philosophers of religion (such as Richard Swinburne and J. L. Mackie!) who dispute over the probabilities of the existence of certain entities; what Cavell means comes out best towards the end of *The Claim of Reason* (p. 441), where he is arguing against the idea that our knowledge of objects is unproblematic while our knowledge of another human being is everything that goes into knowledge of an object *plus* something extra: 'something that, as it were, animates the object': 'This idea of knowledge may indeed have the whole process of perception (of different strata or kinds of being) backwards. It makes equal sense – at least equal – to suppose that the natural (or, the biologically more primitive) condition of human perception is of (outward) things, whether objects or persons, as animated; so that it is the seeing of objects as objects (i.e., seeing them objectively, as non-animated) that is the sophisticated development'. This is roughly what Heidegger was getting at in his claim that things around us are initially *zuhanden* and required to be seen in special ways to become *vorhanden*; and what he was suggesting with his attempts to enchant us

into inhabiting a world in which the interplay of sky, earth, mortality and intimations of the sacred is primordial.

79. *Philosophy and Psycho-Analysis*, p. 160. The context is that Wisdom wants to suggest that 'the difference as to whether a God exists involves our feelings more than most scientific disputes and in this respect is more like a difference as to whether there is beauty in a thing' (p. 159).

80. *Philosophy and Psycho-Analysis*, p. 161.

81. *The Claim of Reason*, p. 441.

82. As Mulhall suggests (*Stanley Cavell*, p. 142), the question is to see whether perceiving objects as 'animated' is anything more than a 'metaphorical' way of talking.

83. *The Claim of Reason*, pp. 451f.

# 7. Charles Taylor's moral ontology of the self

1. Charles Taylor (born 1931), based at McGill University for many years, has published, besides many much-discussed essays collected as *Philosophical Papers* (two volumes 1985) and as *Philosophical Arguments* (1995), three very important books: *The Explanation of Behaviour* (1964), a critical analysis of behaviourism; *Hegel* (1975), the first major study by a philosopher in the analytical tradition; and *Sources of the Self: the making of the modern identity* (1989). He has agreed to give the Gifford Lectures at Edinburgh in 1998/99. For a theological review of *Sources of the Self* see James J. Buckley, *The Thomist* 55/3 (July 1991): 497–509; for a very illuminating discussion of the radically different views of St Augustine held by Martha Nussbaum and Charles Taylor see David Dawson: 'Transcendence as Embodiment: Augustine's Domestication of Gnosis', *Modern Theology* 10 (1994): 1–26.

2. See 'Atomism', first published in 1979, in *Philosophical Papers* (Cambridge University Press 1985) volume 2, Chapter 7.

3. See 'Foucault on Freedom and Truth', first published in 1984, in *Philosophical Papers* 2, Chapter 6.

4. 'Foucault', p. 206.

5. *Sources of the Self: The Making of the Modern Identity* [SS] (Cambridge University Press 1989), p. 3.

6. SS, p. 3.

7. SS, pp. 4–8.

8. SS, p. 10: 'It will be my claim that there is a great deal of motivated suppression of moral ontology among our contemporaries, in part because the pluralist nature of modern society makes it easier to live that way, but also because of the great weight of modern epistemology (as with the naturalists evoked above) and, behind this, of the spiritual outlook associated with the epistemology.'

9. SS, pp. 59f.

10. SS, p. 6.

11. SS, p. 7.

12. SS, p. 8.

13. SS, p. 8.

14. SS, p. 8.
15. SS, p. 8.
16. SS, p. 8.
17. SS, p. 9.
18. *Zettel* (Basil Blackwell 1967): §§ 414–16.
19. SS, p. 10.
20. SS, p. 13.
21. SS, p. 13.
22. SS, p. 13.
23. SS, p. 14.
24. SS, p. 226.
25. SS, p. 226.
26. SS, p. 227.
27. SS, p. 227.
28. Taylor, 'Reply and re-articulation', in *Philosophy in an Age of Pluralism: The philosophy of Charles Taylor in question* (Cambridge University Press 1994) ed. James Tully, p. 226.
29. 'Reply and re-articulation', p. 227.
30. 'Reply and re-articulation', p. 228.
31. 'From Marxism to the dialogue society', in *From Culture to Revolution* ed. Terry Eagleton and Brian Wicker (Sheed and Ward 1968): 141–81.
32. 'Marxism', p. 150.
33. 'Marxism', p. 152.
34. 'Marxism', p. 153.
35. 'Marxism', p. 154.
36. 'Marxism', p. 160.
37. 'Marxism', p. 162.
38. 'Marxism', p. 166.
39. 'Marxism', p. 175.
40. Berlin, 'Introduction' in Tully, *Philosophy in an Age of Pluralism*, pp. 1–3.
41. 'Introduction', 1; Isaiah Berlin's assumptions here are interesting – there are certainly Jews and religious Jews, but are there Christians and religious Christians? And which Christians or Jews would believe in a divine purpose for human beings but not for the entire universe?
42. 'Reply and re-articulation', p. 213.
43. 'Reply and re-articulation', p. 214.
44. 'Reply and re-articulation', p. 214.
45. The best demonstration of this is by a Catholic theologian: see John Macken SJ, *The Autonomy Theme in the Church Dogmatics: Karl Barth and his Critics* (Cambridge University Press 1990).
46. Much of the best philosophy of recent times has gone into discrediting the picture of the subject as an unsituated, even punctual self (SS, p. 514); but when we follow up the footnote we find Taylor citing Maurice Merleau-Ponty, *La Phénoménologie de la perception* (1945), Heidegger's *Sein und Zeit*, Michael Polanyi's Aberdeen Gifford Lectures, and adding that 'the works of the later Wittgenstein can also, I think, be seen in this light'. Taylor has always been open to learning from a much wider range of thinkers than most philosophers in the analytical tradition.

47. See 'Heidegger, language and ecology', *Heidegger: A Critical Reader*, ed. Hubert Dreyfus and Harrison Hall (Basil Blackwell 1992): 247–69, and in *Philosophical Arguments*, Chapter 6.
48. 'Heidegger', p. 247.
49. 'Heidegger', p. 263.
50. 'Heidegger', p. 264.
51. In 'Overcoming epistemology' (1987, reprinted in *Philosophical Arguments*, Chapter 1), Taylor's attack on the moral and spiritual consequences of rationalist/empiricist doctrines, he introduces Heidegger's notion of the clearing, *die Lichtung*, to help get us away from subjectivistic notions of 'experience': the disclosure of the human world is not in our heads but in the space that we inhabit. The *lumen intellectuale quod est in nobis*, of which Thomas Aquinas writes (e.g. *Summa Theologiae* 1a, 84, 5), is not some kind of 'participated likeness of the uncreated light in which the divine ideas are contained', but a share in the space in the surrounding jungle (or Schwarzwald!) that language opens up. In effect, Heidegger's notion of the clearing is another attempt to remind us of the space which enables us to see anything at all according to our lights, let alone illumination from a divine source.
52. 'Heidegger', p. 264.
53. 'Heidegger', pp. 264–5.
54. 'Heidegger', p. 267.
55. 'Heidegger', p. 267.

# 8. *Natural desire for God*

1. Hans Urs von Balthasar, *Explorations in Theology I: The Word Made Flesh* (Ignatius Press 1989), tr. A. V. Littledale with Alexander Dru, p. 194.
2. Many books have been written about the medieval-theological antecedents of modern philosophy but see especially Frank B. Farrell, *Subjectivity, Realism and Postmodernism: The Recovery of the World in Recent Philosophy* (Cambridge University Press 1994).
3. Hans Urs von Balthasar (1905–88), Swiss theologian, Jesuit 1929–50, never held an academic post in theology, not invited to contribute to Vatican II, deeply influenced by the mystic Adrienne von Speyr, worked as student chaplain and publisher; the most prolific of all recent Catholic theologians, with three monumental works: *Herrlichkeit: Eine theologische Aesthetik* (1961–84), translated as *The Glory of the Lord; A Theological Aesthetics* (T & T Clark 1985–91), 7 volumes; *Theodramatik* (1973–83), in course of translation (Ignatius Press 1988– ), 5 volumes; and *Theologik* (1985–7), in course of translation (Ignatius Press), 3 volumes. Among his many other books note his pioneering study of Karl Barth (1951), translated as *The Theology of Karl Barth* (Ignatius Press 1992).
4. *Theo-Drama* IV, pp. 64–5, first published in 1980.
5. 'In a world that no longer has enough confidence in itself to affirm the beautiful, the proofs of the truth have lost their cogency. In other words, syllogisms may still dutifully clatter away like rotary presses or computers which infallibly spew out an exact number of answers by the minute. But

the logic of these answers is itself a mechanism which no longer captivates anyone,' *The Glory of the Lord*, volume I, p. 19 (written in 1961).

6. *Theo-Drama* IV, p. 65; earlier we hear of 'an undramatic philosophism' (p. 53).

7. *Theo-Drama* IV, p. 66. Karl Rahner (1904–84), German theologian, Jesuit 1922, published *Geist in Welt* (1939), translated as *Spirit in the World* (1968), reinterpreting Thomas Aquinas's theory of knowledge in terms of human subjectivity's implicit relationship with the absolute; *Hörer des Wortes* (1941), untranslated, portraying human subjectivity as listening for Christian revelation; and among much else his collected essays *Schriften zur Theologie* (1954– ), translated as *Theological Investigations* (Darton Longman & Todd 1961– ).

8. The best introduction to the controversy is Stephen J. Duffy: *The Graced Horizon: Nature and Grace in Modern Catholic Thought* (The Liturgical Press 1992); it is placed in much longer perspective in the magisterial study by Louis Dupré: *Passage to Modernity: An Essay in the Hermeneutics of Nature and Culture* (Yale University Press 1993).

9. *Natural Theology: Comprising 'Nature and Grace' by Professor Dr Emil Brunner and the reply 'No!' by Dr Karl Barth*, tr. Peter Fraenkel (Geoffrey Bles 1936).

10. *Church Dogmatics* II/1 (T & T Clark 1957, in German 1940), p. 173.

11. *CD* II/1, p. 174. Evidently Barth included Scotland in England or did not regard it as a 'stronghold of the Reformation': he delivered the Gifford Lectures in the University of Aberdeen in 1937–8, based on the Scottish Confession of 1560.

12. See, for a start, Joseph A. Komonchak, 'Theology and Culture at Mid-Century: The example of Henri de Lubac', *Theological Studies* 51 (1990): 579–602.

13. Henri Marie-Joseph Sonier de Lubac (1896–1991), French theologian, Jesuit 1913, war service (wounded 1917), published among much else *Catholicisme: les aspects sociaux du dogme*(1937), translated as *Catholicism: Christ and the Common Destiny of Man* (Burns and Oates 1950); *Surnaturel: Etudes Historiques* (1946, new edition 1991), never translated but see *The Mystery of the Supernatural* (Geoffrey Chapman 1967) and *Augustinianism and Modern Theology* (Geoffrey Chapman 1969). The best study in English is Paul McPartlan, *The Eucharist makes the Church: Henri de Lubac and John Zizioulas in dialogue* (T & T Clark 1993).

14. *Catholicism*, p. 313.

15. Perhaps this is the place to mention Charles Taylor, 'Clericalism', *The Downside Review* 78 (1960): 167–80: 'There is a clear link between the view that this human development is devoid of significance and the view that we have been calling clericalism, and also an important historical link between the dissolution of the laity as a people and the denigration of their task, of secular progress as a whole, a rejection of humanism.'

16. *Gaudium et Spes* § 4.

17. *Ad Limina Apostolorum* (English version, T & T Clark 1969); see Aidan Nichols, 'Twenty-five Years On: A Catholic Commemoration of Karl Barth', *New Blackfriars* 74 (1993): 538–49.

18. *Theo-Drama* IV, p. 76.
19. *Zeitschrift für katholische Theologie* (1939): 371–9.
20. *Cordula oder der Ernstfall* (1966), translated as *The Moment of Christian Witness* (Ignatius Press 1994). Cordula does not make it into *The Oxford Dictionary of Saints*; but she counts as one of the companions of St Ursula: she hid all night in a boat but gave herself up to martyrdom by the Huns next day, according to the immensely popular Legend of the Eleven Thousand Virgins (a misreading of the numeral XI in a tenth-century fabrication), all supposedly of British origin, martyred at Cologne.
21. *Theological Investigations* [TI] 4 (1966), pp. 180f.
22. TI 9 (1972), pp. 38f, from a lecture given in Chicago in 1966.
23. Fergus Kerr, *Theology after Wittgenstein* (Basil Blackwell 1986), pp. 10–14.
24. Gerald McCool, *A Rahner Reader* (Crossroad 1984); Rowan Williams, 'Balthasar and Rahner', in *The Analogy of Beauty: The Theology of Hans Urs von Balthasar*, ed. John Riches (T & T Clark 1986); and many others.
25. TI 4, p. 187, a warning first published in 1960!
26. Karen Elizabeth Kilby, *The Vorgriff auf esse: A Study in the relation of philosophy to theology in the thought of Karl Rahner* (Yale University unpublished PhD thesis, 1994).
27. J. A. DiNoia, 'Karl Rahner', in *The Modern Theologians*, ed. David F. Ford (Basil Blackwell 1989) volume 1: 183–204.
28. Nicholas Healy, 'Indirect methods in theology: Karl Rahner as an ad hoc apologist', *The Thomist* 56 (1992): 613–34.
29. DiNoia, 'Karl Rahner', p. 194.
30. Kilby, *The Vorgriff auf esse*, p. 179 n. 3.
31. Michael Purcell, *Mystery and Method: The Mystery of the Other, and its Reduction in Rahner and Levinas* (University of Edinburgh unpublished PhD thesis 1996).
32. R .R. Reno, *The Ordinary Transformed: Karl Rahner and the Christian Vision of Transcendence* (Eerdmans 1995).
33. TI 16 (1979), pp. 227–43.
34. Stanley Cavell, *Must We Mean What We Say?*, *A Book of Essays* (Charles Scribner's Sons 1969), p. 61.
35. TI 11 (1974), p. 101.
36. TI 11, pp. 68–114.
37. 'Whereof one cannot speak, thereof one must be silent', the final remark in the *Tractatus Logico-Philosophicus*, in C. K. Ogden's version (1922): the only remark by Wittgenstein that Rahner seems to have known.
38. TI 4, p. 53.
39. TI 4, p. 58.

# INDEX